SEX
DRIVE

By the Same Author

Biche
Sucking Shrimp
Trix
A Partial Indulgence

SEX DRIVE

STEPHANIE THEOBALD

ON THE ROAD TO A PLEASURE REVOLUTION

Unbound

This edition first published in 2018

Unbound
6th Floor Mutual House, 70 Conduit Street, London W1S 2GF
www.unbound.com

This book is a work of non-fiction based on the experiences and recollections
of Stephanie Theobald. In some cases, names of people have been changed to
protect the privacy of others.

Text design by PDQ

A CIP record for this book is available from the British Library

ISBN 978-1-78352-681-9 (trade hbk)
ISBN 978-1-78352-683-3 (ebook)
ISBN 978-1-78352-682-6 (limited edition)

Printed in Great Britain by CPI Group (UK)

For the Wizard of O,
Betty Dodson

In times of war – and it's always a time of war – women especially need to seek out more pleasure. Because it's the first thing they steal from us. You have to find a way to dissolve into hedonistic pleasure, you have to pander to your worst instincts.

Lydia Lunch

PROLOGUE:
SADDLING UP

London, 5 October 2014

Sunday morning in bed. Only crumbs remain on the croissant plate and, any minute now, he is going to start looking at me in that way. It's become a routine on Sunday mornings after breakfast in bed and it does make sense. Women's magazines say it all the time: if you've been together for a long time then you should do it even if you don't fancy it, because it brings you closer together.

So I do do it. Only I'll probably be thinking of the sixty-six-year-old art dealer I had an affair with a few years back, although actually I wasn't always present with him either. Sometimes I'd teletransport away from his boat on Chiswick Pier over to an imaginary barrister's office in Lincoln's Inn Fields, where I'd be submitting to a pinstriped lawyer type. Yet within that fantasy, I'd soon have to be back at the flat of the real-life dirty blonde from Harvey Nichols I'd recently bought perfume from. In my head, we'd become lovers and wouldn't she punish me good and proper when she found out what I'd been up to with the lawyer?

So there I was, lying in bed on Sunday morning, wondering who the hell I was about to have sex with. Over the past few months, the sight of croissants has served to fuel my midlife crisis like the dogs and Pavlov. Wasn't it dishonest to have sex with someone while thinking about doing it with someone else? How did you carry on having sex in a long-term relationship, and what was this 'poly' thing everyone was talking about? We'd been together for ten years but we didn't have children, so there was nobody to hurt apart from ourselves. Maybe he'd be better off with someone who didn't make him feel like a freak for wanting sex. Maybe not wanting sex was part of the perimenopausal thing. Yet I dreamed about it all the time.

Mainly, I wondered, is sex important? Is it really bad for you if you don't have it regularly? I hadn't broken out with fangs and scales just yet, and my friend in Cannes hardly ever has sex with the father of her three children. 'Sometimes it just strikes me as so absurd, all that rumpy-pumpy bestial jerking, when you could be painting a picture or something.' She seems to have sublimated her urges with vegetables. She's always sending me emails about the amazing produce ('baby broad beans, tiny artichokes and Perroquet tulips') that she's bought from the local market.

I'd talked to other friends about my dilemma. The magazine editor looked worried and said, 'Relationships do go through difficult patches.' (People hate it when their friends split.) My PR friend warned, 'Stay with the devil you know!' which is rich, because she fantasises about her gym instructor every time she does it with her husband. My TV friend told me to, 'Have your cake and eat it!' (She's desperate to have an affair with a guy in her office and if she didn't have kids she'd do it 'like a shot'.) My twenty-four-year-old poet friend said, 'Go for it – you've not been happy for a long time. But you have to be honest with him.'

And I have been. More or less. The following Sunday, as I lay on his shoulder after the plate of crumbs and the ensuing sex, I managed to stammer something like, 'I will always know you.' It felt like a lever, like the first bit of levering had taken place, which one day would uproot the jammed stone and send it rolling down the cliff. It was a feeling of moving something, but it was frightening too. There was a silence and then he joked that we could be like Vita Sackville-West and Harold Nicolson, the glamorous bisexual literary couple of the 1920s and 30s, who exemplified polyamory before the word was invented. I cheered up then. I said that yes, I'd be Vita having sex with Virginia Woolf while Hadji would sit in his club in St James's smoking cigars with Winston Churchill (I didn't want to think too much about what my Hadji would actually get up to).

And then joking wasn't enough. Something needed to burst through. Maybe I didn't want an affair. Maybe I wanted a whole new life. The following weekend, I found myself in the kitchen with the man who used to be known as 'the brute boy of British fiction', surrounded by all the things that were making me feel buried alive: the BBC Radio arts review show, the roast chicken in the oven, the prospect of croissants the next day. Something came to a head. All year, I'd been hungry for stories of people splitting up: how did they do it? What words did they use? How did the conversation start? Someone said, 'Wait until next time you're having a row, it'll come naturally.' But in the event, I just started to cry. I'd never cried wolf in all our years together and now something terrible was coming out of my mouth: 'I was thinking that maybe we should split up.'

It felt as though I'd poured poison into his drink. He didn't drop down to his knee and say, 'No! Anything but that!' He nodded and said, 'Yes.' We were both in shock. He ran me a bath and brought me chocolate and wine and lit candles. I lay in the warm water thinking, *The poison will trickle into his guts. Soon it will start to have an effect.*

At the beginning of November, I flew to New York to visit some old friends and ended up bedding the art director of a US glossy followed by a night with a badass chef from a restaurant in the Meatpacking District. On my return to London, a week later, I was delirious. I had a meeting with my bank manager and I was thinking of saying to him, 'I want to talk to you about orgasms!' because I was back in the sexual saddle after such a long absence. I was seeing the world through a phantasmagorical sea of stirred desire and deranged memories: a stuffy apartment, orange décor, a pierced clit, a leather belt. The selfish, slippery, feverish mind of the born-again sex junkie.

Only I was a big phoney. I didn't actually have an orgasm with the art director until she was safely in the bathroom the next morning (Americans take ages in the shower). And I only climaxed in the badass chef's orange apartment when she left the room to answer the phone in the early hours. The next morning, I played distractedly with her breasts on the couch because I felt I should try and get turned on again. After a while, she said, 'Let's go get bagels.'

Getting back into the sexual saddle isn't as easy as you think. The fact was that after being in a monogamous relationship for so long, I wasn't sure how to sit on the horse any more. And yet I knew I needed to come alive again. I'd never been a shrinking violet about sex. Much of my journalistic reputation over the past twenty-five years had been based on it, writing about attraction to both men and women. Some people gain confidence from work, some from sport, some from trophy husbands. But for me it had always been sex.

And then I found something I'd written in my diary in my late twenties. I'd just been chucked by a girlfriend and when I'd calmed down, I observed, *I need some masturbation time.*

Some TLC for my own body. To try and remember my own body. Wanking off and eating straw always seems to be the starter for any creativity I have.

'Wanking off and eating straw' was shorthand in my twenties for afternoon autoerotic sessions when I was bored or looking for inspiration. After rutting under my sheets for fifteen minutes at a time several times a week, my bed resembled a stable that needed mucking out. I always felt guilty afterwards because all the wage slaves were in their offices working away. Mainly, I felt like a peasant because having real sex with good-looking people was what you were supposed to be doing.

But now I start to think that masturbation might be good for me. That it might be the way out of this mess – jump cords to a new life. The Victorians used to trot out that line from Juvenal about *mens sana in corpore sano*, a healthy mind in a healthy body, but what if a healthy body were the fruit of a dirty mind?

So I started to masturbate. A little bit every day when Hadji was out at his office. And the more I masturbated, the more I wanted to masturbate – not just touching and rubbing, but fantasies too. Filthy craven sex with strangers: men and women, old and young, posh and common, inter-epochal. The secret films I ran in my head when I was alone and naked in bed would be shouted out of Sundance, but at least they were honest. They were possibly the only things I had ever created not to impress a boss or an editor or to gain the approval of a lover. Maybe they could teach me something. And now that I was spending more time alone with myself, I was remembering my own body. And it was pissed off. There was something it wanted.

One night when Hadji came home, I'd forgotten to put my vibrator away. There was something like relief in his

5

voice when he came into the kitchen and made a joke about something he'd found on the bed. I felt embarrassed. Then I thought, *Wouldn't it be great to be honest about your desire? To take time out to discover what your desire really is?*

There were inklings of a plan forming. I wasn't sure how to put it together, but I knew it would involve America. Growing up in drizzly Cornwall in the 1970s, I knew America would be my salvation. It was about bubblegum and riding horses and not having to be 'ladylike'. And when I finally made it to New York one summer as a student, I wasn't disappointed. I learned that America made you stop being shy. It made you unashamed to ask for whatever you wanted. I was excited to learn that there was such a thing as an 'everything bagel' and after a while that didn't seem such a greedy concept.

I decide to fly back to New York in the New Year. I need to get away from everything I know to figure this out. Besides, the chef has been emailing me. When I tell her that I'm thinking of taking a fantastic voyage into my own body, she doesn't laugh. She tells me she knows a bunch of sex-positive feminists from the 1970s. Some real characters. She's happy to introduce me.

A lot was still up in the air, but luckily I was about to meet an eighty-five-year-old pot-smoking masturbation addict. She was going to set me on a path that would change my life forever.

MEETING PINKY TUSCADERO

There are eleven women stark naked in a room in a New York apartment. Ten of us are lying with our legs spread, a metal dildo in our vagina, a purring vibrator on our clitoris and our left hand stroking our breasts, which glisten with almond oil. 'Your left hand is your lover,' the naked eighty-five-year-old lady barks as she patrols the room with her own massive vibrator, which sounds like a cement mixer and resembles an old-fashioned kitchen device.

It's the first week of January 2015 and I've flown back to New York to try and perfect my orgasms with the help of the badass chef. Let's call her 'Virginia'. The fast-paced seafood restaurant she works at reminds me of my thrilling student summer as a twenty-year-old waitress in the Dallas BBQ on West 72nd Street. Yet even though I have now popped a pretty good fantasy (semi-public sex under the raw bar before the other chefs came in), I didn't come. I'm convinced that there's something wrong with me. Am I too tense? Is there something wrong with my wiring? Am I too stuck in my head?

In between bouts of sex where I take ages to come, Virginia suggests I interview a woman she's heard about called Betty Dodson, who's revived the women-only masturbation masterclasses she created in the 1970s.

A pioneer and a renegade, described as 'one of the early feminists' by Gloria Steinem and as a 'misguided career masturbator' by Germaine Greer, Dodson wrote the world's only bestseller to date about female self-pleasure. *Sex For One*, originally self-published in 1974 as *Liberating Masturbation*, came out of Betty's observation during her orgy years in the 1960s that many women were faking orgasm. It was an insight that launched her on a lifetime's crusade.

When I go round to her apartment one freezing January afternoon, I meet a woman with a mouth like a sailor and the easy manner of a wisecracking Scorsese character. She looks amazing for her age. More sixty-five than eighty-five. Her secret, she quips, is: 'Masturbation, pot and raw garlic.'

She explains that she's revived the classes, which she terms 'Bodysex', because today's young women are way more at sea about their bodies than their 1970s counterparts. 'Most of them haven't even seen their genitals in a mirror. You show 'em and they go "eek!" or "ugh".'

I've done some interesting journalistic assignments in my time: taken the Amazonian hallucinogenic ayahuasca, attended a goddess workshop in Wales and a black Mass in Paris, but Betty's masturbation masterclass sounds fascinating. I say I'd love to come to the next one and ask her why she keeps doing them. She looks at me like I'm an idiot. 'The sounds, the sights, the smells,' she says. 'Women are so beautiful: fat, skinny, one tit gone. No wonder I keep doing it. Why do you think I look so good?'

And yet, down here on the carpet, I'm having some performance anxiety. It's finale time of day two where, having learned the nuts and bolts of our genitals on day one, we are now expected to masturbate to orgasm together. We've only been going about thirty seconds and Maria, the Spanish lawyer, has come already. This is followed by a cry from

Ingrid, the vet from Norway, who begins to climax with a soft, musical moaning, as if she's auditioning for an *Emmanuelle* movie. Do women really make that sound when they come? Clearly they do. Now that Spain and Norway have come and the only other European person in the room is me, Betty's logic is that I should be next in line. 'Come on, London!' she roars. 'Fake it!'

Yesterday wasn't without its pressures either. I arrive late at the rent-controlled apartment on Madison Avenue where Betty has lived since 1959 and glimpse women of varying shapes and sizes sitting naked in the next room. It feels like an X-rated Tupperware party. There's no offer of a dressing room, so I just strip in the hallway and go into the main room lined with glass dildos, Betty's drawings of erotic couplings and eleven naked women sitting in a circle. Betty tells us we are re-enacting an ancient ritual of women sitting together and sharing experiences. Luckily, she doesn't use that new spiritual-speak about 'mindfulness' and 'soul connection'. She says, 'When you look around the circle, you let go of the bullshit image they pump into the marketplace with the fashion magazines and the Hollywood movies and the fuckless porn. The biggest problem for women is our body image and it starts with our vulvas. We think – all of us – that there's something wrong with them.'

It's taking a while for us to see through the bullshit image. From a Rubenesque student to a Sandra Bullock lookalike and Maria the Spanish girl with her legs confidently splayed, we're all taking sneaky peeks at each other's pubic and breast areas.

Betty explains that Bodysex came about through the now-forgotten 'consciousness-raising groups', feminism's bush fires of the 1970s, where women would meet to talk honestly about what was really happening in their lives. Betty felt the need to form her own group after a while, since she found that a lot of women in the CR groups she went to were just bitching about men. She believed there were more important issues.

'I felt that sex was a top-priority feminist issue. Gloria Steinem thought it was a private matter.'

And then we're on to the action. After an opening exercise where Betty asks us to put our fingers slowly up our nostrils to demonstrate what a sensitive matter penetration is, she asks each of us two questions. One: what do you feel about your body? Two: what do you feel about your orgasm? The Rubenesque student, Lois, who at twenty is the youngest in the group, says she ejaculates, but she's not sure if she comes. Business consultant, Erica, thirty-two, says she can only come using her vibrator, not with her boyfriend's penis. She's worried that she's 'wired wrongly'. Miranda, forty-eight, is dating a trans man who says he's 'jealous' of her vibrator, but that's the only way she can come, as she has vulvodynia, a medical condition that makes vaginal penetration painful. Sandra Bullock, forty-one, a yoga teacher, is worried that her labia lips are too long. The common denominator is that, as Betty predicted, we all think something is slightly wrong with our sexual parts.

Betty announces that it's time for 'genital show-and-tell', which is where we look at our vulvas under an anglepoise lamp in a make-up mirror. The vulva is the correct name for the female genitals, Betty is at pains to tell us. The word encompasses the full works: the inner and outer lips, the clitoris, the vagina, the urethra. She gets incensed at the way so many women misuse the 'vagina' word. 'The vagina's the goddam birth canal!'

Betty is the first to take to the stage. 'Look carefully now,' she jokes. 'When's the last time you saw an eighty-five-year-old snatch?'

She spreads her legs and, once you get over the grey hair, Betty doesn't look much different from what I recall my vulva looks like. She goes on to explain that the vagina is not a hole at all but a muscle. She squeezes hers in and out. Lois opines that it looks like a rose with folds and petals, but it reminds me of the 1970s opening credits of *Doctor Who*, a scary spiral tunnel that goes on and on.

Betty then demonstrates a vulva massage, which she says is 'like a ballet', only with almond oil. She is scornful of expensive commercial lubricants. Throughout the weekend, Betty says things like, 'I went through the sexual revolution using almond oil,' which makes you feel as though this might be 1968 and Janis Joplin is going to walk through the door at any minute.

It's mesmerising to watch Betty do the vulva ballet. 'It's very important to maintain a relationship with your genitals,' she insists, pointing out her urethra, or pee hole. She tells us to cup our hands and smell the scent of our vulva. 'I always taste myself before lovemaking, for reassurance. It's the equivalent of testing your breath to see if you want to brush your teeth.'

Then she says, 'Can you see the Virgin Mary?'

'Oh yeah,' Sandra Bullock nods, looking intently at Betty's bits. 'The clitoris – that's the face, right?'

If I was going to be pernickety, I'd say that Betty's bits remind me more of the Ku Klux Klan, but then she's calling us up, one by one, for our turn as prima ballerinas.

There's minimal fuss involved in moving around this room where Betty threw orgies in the late 1960s. 'There's no furniture that can't be moved,' she says (although the loo-door handle soon becomes greasy with almond oil as women nervously tiptoe in to prepare for their big solo).

Betty's message for women today is the same as it was back then. 'You have to run the fuck,' she keeps telling us, meaning

11

that women need to take control of their own orgasms and stop worrying if they're being sexy enough for their partner. Masturbation is not a second-rate sexual activity – it liberates you from what Betty sees as the yoke of romantic love. On a practical note, it's also good for relationships, because why should you expect your lover to get you off if you don't know how to do it yourself?

Over the course of the next three hours we see angels, wizards, hearts, kites and flowers in our pussies. Vulvas, she tells us, come in all shapes and sizes. 'You get Baroque ones, Renaissance ones, Gothic. I had a young girl here recently who was art deco. Pretty little thing. Just simple lines.' Sandra Bullock has a frisée-lettuce look about her inner lips. Lois says they remind her of a crinoline. Sandra Bullock does a lot of sport. She says she's often thought of cutting them off, as many athletic women do, because they claim they get in the way.

At one point, Betty tells me to stop frowning, but I'm not frowning – I'm feeling wonder. I started out the genital show-and-tell wondering who was going to be the dunce of the class, i.e. who would have the most ugly pussy – but there is no ugly pussy. We look at different vulvas, less than a metre from our face and people say things like, 'Oh, it's adorable,' or, 'Oh look, another angel!' As I look at the variety of cunts that pass before the mirror: large clits, asymmetrical inner lips, pussies pink or edged in brown, skin tags, rose-shaped vaginal entrances, it strikes me that the vulva is a massively complex area. A Lamborghini to the penny farthing of the male genitalia. 'Men just have a couple of balls and a tube!' Betty jokes, adding that a woman has 8,000 nerve endings in her clitoris compared to 4,000 in a man's penis.

The genital show-and-tell is not sexual and it's not clinical. It's more a feeling of sisterhood. Real 1970s stuff. I feel moved. And angry. That it's taken me until I'm forty-eight to realise that my pussy is something to be proud of. That it's just like every other woman's – unique and odd-looking and more beautiful the longer you look at it.

After Lois's turn in front of the mirror ('Woah! That's a big clit, girlfriend!' says Betty, sounding very much like a size queen), it's my go. I'm surprised that I don't feel too self-conscious, although I curse myself for my shoddy shave job when it's become clear that most American girls use laser hair removal. I have got into a habit of looking at my vulva in a make-up mirror, but this is the first time I've ever seen my pee hole. I also realise that Virginia's 'pierced clit', which I've been bragging to my friends about, is actually a pierced 'clitoral hood'. I am told I have heart-shaped inner labia (inner lips are the big issue when you get into pussy gazing). When Sandra Bullock croons, 'Oh they're so small!' I want to hug her and say, 'But I love your frisée lettuce!'

I know. You had to be there.

Betty then asks me what I want to call 'her'. Everyone has to name their vulva. By the end of the day we have christened Regina, Santa, Minx, Chakra, Siankiki, Clementine, Gabby and Tonks, after the witch from Harry Potter. For my own vulva, I draw a blank, so Betty offers 'Pinky' because of the virginal colour. That sounds a bit femmy to me and I hesitate before Carlin, Betty's business partner and workshop assistant, says, 'How about Pinky Tuscadero?' referring to the Fonz's hell-raising biker girlfriend from Happy Days. I have no recollection of this character, but I go for it because I'm keen to put my legs back together.

Carlin Ross, forty-one, is a former corporate lawyer who has brought the Bodysex business up to date. The weekend costs $1,200 and since 2014 you've been able to take the Betty Dodson Certification Program, and go back and teach women in your own country how to have good sex with themselves. By 2018 there would be thirty-five women in eight countries and seventeen US states teaching Betty's method of self-love. The women are from all walks of life. The only difference between today's workshops and those in the 1970s is that they've replaced flyers and phone calls with social media and emails.

At the end of the first day, we students reluctantly put our clothes back on and go to an Irish bar near Times Square. A Canadian, Natasha Salaash, thirty-seven, starts to talk about her recent sexual awakening. She's recently out of a seventeen-year-long monogamous marriage.

'I have five kids, I make my own bread, I keep chickens, I work with children. I'm "respectable", but I think that lifelong monogamy is such a load of bullshit!'

Natasha thinks that starting to work out at the gym might have been the catalyst for her 'awakening'. 'I felt like a wheel. I had all these spokes, but I was neglecting so many of them.' She stresses that she's not against monogamy per se. 'I just think that a lifetime of it is not for me.' She describes masturbation is a 'lifeline'. She tries to do it for thirty-five minutes every day so that it becomes a sort of sexual meditation.

It's great to be talking so openly about wanking. We talk about how we did it as kids. Norway confides that she used socks pressed against her clitoris and I did a similar thing with Jemima, my stuffed doll with orange-wool hair, also seen on the children's 1970s UK TV show, *Play School*. Poor Jemima. She had a usefully large head.

Natasha makes the good point that, 'Masturbating's not the hard part. It's touching your body and loving it that's most difficult.'

I take a subway back to my fashion-writer friend's apartment, where I'm staying tonight. She's sitting on a designer couch talking about Marc Jacobs' great new collection and I'm nodding, secretly wondering what her vulva looks like under her Chanel dress. Men see other penises every day in public urinals, but I bet you don't even know how big your clitoris is or if your inner lips resemble a rose or an angel.

The next day on the subway back to Madison Avenue, I see Betty's vulva advertised on the wall of the carriage: a browny swirl with the face of some biblical character in the middle. As the train judders to a halt, I realise it's actually a picture of a dollop of peanut butter. I get off the train and walk down the street, vaguely worried that I now appear to be hallucinating female genitals.

When I arrive at Betty's apartment, it's D-Day or, rather, Big M day. All eleven of us are going to masturbate in a big circle. Betty points to Carlin, who she calls the 'stunt cunt' and who slowly inserts a stainless-steel tube the size of a large cigar into her vagina. This is the Betty Dodson Barbell, 'a vaginal exerciser that doubles as a dildo', which sells for $130 on Betty's website. As we watch Carlin breathe deeply, Betty tells us that breathing teaches you to tolerate higher levels of body sensations. Then Betty tells us to, 'Start your engines!' and goes to lie next to me with her huge cement-mixer vibrator (the Hitachi Magic Wand), because she says you need a bit more force when you get older. It is weird lying next to a masturbating eighty-five-year-old lady. If Betty looks more like sixty-five than eighty-five, she looks more like a fifty-year-old when she's pleasuring herself. A pink glow comes over her face. But I'm distracted from the octogenarian's ecstasy by the sound of Spain and Norway coming. And then the yell of, 'Come on, London, fake it!'

I get back to work, fishing around in my head for some suitable fantasy and then suddenly I feel Sandra Bullock's foot on mine. I'm slightly worried about being the dirty old bisexual at the party. I don't think we are supposed to eroticise our fellow wankers. Still, Sandra's lying next to me and the sensation sends a rush of energy through my body. I decide to cast the vibrator aside and go for manual stimulation. Suddenly I see the cleavage of the barmaid at the Irish bar last night and that starts something off. Then Norway starts to come again (or is that still the noise from her first one?), and then I hear Natasha on the other side of the room (she's using the manual method too), followed by groans from Sandra Bullock. It's impossible not to get pulled into the wave of sexual energy spinning round the room.

I climax and then I hear Betty say, 'You're not done yet, honey!' She takes the vibrating rolling pin of her Hitachi Magic Wand, snaps a condom on the head and I see it heading towards my clit. It feels like I'm being electrocuted, but I think I'll go with it because this is, after all, the legendary Betty Dodson and she must know what she's doing. I don't hold my breath or pull back and suddenly, I don't think any more. The vibrations buzz through my body and soon I'm in outer space, having some mad cosmic orgasm. I'm aware of Betty's evil laugh and the fact that I'm writhing around on the floor making this moaning, wailing sound that even I don't recognise. But I'm beyond caring what anyone thinks. It reminds me of the time I snorted a line of heroin at a party and spent the night floating around the Garden of Gethsemane 2,000 years ago.

Afterwards, I wonder if, like young Lois, I've never had a proper orgasm in my life either. Betty's now moved over to the twenty-year-old with the Hitachi Magic Wand, and Lois can't stop coming. It looks as though she's giving happy birth. She's laughing uncontrollably, as we've all been doing at the end of our orgasms – something that rarely happens when I masturbate on my own.

Afterwards, Sandra Bullock says, 'It feels like free drugs!' and Natasha says, 'I feel like I'm drunk.' When Lois says, 'I don't know why I'm laughing so much!' Betty retorts, 'Silly girl – you're orgasmic!'

Betty doesn't seem surprised by the radical feelings going through our bodies. 'This is what people don't know,' she says. 'This is female sexuality. Men, they shoot their load, they gotta have a nap, they gotta have a sandwich. But we are endless.'

And the afternoon's not over yet. We're told to get on our fronts and start the 'pillow hump'. This is a trademarked Dodson technique that Betty developed in the 1970s, along with her workshops where women carved dildos out of courgettes. We don't get on to vegetables today, but we learn that the pillow hump is for women who prefer to get off on their front. I feel as if I'm still tripping from the Hitachi Magic Wand experience, but I'm confident in this position, as it reminds me of what I did with Jemima all those years ago. In spite of the rug burn under my knees, I feel a glow of pride as Betty shouts out, 'You're a pig, London! A pig!'

TOWARDS THE CLITORIS
OF AMERICA

The main after-effects of Betty Dodson's masterclass were that a) I could now come much quicker and b) my sexual fantasies became much dirtier. Mainly though, I wanted to have another of the heroin orgasms, and I got a taste thanks to a charismatic former actress and her sexual-politics-meets-showbiz school of feminism.

Regena Thomashauer, aka Mama Gena, has become a multi-millionaire thanks to a philosophy that promises an escape from the doom and gloom of current feminism. It's at her New York workshop that I first hear the phrase 'fourth-wave feminism', which, as one nineteen-year-old student tells me enthusiastically, is about, 'stopping bitching about men and reconnecting with your body'.

When I arrive at the NYU Skirball Center for the Performing Arts, the women lining up outside look like they normally spend their Saturday mornings shopping for handbags at Bergdorf Goodman. Inside, there are pink boas draped everywhere and beaming women wearing T-shirts saying '8,000 nerve endings at your service' (that figure again, referring to the physiology of the clitoris). These are Mama Gena's volunteers. They tickle us with pink feathers when we arrive, saying, 'Welcome to the party, sister goddess!'

But I soon watch impressed as Mama Gena herself strides up and down the stage in maroon Dolce & Gabbana, whipping them up into a frenzy. The fifty-seven-year-old author of a *New York Times* bestseller called *Pussy* talks of a female 'pleasure revolution,' declaring, 'You're not a victim, you're a vixen!' She urges the women to get to know their vulvas 'better than the back of your hand!' and I end the weekend by flashing my breasts to over 600 cheering women.

In spite of the chignons and the designer dresses, there is an implicit 'spread the love' hippie message going on at the Mama Gena weekend. The idea is that once you've unlocked your own power, you have a responsibility to light up the next woman. A lot of sharing takes place, with one Catherine Deneuve lookalike admitting to the room, 'I have this sense that I have no right to even know what I want. Even though intellectually I know I do' (gasps from the audience). When emotions get too dark, Mama Gena cues a 'dance break', where we get up and boogie to anything from Lady Gaga's 'Born This Way' to 'What a Feeling' from *Flashdance*. My favourite bit of Mama Gena life coaching is when she recommends getting up every morning, dancing naked in front of a mirror to an angry song, followed by a naked dance to a sexy song and then, with that whirling-dervish energy stirred up, going into the office and socking it to them.

I flag slightly in the afternoon and sit in the audience, smelling my hands and wishing I was back in bed with Virginia. I snap back into the room when Mama Gena tells us we're all going to get on stage to 'walk a runway' to demonstrate that we're proud of our bodies. My cheese alert sets off, and then a woman stands up and talks about how she survived breast cancer, showing us her reconstructed breasts. I feel angry and sad all at once. Someone I know died recently of breast cancer.

So when it's my turn to walk the runway, even though my legs are wobbling and even though the soundtrack has become the unbearably cringy 'I'm Too Sexy' by Right Said Fred, I resolve to test quite how proud of my body I am by taking my top off. Following the line in front of me onto the huge stage, I start lifting my T-shirt over my head. I'm aware of a murmuring from the crowd and when I come out into the air again, I see bright lights and hundreds of faces. Now centre stage and wearing just a clatty black bra, I clutch the T-shirt in my right hand and make myself stop and look at the audience. When I start to fumble around with my bra clasp, a ripple of something starts in the crowd. It's that sisterhood thing again. When the ripple rises up high towards the roof it excites and petrifies me, but I think of my friend who died of breast cancer. I close my eyes and release my bra. Cool air hits my naked breasts and I hear a massive wave of *woo hoo!*s coming from the auditorium. When I open my eyes, I see a blur of cheering women and I lift my arms into the air because I'm curious to see how high I can whip this energy up. I soak it in and have a brief revelation of what Mick Jagger must feel like on stage – it's a massive rush, but it's not sexual. Actually, I guess it could be really sexual. In fact, who knows what you could do with energy like this?

When I get to the other side of the stage, I wish I'd had a mike so I could have said to the women in the audience, 'Get your fucking tits out! Where else are you going to have a chance like this?' Mama Gena is standing there with her mouth open and I float back to my seat with a mass of hands patting my back and voices saying things like, 'That was awesome!' I walk back to Virginia's on a massive high of jet-lag-meets-sleep-deprivation-meets-loads-of-sex-meets-taking-your-top-off-in-front-of-600-women. I'm not surprised when I stop off at the bagel store and the man serving is really nice to me. When I order an everything bagel, he gives me extra cream cheese. I tuck into the sesame, poppy seed, onion, garlic, caraway and salt bagel, asking myself how much extra cream cheese I'd get if I could afford the $12,000 Mama Gena course that involves a trip to Paris to see what nineteenth-century French courtesans can teach modern women about lighting themselves up.

I start to wonder how many more of these avant-garde sex women there are in America. What if I cobbled together a story so I'd have an excuse to meet some more of them? Go on a sort of sex drive across America in search of the ultimate climax? Forget croissants – how about the everything bagel of orgasm? It's been surmised that 'clitoris' comes from the Greek for 'little hill', *klytis*, but what if I were to make it all the way to the top of the rock? I have an idea that California would be a good place to drive to, but my plan doesn't get a precise location until a few days later, when Virginia and I are walking down Eighth Avenue. Things are going well between us, despite the fact that working in a professional kitchen seems to have made her obsessed with neatness and hygiene. When she's at home she's often armed with paper towels and a spray bottle of Windex.

'You're such a clean freak,' I tell her. 'Lucky you've got a dirty mind.'

'You're welcome,' she drawls, pointing to some icicles dripping in the sunshine from the 14th Street subway-station railing. I love that a gritty New York chef is so good at noticing natural beauty.

'Yeah, well,' she shrugs, 'I don't just want to be in my head. I want to be connected to my heart too.'

'Heart,' I scoff. 'So American!'

'OK,' Virginia groans. 'We're done with this conversation.' She waves suddenly to a kittenish woman on the other side of the street and we cross over to a Bianca Jagger-esque beauty in her sixties called Veronica Vera, or 'VV' to her friends. It turns out that VV used to model for Robert Mapplethorpe and she now runs a business out of her Chelsea studio apartment called Miss Vera's Finishing School for Boys Who Want to Be Girls. Virginia got to know VV when she used to come by the restaurant with a bunch of friends from a group called Feminists for Free Expression. The group challenged the blanket claim of anti-sex feminists such as Andrea Dworkin and Catherine MacKinnon that pornography was degrading to women. Other core members included porn-star-turned-performance-artist Annie Sprinkle, pioneering feminist pornographer Candida Royalle and kink tantrica, Barbara Carrellas.

The two of them stand chatting as I watch dogs walk past in purple snowshoes and half listen to their conversation, which soon turns to Betty Dodson (all the sex women know Betty). VV, it seems, is all up for fourth-wave feminism. She explains that some of the audience, both older feminists as well as the more PC Millennials, gave Betty a hard time at a recent conference talk about orgy etiquette. 'Betty was saying that if someone grabbed your ass at an orgy back in the day, it was no big deal. You'd just tell them, "Don't do it next time." And the people at the conference were disgusted. They were all, like, twittering this mean stuff about Betty.'

She sighs. 'I guess people can get into their anger around sex more easily than their pleasure. People don't realise. The 1970s were different times.'

VV makes New York of the 1970s sound amazing. 'I'd wear a sheer blouse with no bra and you could walk down the street like that. No problem.' She reminisces about being Annie Sprinkle's partner in crime back in the day. She'd met Annie at Club 90, a sort of porn star support group which took place at Annie's flat at 90 Lexington Avenue. VV was at the centre of the New York sex world in the 1970s and 80s. She appeared in porn films, made cable sex shows and advocated for prostitutes' rights. In the early 1980s she and Annie would go to the Hellfire Club, a central piece of New York's kink nightlife back then, at 9th Avenue on 14th Street. 'It was the kind of place you could find yourself drinking a lot of beer then pissing on guys.' She'd usually wear leather because, 'You wanted something you could wipe off easily afterwards.'

She wrote about her adventures in *Penthouse* magazine, where she became a contributing editor in the mid-1980s. VV points out that she and her friends thought of themselves 'more as idealists than swingers. We believed that erotica could be part of the sexual revolution.' She was helped in her journey by the religion she was raised in. 'Catholicism turns guilt into an aphrodisiac,' she points out, before lamenting that New York has become too corporate to be any fun as a sex city. 'When you get into power, people stay more straitjacketed, because nobody wants to lose control.'

Just as Rome was supposedly the hotshot city but Pompeii was where all the kinky brothels were uncovered, VV insists that San Francisco runs rings around New York on the sex front. Her eyes shine as she talks of how San Francisco was the town evocative of the gold rush, bordellos and cowboys, as well as Miss Kitty, the saloon keeper from the 1960s TV show *Gunsmoke*, who had 'a bustle skirt, a plume in her hair and a heap of sass'. She quotes Annie Sprinkle, who believes that San Francisco is 'the clitoris of America'.

Now I know exactly where I'm headed.

FUEL FOR THE JOURNEY

I've written to Hadji, telling him that I'm going to write a book about masturbation. I don't quite know what I mean by this yet, but I know that there's some mystery I need to get to the bottom of.

Of course, there are complications. My one-night stand with Virginia has spilled over into a full-on affair. Lying by day in her bedroom as it snows outside feels like being in an opium den and I am stoned on love. I lie there after she's gone to work at the restaurant, lulled by the hiss of New York apartment radiators and the sight of the falling flakes outside. Snow, I write, is like love: beautiful, squally, slushy, relentless. You think it will never stop, but then one day it does stop. You're never sure when it will snow again.

Betty Dodson gives me short shrift when I email her about how I'm spending my days in New York. 'Stay in the moment, honey,' she warns. 'Don't project. If you want to talk about hot sex, the first three months is a pretty good run. If you're really good at it, you might make it stretch into a year.'

She's given me a copy of her memoir, *Sex by Design: The Betty Dodson Story*, and she seems very down on lovey-dovey stuff. A huge bee in Betty's bonnet at the masturbation weekend was the possessive and, *ergo*, evil nature of romantic love. 'It's brainwashing crap. A form of mental illness. Take a shit or jerk off. Have a nice stiff drink!' She launched into a warbly line from 'Some Day My Prince Will Come' followed by exclamations of 'Puke!' and 'Barfarama!' before returning to the matter in hand: her vulva ballet.

I admit I have started projecting a bit with Virginia. This morning in bed, she talked about buying a house somewhere rural in upstate New York. When she said it would be cheap enough to have a garden, I immediately imagined living there with her and growing lettuces. I suppose lettuce signifies security, because even I realise that a life of sex on the sly in restaurants has its limitations. Betty implies that I mustn't let the lettuce take over. 'Romantic love is the heaviest drug on the planet and we make permanent, long-lasting bad decisions because of it.' She concludes her email by warning that, 'Even with the best lover, it will become boring unless you have other partners.'

I'm not aware of waiting for my prince to come, but as a child I do remember thinking that my parents' story was very romantic. My mother came from a family of middle-class teachers and my father's parents were working-class people who'd made money in fish and chips during the Second World War. They met on a blind date and it was love at first sight. They moved to Cornwall, where my father set up his own fish-and-chip restaurant and for the first seven years of my life I lived above it with them and my two brothers. My poor mother, with her state-of-the-art Laura Ashley wardrobe and her *coupe sauvage* (Cornwall's only Vidal Sassoon-trained hairdresser resided in the locality), living above a chip shop. For me, a school uniform smelling of cold batter was a small price to pay for on-tap chips and banana splits and middle-aged waitresses telling saucy stories after the lunchtime rush. But they called each other 'darling' and they showed public affection. And whenever I saw my father, the back of his hands covered in fat splash blisters, stroking her frill-trimmed wrist, it was the most happy-making thing I'd ever seen.

Still, I can't deny that Betty's anti-romance angle is attractive. Although I've decided that solo sex is going to be the theme of my journey across America, I suspect that a prolonged period of masturbation will spill over into a desire for sex for two. Using Betty's logic, having sex with other people would be a political thing to do. A form of spring cleaning. Making sure I don't fall into the mental illness of monogamy.

Plans for the trip are slotting into place. A Facebook friend of a friend in San Francisco has offered to put me up for a couple of weeks and I've decided who my first two interviewees are going to be. The first is VV's friend, the cult superstar of every gender-studies student: Annie Sprinkle. The second is Joycelyn Elders, the first African-American Surgeon General of the United States, whose career was cut short by a masturbation scandal.

Annie is very friendly by email. The sixty-one-year-old says that when I get to San Francisco, she'll take me on an 'ecosexy tour of the hills with a masturbation twist'. I'm very excited to meet her. People always talk about her large breasts but, more interestingly, she was denounced by Republican senator Jesse Helms on the floor of the US senate in 1989 for her government-subsidised theatre show, where she re-enacted a 'sacred prostitute priestess masturbation ritual'. I think back to my breast-flashing at the Mama Gena weekend and wonder how much more energy must have been buzzing round the theatre during that performance.

Joycelyn Elders has an incredible story. She grew up picking cotton and was fired by Bill Clinton in 1994 for saying, while the AIDS crisis was still raging, that masturbation should be talked about in schools. This is ironic, as Clinton later used auto-eroticism to save his skin when his presidency ended with a scandal surrounding White House intern Monica Lewinsky. He insisted that he 'did not have sexual relations with that woman' because he sometimes masturbated his way to climax, so it wasn't real sex.

I buy a plane ticket to Arkansas, where Dr Elders lives. It's probably best if I leave New York by the end of January. For one thing, if I stick around here, I might lose my nerve. My mental freak-out list includes:

a) The fact that I haven't even sold this book yet. 'Brilliant!' my TV friend tells me. 'They call that "jeopardy" in the television world.'
b) I have twenty $100 bills in my suitcase to last me for my three-month trip.
c) Is it really a good idea to drive across America on my own? My friend in Cannes says, 'Wow, that's very daring of you. Have you seen *127 Hours*, where the man goes climbing alone in a canyon in Utah and has to cut his arm off?'

Luckily, there is an underlying malaise that goes even deeper. Even after Betty Dodson's workshop, I suspect that something's not quite right with my body. Like, why do I make fantasy scenarios in my head even when I'm having sex with Virginia? I'm never sure exactly how many people are in bed with me and her when we're together. The other day, I was sucking her clit ring as I was being penetrated by the cock of an ageing playboy who'd looked at me from a taxi at the lights in Times Square. And I've recently experienced the desire to be whipped. I've always liked it lightly on my butt, but now I like it harder and on my back too. Is this the 'dirty' sex, as opposed to the 'clean' sex that we used to talk about at my convent school? When the furious face of Mother Eugene fades out, it strikes me that flagellation is actually therapeutic. It wakes your body up and puts your mind to sleep. I can't think about next month's mortgage payment when a leather belt is demanding my attention. I'm convinced that there must be other ways to shut my mind off during sex. I tell myself that I need to make this trip to find out what they are.

Sometimes I talk to Hadji on the phone. He's being very good about my midlife crisis. If I was in a long-term relationship with a woman, there'd be a lot more drama. He seems to be doing his own getting-into-his-body thing by attending loads of tai chi courses. In some ways, he's more like a lesbian and I'm more like a gay man. I'm always ranting on about how it's really hard to get laid if you're a lesbian, while even in the smallest place in the world there are always gay ruins where men can have encounters at three o'clock on a February afternoon if they want. Hadji's not interested in this. He says, 'There's a lot of bad sex out there if you're a gay man. And I don't want a lot of bad sex. I want a little bit of good sex.'

I, meanwhile, am thrilled by the prospect of having loads of bad sex, although I feel a twinge of sadness when Hadji sends me emails from London telling me about things like the leek soup he's been cooking. Virginia sends me text messages saying she's fantasising about putting her cunt over my face. Both things I love, but sometimes it's exhausting having the two of them in my head.

I'm actually looking forward to beginning my trip because the high of the Betty Dodson workshop is starting to pale. Annie Sprinkle believes that when it comes to masturbation, there is the gourmet variety and the fast-food variety. Yesterday's 'homework,' as I'm now calling my experiments with solo sex, was definitely fast food. I got out my phone, logged into a free porn website called Xhamster and watched two pasty plumbers getting up to no good in a cheap hotel room. I'm not sure why I think they're plumbers. One of them paced the room nervously as he waited for his mate to finish doing the woman on the bed. It's moronic and it turns me on. My orgasm is a short, intense shudder.

I feel seedy afterwards. Like Elvis, lying in his bed surrounded by joint butts and cheeseburger wrappers. After Betty's workshop, I thought that I'd always have incredible orgasms. Xhamster is one of the sources of fuel for my burger grill. Categories include: Big Boobs, Interracial, Swingers, Lesbian, and Creampie, but I always go straight to the Amateur section. The people are not oil paintings, the men are working class (and I do like a plumber fantasy), but mainly I like the fact that the women seem to be into what they're doing. There are more genuine female orgasms and more normal embarrassing stuff: hair over the face, ridiculous expressions, embarrassing noises.

A recent scene was between a chubby Asian woman and a muscly black man. The Asian chick was making these tender, squeaking noises, which ideally you don't want to make and that you never hear in professional porn. You could tell that the black guy was affected by her authenticity, even though you suspect he'd never have admitted later to his mates in the pub that he'd been turned on in a weird, sexy way while shagging a big Korean girl in a Xhamster porn video.

The other fuel source comes via a taste I have for eighteenth-century pornography. I especially like the pictures that accompany the 1797 Dutch edition of the Marquis de Sade's *La Nouvelle Justine, or the Misfortunes of Virtue*. Unlike contemporary porn, eighteenth-century erotica leaves much up to the imagination while still managing to be very politically incorrect. The Sade pictures show acrobatic group sex in rococo drawing rooms; cages and winches and candelabra; priests inspecting female gash in disgusted awe; virile, bewigged gentlemen whipping piles of naked ladies – and all of it captured in the shadowy silence of a black-and-white engraving.

Still, while I can see that eighteenth-century porn might be considered more of a Jamie Oliver burger than a Big Mac, we're still talking fast food. Xhamster and the Marquis de Sade are certainly not tickets to the 'prolonged ecstatic state accompanied by the sensation of champagne bubbles dancing under the skin' that kink tantrica Barbara Carrellas promises in her book *Urban Tantra*. She's one of the final people on my list to talk to before I leave New York. I arrive too early outside her East Harlem apartment and as I walk along a stretch of virgin snow in front of her block, I go into a weird trance. It's one of those falling-between-the-cracks moments that sometimes happens when you travel: I walk along slowly, I look at the snow, I crunch my army boots into the white crystals. Just snow and boots and crunch. It's very restful.

When I finally buzz, the door is opened by a woman with pink hair and wacky glasses. She seems very confident. Another Catholic girl, she started out life as a Broadway theatre manager. She and her lover of the time, Annie Sprinkle, got into tantra during the height of the AIDS crisis of the 1980s, when sex equalled death. 'Tantra,' she says, 'raises its head every time the question is raised: there must be something more to sex.'

Her interest in sex was first piqued as a child on the day of her first Holy Communion. She'd been very excited about tasting the holy bread because, 'The nuns would get all flushed and excited. Talk about how the body of Christ was going to come into your body. I thought something magical was going to happen.'

But when the priest put the wafer on her tongue and nothing happened, she was furious. The only way she found comfort was climbing the maple tree in her backyard.

'I remember straddling rough bark in my underpants. The experience with the tree was far closer to feeling God inside me than any religious ritual had promised.'

The nearest I got to a maple tree as a kid was my weekly horse-riding lesson. My mother recently confided that I had horse-riding lessons instead of piano lessons because my parents couldn't afford both and, 'I didn't want you to be in your books all the time.' Meaning she wanted me to escape my head and remember my body. I was very moved when I heard this. Maybe if I'd had piano lessons instead of the horse lessons, I'd be in some chamber orchestra right now rather than writing a book about masturbation, but still. Riding a horse up a bank in the woods is a perfect way to discover the wonders of a clitoris. My hippie hairdresser friend says she never masturbated as a kid because she had a horse, and I can see what she means.

Barbara Carrellas did Betty's masturbation workshop back in 1990 and says it was a 'revelation', but the masturbation classes she teaches now have a very different emphasis.

'If Betty did one thing for the rest of her life, you know what it'd be: Bodysex and vibrators and clits. For a twenty-four-year-old, it's great to have a grandmother like Betty showing her what to do. It's about a lack of knowledge.'

But Barbara's clients are often older and feel they need 'another way in'. She and Annie Sprinkle developed something Carrellas now teaches, called 'energy orgasm'. This is achieved by breathing and no genital stimulation whatsoever. 'You're thinking of moving your energy up your body via your breath.'

She gives me a solo tantric exercise to try at home. She tells me to start masturbating ('use the truck-driver fantasy, whatever') to get almost to orgasm and then to 'breathe that "almost-orgasm" into your heart. Do it again. Get almost to orgasm and then breathe the almost-orgasm into your heart. Your heart will start to feel like it's orgasming. By the third time, let yourself come both in your clit and your heart.'

And that, apparently, is basic tantric sex in a nutshell. 'Because right there you've got breath, sensate focus and moving energy around the body.'

I take the subway back to Chelsea, wondering if I'll use plumber or trucker fantasies to get to almost-orgasm. Even thinking about these two options makes me feel uneasy. I would really like, one day, to be able to have an orgasm without having to conjure any tacky porn imagery in my head. Naomi Wolf claims in her book *Vagina* that porn desensitises your pussy, but maybe it's rather that it shrinks the imagination. Because at some point, you have to ask yourself: Is this really my fantasy or am I becoming addicted to someone else's dream world? When I told Betty that I worried about having dirty thoughts, not just when I masturbated but also when I was having sex, she told me not to worry. 'Fantasy focuses the mind,' she said. 'The dirtier, the filthier, the better.'

Even so, it strikes me that porn takes you away from your body, and I want my journey across America to be a trip into my own body. I determine to stay away from hamburgers and aim for something a bit more organic and healthy.

I have an early night with a view to trying out the heart wank first thing tomorrow.

ROADSIDE ASSISTANCE

But when I wake up the next morning, it feels as though there are nails spiking my Lamborghini tyres. I would cry if I didn't have to run out and interview a neuroscientist about female orgasms.

I take the train to New Jersey, trying not to notice the needle pain in my clit if I sit in the wrong position. God, I've forgotten how pain can bring you down. I had a particularly bad bout of this complaint ten years ago when I was about to turn forty. An alternately stinging, aching, throbbing, burning pain that didn't go away. It was very embarrassing going to the doctor, even though I knew a vulva was an organ just like a heart or a lung. And it's ironic that this is the morning I'm going to interview Dr Barry Komisaruk, seventy-three, a Bronx-born neuroscientist at Rutgers University, who has been studying female sexual pleasure since the 1980s.

The thing that fascinates Komisaruk is that many of the areas of the brain that light up when pleasure is experienced are the same areas that light up with pain. Which raises the question: what is the difference between pleasure and pain? 'There's some fundamental commonality between pain and orgasm,' he tells me in his office. 'Orgasm has a potent pain-blocking action. It's something I'm looking into.'

I sit in the chair, wondering if it would be rude to tell him about my on/off clitoris problem. Komisaruk is best known for his 'orgasm tapestries', where women lie in an MRI tube and masturbate until their orgasm illuminates different parts of their brain. There's a picture of one of the tapestries on the wall of his office. It looks like sexy curtains in some glamorous oriental brothel. He says that technology's not yet advanced enough to work out which neurons produce pleasure and which produce pain.

He is also known for his research showing that women with severed spinal cords can still experience orgasm via vaginal stimulation. This is due to the vagus nerve, which forms a direct pathway from the vagina and cervix to the brain, bypassing the spinal cord. He takes an interesting approach to diminishing pain: heightening pleasure. He has already discovered that the female pelvic nerve produces a peptide called vasoactive intestinal peptide (VIP), which is released into the spinal cord during vaginal stimulation. The peptide is also a pain blocker, specific chemical parts of it being more effective than morphine, and he's patented it.

Komisaruk is following a tradition of doctors who believe that orgasm contributes to female health. By the time of the Greek physician Galen (AD c. 129–200), manipulating a woman's vulva to orgasm had become a common treatment. Galen suggests rubbing a woman's genitals until she experiences what he describes intriguingly as 'the pain and pleasure' associated with coitus. By the nineteenth century, Jean-Martin Charcot was regularly bringing women to orgasm at the Salpêtrière hospital in Paris to rid them of 'hysteria', from the Greek word for uterus. Other doctors soon followed suit, the only problem being that many of them found vulval manipulation distasteful and time-consuming. Luckily, around 1880, the first electromechanical vibrator was patented by the

English doctor and inventor Joseph Mortimer Granville, and a whole masturbation industry sprang up. Doctors advised hysterical women to come in for treatment once a week for the equivalent of around £40 today.

But after the 1920s, vibrators went underground, not to re-emerge until the 1960s. This might have had something to do with their appearance in early porn films, changing their image from the medical to the sexual. And as Komisaruk knows, female sexual pleasure per se comes weighted with all sorts of taboos.

Yet if scientists can properly understand the way that the genital system gets to the brain, they can start to 'understand pathologies where there is a blockage. Say, in people who don't have orgasms – where their system is blocked and why.' Since I did this interview, Dr Komisaruk has published a paper about how the brain lights up when a woman is merely thinking about having an orgasm as opposed to physically stimulating herself or letting someone else do it. He's also published a follow-up to the original orgasm tapestries he did in 2012. The first study looked at arousal in the brain during orgasm, while the new study shows the difference in activity of specific brain regions at orgasm compared to their activity immediately before orgasm, i.e. it considers what the specifically 'orgasmic' brain regions are. Some regions become uniquely activated during orgasm. These include the angular gyrus and the operculum. The paper notes that the right angular gyrus has already been implicated in out-of-body experiences, suggesting that this is why people talk about altered states of consciousness when they try to describe what happened in bed last night.

Komisaruk is exasperated that enjoyable sex is still seen as a scurvy topic. 'Pleasure plays a crucial role in sustaining life. It ensures that life and species-preserving behaviours get performed. And yet there's virtually no research done on how pleasure is produced by the brain.'

There are apparently more than eighty structurally delineated regions of the brain. The ones I like the sound of are the hippocampus (responsible for memory and fantasy), the cingulate cortex and the insular cortex (especially activated by pain and orgasm), and the nucleus accumbens (a big player in pleasure). Komisaruk tells me not to get too obsessed with the pleasure side of things. That the brain isn't just some crazy playground. 'Inhibition is very important,' he underlines. 'Without inhibition our body movement would be spastic. For gracefulness and precision of movement you need inhibition. It's as essential as the brakes in a car.'

Yet in spite of all his pioneering work, he still has trouble securing grant money. 'Everybody wants to know about sex, apart from federal grant agencies,' he says with a sigh, explaining that the title of one of his grant applications was 'Vaginal Stimulation-Produced Analgesia'. He was told by the grant agency that he would only receive the funds he'd asked for if he changed the title.

'I said, "Let me guess."' He bit his tongue, though, and secured the funds by taking out the offensive word 'vaginal', and renaming the study 'Stimulation-Produced Analgesia'. 'I think the grant agency was concerned it might be accused of wasting taxpayers' money.'

Like Tiresias, the blind prophet, Komisaruk believes that the woman has the greater part of pleasure in sex. Tiresias had to live for seven years as a woman to discover this truth, but Komisaruk knows it simply because, 'Women have more genital sensory-nerve pathways than men.' And, *ergo*, more chances to malfunction.

He's delighted when I tell him I'm soon to meet Joycelyn Elders in Arkansas. 'Give her my best regards,' he says, brightening up. He adds that the Joycelyn Elders Chair in Human Sexuality has just been established at the University of Minnesota in honour of the rebel former government official.

I ask him if his research participants told him what their fantasies were in the MRI tube. When he says that one imagined her lover 'whispering sweet nothings in her ear', I mention the 2009 'Bonobo Porn' study by Canadian scientist, Meredith Chivers, about what really turns women on. Many of the women in Meredith's study claimed that it was 'sweet nothings', but thanks to vaginal sensors, it was revealed that they were really being aroused by . . . I can't remember the specifics.

'By . . . like, the idea of some big muscly plumber. That was really what turned them on.'

'The plumber?'

'Or some big muscly whatever. The point is that women often lie about what turns them on.'

I take the subway home, thinking about pleasure and pain and Annie Sprinkle's friend, Joseph Kramer, a San Francisco-based sex coach who teaches men how to masturbate better. Some men's pleasure becomes so great that they become frightened and interpret it as discomfort. Kramer believes that often it's not pain they are experiencing but rather a 'high erotic state'.

'Most people say, "I can't take it," and I'm like, "What can't you take?" What they mean is that they can't take the pleasure.'

I have an early night, weighing up plumbers vs. truck drivers as fantasies, but I fall asleep before I can decide. When I wake up the next morning, the needle pain in my clitoris has disappeared. Life's a doddle when pain stops. I remember how you forget about it at once and become almost ludicrously optimistic.

MEETING THE WIZARD

Before I leave for Arkansas to meet Joycelyn Elders, Betty Dodson invites me back to her apartment to hear my plans for the trip. I bring her a late Christmas present, but when she opens the pale blue Fortnum & Mason box containing two sugar mice, she growls, 'Sugar, huh? No wonder you Brits have terrible teeth.'

She puts the mice on the bookshelf next to her desk and over one of her famous 'stiff drinks' (vodka and pink grapefruit juice) that protect from the poison of romantic love, she tells me what she thinks of my interview candidates. She approves of Annie Sprinkle. 'She's great. She's got these humongous tits.' She likes Barbara Carrellas too, 'She's crazier than a loon.' She even OKs an organisation called the Raëlians, who believe that the aliens want us to masturbate. 'Frankly,' she says, 'I prefer the ET people to the Jesus people.'

The person she's suspicious of is Joycelyn Elders. 'She's going to be boring as shit,' she pronounces. Betty's line is that she has been talking about masturbation for fifty years, while Elders' comment, which sent headlines around the world, was 'a fluke'. Yet it strikes me they have a lot in common. Like Elders, Betty Dodson hails from the sticks. A dyslexic farm girl born in Wichita, Kansas, in 1929, Betty came to New York City in 1950 determined to become the world's greatest fashion illustrator. But fashion disappointed her and then she married an advertising executive called Frederick Stern, who turned out to be a chronic premature ejaculator.

Betty admits she was raised as a 'romance junkie' who grew up 'mainlining *Vogue* and *True Romance'*. Her teenage masturbation fantasies, she reveals in *Sex by Design: The Betty Dodson Story*, revolved around imagining herself with 'no fat, no acne, no braces on my teeth, perfect hair and a knockout of a nightgown'. Her orgasm would come when she dropped her nightgown to expose 'my naked loveliness for my husband'. She finally plucked up the courage to divorce Stern in 1965 and found herself, at the relatively late age of thirty-six, plunging into the world of sexual discovery.

She soon met a forty-two-year-old English professor from New York University, Grant Taylor, who, like her, was sexually starved after a bad marriage. 'He wasn't the most handsome, or virile or buff, but, oh God, he had a dirty mind.' The two of them began a sexual rollercoaster ride. Grant suggested she try his electronic scalp massager on her clitoris and reassured her that her inner asymmetrical labia weren't deformed, as she'd believed, by showing her some 'split beaver shots', fashionable in the porn mags of the day.

Betty doesn't strike me as a natural 'swinging from the chandeliers' type. At her first sex party in 1966, she nervously folded her new lace underwear under a chair ('a typical Virgo at an orgy') before venturing into the main room and having sex with a man who looked like Balzac.

Little did she realise how important the orgies were going to be. She hadn't yet discarded her original dream of becoming an artist. In the late 1950s, she'd put herself through the best art schooling available in New York City: the National Academy of Design and the Art Students League. In 1968, she made a spectacular New York debut with a show of gigantic heterosexual nude couples having sex. On the opening night Diane Arbus took pictures, *Women's Wear Daily* commented on Betty's 'dominatrix' outfit (Betty didn't realise back then that carrying a riding crop around with you has certain connotations) and within the first two weeks more than 8,000 people had flooded into the Wickersham Gallery next to the Whitney to see what the buzz was all about.

Buoyed up by success, Betty decided to put on a second show dedicated to masturbation. Friends said she was nuts, that the drawings wouldn't sell and when her dealer saw the massive pictures he would only agree to hang two of them. On the opening night, guests were greeted by a six-foot drawing of Betty's friend, legs apart, clitoris erect, approaching orgasm with her vibrator. The naysayers were right. The drawings didn't sell, her gallerist dropped her and Betty was labelled a pornographer, as opposed to an artist and a feminist speaking out for sexual liberation. But she looked on the bright side, calling it 'an invaluable experience in sexual consciousness-raising'.

She was already being drawn further away from art and towards the growing feminist movement. In 1970, she attended her first National Organization for Women (NOW) meeting, America's most popular feminist organisation of the time, founded in 1966. She had been excited to learn that the group's co-creator and her heroine, Betty Friedan, was going to address the crowd. When Friedan's *The Feminine Mystique* came out in 1963, it had given Betty the courage to remain committed to her art instead of becoming a mother. But, Betty notes in her book, she was horrified that day to learn how middle-class many of the women from the movement were:

> As she spoke, it gradually sank in that she was wearing gobs of makeup, had an elaborate hairdo, and was

dripping expensive jewelry. I'm not sure what I expected, maybe an Amazon with shining breastplate and a spear, anything but the wealthy-matron-from-Westchester look.

She reread *The Feminine Mystique* and was shocked to see that she'd forgotten about Friedan's views on women who enjoyed casual sex. Freidan refers to them as 'Peter Pans, forever childlike, afraid of ageing, grasping at youth as they searched for reassurance in sexual magic'. One by one, Betty's heroines began to topple. She was disgusted when Kate Millett's *Sexual Politics* came out later in 1970 on discovering that Millet had attempted to discredit the American writer Henry Miller by quoting the author of *Tropic of Cancer*, saying, 'The great artist is he who conquers the romantic in himself.' Betty agreed with Miller all the way on that one. Then, in the spring of 1971, she was invited to meet the movement's feminist star, Gloria Steinem, in her grand East Side apartment. Steinem was 'immaculately groomed' and the other women present struck her as 'Wall Street-wife types'. Betty felt she couldn't bring up sex in a setting like this.

But Steinem was intrigued by Dodson and in 1973 invited her to write about masturbation for *Ms.*, her new magazine, which had become the unofficial voice of feminism. Betty was thrilled, deciding to write the article in a 'hot feminist porn voice that would get *Ms.* readers beating off in abandon'. Steinem didn't go for it. She told Betty to 'tone down' the article and make it more academic. She said that while it was good for the feminist movement to have its own 'female Portnoy', Betty needed to appeal to a broader audience.

Betty was outraged to be likened to a 'female Portnoy'. Her message wasn't about feeling guilty at masturbating, like

Philip Roth's neurotic hero, but on the contrary revelling in it. She did tone the story down, but Steinem rejected it again, believing it to be too radical. Infuriated, Betty created her own pamphlet entitled *Liberating Masturbation*. She paid for the printing, packed up hundreds of copies in brown-paper envelopes and, in 1974, mailed them out to the housewives of America. Betty's instincts were right. There was a massive readership for un-fancified writing about female self-pleasure. In 1986 Random House bought up *Liberating Masturbation*, repackaging it as *Sex For One*.

Betty doesn't bear Steinem any grudges. She used to refer to her fondly as 'the General', although Gloria used to berate her, saying, 'Betty, I really wish you wouldn't call me that.' Betty sees her as a 'very shy woman who got thrown into the spotlight because she was beautiful and thin. And women worship beauty and thinness even more than men.'

She takes another slug of vodka. 'I think your trip sounds good,' she says. 'You're going to meet some good people.'

I tell Betty my idea about how the trip feels like setting out on the Yellow Brick Road. I add that I feel like the Cowardly Lion. I'm a Virgo too. Always forcing myself to be brave.

'I wouldn't use *The Wizard of Oz* as a metaphor,' she frowns. But I figure that Betty, like Dorothy, is from Kansas, so maybe that's why she's not into the idea. I ask her if prolonged masturbation homework is going to make me end up wanting to have sex with other people. Of course it is, she says. The secret, she reminds me, is not to get caught up in any of the 'romance shit'. She admits that it took her 'soul searching and bitter tears' to get to the point of enjoying sexual friends rather than one romantic lover at a time. At one point in the 1970s, she stuck a quote by Bertrand Russell on her kitchen wall to help her with her feelings when she and Grant decided to 'open up' their relationship.

The note, with changed pronouns, read:

Jealousy must be regarded not as a justifiable insistence upon one's rights but as a misfortune to the one who feels it and a wrong towards its object. When possessive elements intrude upon love, it loses its vivifying power. She who fears to lose that which makes the happiness in her life has already lost it.

It seems quite a Virgo way of dealing with jealousy, but I don't press Betty on this. Instead I whine, 'But Betty, I wish it was still the 1970s. You used to go to all those orgies and now there aren't any!'

'Sure there are,' she says, telling me she knows a woman who runs great events in San Francisco. She tells me to call them 'play parties' though, not 'orgies', because 'orgies' brings up ideas of sexist men and eating too much food. Then suddenly she seems hurried. I wonder if she has a 'play date'. Or a need to masturbate urgently. She accompanies me to the door, chuckling as I put on my leather coat, my army boots and my Russian black fur hat.

'So butch,' she drawls. Then she turns serious. She grabs a pink scarf from a peg on the wall. 'You want this?' She tells me it was made by Sheila Shea, her 'fuck-buddy friend' from the 1970s who helped her with the admin side of the original Bodysex workshops. My reaction is: scary pink scarf. But my instinct is to accept it. It feels like a good-luck charm to keep me safe on the road. Like the Good Witch of the North giving Dorothy the ruby-red slippers or Athena giving Perseus a polished shield on his way to slay the Medusa (although maligned, vagina dentata Medusa is going to be this trip's patron saint).

'Betty,' I say as an afterthought. 'Do you think that San Francisco is the clitoris of America?' Betty gives me a dirty look. 'San Francisco might be the clitoris,' she growls. 'But New York is the grounding dildo.'

With this piece of wisdom ringing in my ears and with a scratchy pink scarf wrapped around my neck, I step out into the Madison Avenue deep freeze.

BEDTIME STORIES

On my final day in New York, I lie on Virginia's bed, naked but for a pair of black lace knickers. Virginia is prepping for lunch over at the restaurant while I flick around in my head for a good story in what Betty terms the 'fantasy Rolodex'. Donatien Alphonse François, Marquis de Sade, had something similar, which he termed his *Almanach illusoire*, or a calendar that noted the frequency and quality of his forays into solo sex. By 1 December 1780, after two years and three months of imprisonment in Vincennes for crimes including sodomy and attempted prostitute-poisoning, he records 6,536 incidences of masturbation, or an average of eight a day.

I imagine that Sade's fantasies were quite precise if his prison-food shopping list is anything to go by. He'd fly into queeny rages if his wife, Renée-Pélagie, got anything wrong. 'The Savoy biscuit isn't at all what I asked for,' he fumes in a letter dated 16 May 1779. 'I wished it to be iced all the way around its surface, on top and underneath.'

This reminds me of an early fantasy I had about having sex with Donatella Versace. The frontal zip of her silver cocktail dress had to be four inches above her right knee before I could come. Right now, I'm trying to masturbate myself to almost-orgasm and then hold back, as Barbara Carrellas counselled. As always, once I get to the place when

I start to feel turned on, I relax. I think, *This is amazing. Why the hell don't I masturbate more often?* But then logistics start to complicate things. For instance, does the Iranian man from the bar need to have a shower before we go to bed? I passed a bar today where a man, Iranian maybe, was touching a woman he clearly didn't know on the exposed skin at the back of her dress. He reminded me of the fat Hogarthian repulsive that Betty has hung on the wall of her office. I put the dildo inside me. Just a bit. Just at the entrance. I gasp. I make myself wait. Slowly. And then I want more. A dildo makes you feel like you are being taken. Penetration is a big deal. It's easy just to do what Betty calls 'clit stim', when you're masturbating, but adding a dildo will take things up a notch.

I'm nearing the almost-orgasm stage, so I stop and scribble in near-illegible writing on a Post-it note pad by the pillow, 'Is there clean sex and dirty sex?' (I'm still not sure of the best way to record my 'research'.) Then I touch my body, slowly, feeling out the mood of my breasts, my belly, Pinky Tuscadero. When I lay my hands over my cunt, I make a deep sigh of relief. It feels safe to have my hands on my pussy. At times like these you realise that your cunt really is the centre of your body. I start stroking my clit. I do a bit of a vulva ballet and smell my hands. Lemon and cow parsley with a slight tang of urine, but I can't be bothered to get up and wash. I usually close my eyes when I masturbate. I keep them open now and look down at my – what do you call it – mons Veneris? A female sex body part with a name like something off the *Antiques Roadshow*. Like 'pudenda', meaning literally 'parts to be ashamed of'.

I notice those two grey hairs that I keep meaning to pull out. I think they look ugly. I was ashamed when I saw Virginia looking at them. But now we're all on our own, I don't mind.

I remember what Natasha said in Betty's workshop about how the hardest thing about masturbation is getting intimate with your own body. Virginia said I was 'very cuddly', which I wasn't sure if I liked. But now I can see I'd be nice to hold. I think of the sex I had with her, rubbing my face between her big breasts, getting turned on by the idea that this is a porny thing to do, that this is what men are allowed to do. The idea of being crushed to death by breasts. I feel my bum. A bit wobblier than I'd like, and I need moisturiser. As a child, when I used to experiment at nights, I'd feel the flesh on my hips and I'd think there was too much of it. That I'd have to lose that by the time I grew up or no man would want me. I'd been infected by that 1970s advert for Kellogg's Special K. 'Can you can pinch more than an inch?' the voiceover man asked a smiling wife as she brought her husband out his morning breakfast cereal. I recently learned that Dr John Harvey Kellogg came up with cornflakes in 1878 as a bland foodstuff intended to quell sexual desire in the young. At one point, he advocated applying pure carbolic acid to the clitoris of overexcitable girls if the breakfast cereal didn't do the trick.

And then suddenly the Iranian's in bed with me and the shower question comes up again. I can't decide, so I teletransport to the spaceship where the Raëlians hang out. I've been in email contact with a French woman called Nadine Gary, who describes herself as a Raëlian 'priestess'. She runs the Raëlian chapter in Lake Las Vegas. I imagine her as a beautiful Frenchwoman with a Brigitte Bardot accent on the spaceship with Raël himself. Wet. Wetter. I gasp from a place somewhere inside my vagina and behind my belly. The dildo slides in more easily, further in it goes and I remember why I'm bothering to perform this action while I could be out having a nice holiday in New York City.

I've seen pictures of Claude Vorilhon aka Raël from the 1970s. He wears space-age robes. Right now in my fantasy, he is wearing a Courrèges-style white satin tunic with geometric shoulders and Marilyn Manson eye make-up. He will be having a special Saturday-night UFO swingers' party. Beautiful Nadine with her Brigitte Bardot accent will say to me, 'I think you like sex. Let us have sex' (hopefully she won't say, 'Let's make love'). Then she'll go, 'Raël wants to meet you personally.'

The truth is that you never know what's going to happen in your head when you start to masturbate. It's like that challenge in *Masterchef* where the chefs lift the lid on a mystery box and find they have to make dinner from a tub of gherkins, some glacé cherries, a jar of peanut butter and a couple of crayfish. Who knows what will come out in the end? The only certainly is that whatever does emerge in the privacy of your head shouldn't be thrown in the bin. It might not win a TV show, but you should look on it as your own personal masterpiece.

This particular 'homework' session begins with an engraving from the 1797 Dutch edition of Sade's *La Nouvelle Justine, or the Misfortunes of Virtue*. Back in London, I snapped a few of them with my phone from my copy of the Taschen *Erotica Universalis*. In this one, a monk at an altar sucks the anus of a naked girl in an elaborate wig as a young man prepares to mount the monk from behind. Above them is a statue of Mary and the baby Jesus with his arm outstretched as if he wants to join in too. I wonder if my convent-school education is responsible for my taste in this kind of anticlerical porn. If Betty got her sex education from split-beaver shots in porn magazines of the 1970s, then 1 Corinthians was my first *Erotica Universalis*. The salivary way dear Sister Angela pronounced 'homosexual perverts' and 'sexual immorality' just left you wanting more.

Convent-school girls develop particularly fertile fantasy lives. It's not so much about fancying nuns (yuck), it's more about the pervading atmosphere of fear and darkness courtesy of flocks of old women in black robes hovering in every corridor, infecting every corner of your mind. A convent girl develops interesting fetishes because tiny things are deemed worthy of being sent to hell for – for example, peeing into the snow on the hockey pitch – and imagine what constant rumours of blue knicker inspections do to a young girl's head. Scaly old-lady fingers flicking up the side of a kilt, furious eyes bearing down on the 'parts to be ashamed of' in the lugubrious light of Mother Eugene's office. It is clear to me why Catholic girls later go on to become so good in bed (a theory of mine). The first time I ever slept with a woman, I was extra-thrilled by wondering what the nuns would say.

It was a girl at the convent who taught me about the power of an exposed vulva. Even at seven, she was acting like a brunette Courtney Love. One lunchtime, on dreaded stew and lettuce day, she sat in the dining room, feet on her chair, kilt hitched high, thighs sprawled apart, heels of her outdoor shoes (deducted house points right there) wedged against a pubis covered in non-regulation floral nylon. The sneer on her lips dared the nuns to try and make her eat her disgusting lunch and, incredibly, they didn't. The miracle of the flashed crotch. More thrilling than the threat of underwear inspection was the sight of that floral nylon-clad pussy, positioned in flagrant rejection of every 'ladylike' convention we'd ever been indoctrinated with. At that moment in the dining room, the naughtiest girl in the school became the most powerful girl in the school.

When I got home, I sat on an armchair in front of *Blue Peter*, my legs splayed and my genitals pointing straight at the TV like some seven-year-old Patpong bar girl in Bangkok about to shoot table-tennis balls. I was aware of a warmth, a force coming from this newly discovered part of my body. I couldn't quite put my finger on why what I was doing was bad, but I knew it was. My regulation blue gusset seemed to be growing in size and importance, becoming bigger than the room, taking over the room, turning the room brighter and lighter but more blurry and distorted until it was impossible to concentrate on *Blue Peter*.

I realised that if I slid down in the chair and opened my legs wider, the feeling became even more thrilling. I was gradually moving into nineteenth-century French neurologist Jean-Martin Charcot's famous arched-back posture of hysteria, which we'd call today the sexual climax position. My mother started coming into the lounge more frequently, looking suspiciously at Valerie Singleton telling you how to make an Action Man bed out of a shoebox. She finally turned to me and said, 'Stephanie, put your legs together.' It was a light admonition, as if I'd made a slip-up with my table manners.

The 'down-there' mystery was reopened later that summer when I found myself in a hollowed-out bramble bush on the banks of the hockey pitch with some school friends. The hot, prickly tent held the sound of bees, the smell of musky grass, the sight of blue summer dresses pulled up to the waist, blue knickers around ankles. Six *Doctor Who* mini monsters. Exposure was actually not that easy – you had to be good at crouching. Fern showed hers first. She had something white in hers. Emma and I both had one hair each on our outside bit. Then someone said she didn't want to show hers and that broke the spell. We ran out of the bush, up to Miss Corbett, my favourite teacher, who was patrolling the hockey pitch that day as she conducted a nature walk. I felt extraordinarily bumptious as Miss Corbett started pointing out pink campions and buttercups and cuckoo spit to the other girls and thought excitedly, *We must never do that again!*

The tuned-in people in the 'Century of Lights', as the eighteenth century was known in France, saw pornography as progressive because erotica in France was frequently anticlerical. Most liberal gentlemen of the eighteenth century – the Marquis de Sade's priest uncle, for instance – had libraries stocked with seventeenth-century favourites (Molière, Racine), major texts of the Enlightenment (Hobbes, Montesquieu, Rousseau), erotic classics such as Aretino's *Postures*, and more contemporary 'philosophical' erotica. This consisted of lurid sex scenes followed by serious pillow talk about hedonism, the corruption of the Church and the liberating power of reason. It's a great mix, actually. You're drowning neither in smut nor philosophy. Bestsellers included *Venus in the Cloister* and, one of Sade's favourite salacious reads, *Thérèse the Philosopher*, attributed to the Marquis d'Argens in 1748.

In a Catholic country like France, transgression of sacred boundaries assured maximum titillation and explains why nunneries and church property were usually the backdrop for debauches. The eponymous teenage heroine of *Thérèse the Philosopher* has her sexual appetite whetted when she spies a lascivious priest flagellating her friend Eradice before fucking her doggy-style with the 'venerable rope' that holy Saint Francis wore around his habit. Sometimes I find these dynamics even more exciting than two Xhamster plumbers grunting away in the Premier Inn.

Wielding his rope-dildo relic, the priest tells Eradice that to achieve spiritual ecstasy with God she needs to forget her body by submitting to his 'mortification exercises'. Yet although he has told Eradice that he's using the 'venerable rope', to mortify her with, Thérèse, from her vantage point, sees that the priest is actually using his 'red snake'. The difference is academic to the unsuspecting Eradice, who pants, 'I see . . . the angels . . . harder . . . don't stop . . . I feel the ro-ro-rope . . . I can't hold back . . . I am . . . dying.'

This scene nearly always turns me on, but today, here in Virginia's bed, the *Masterchef* mystery box inexplicably diverts me to the Raëlian spaceship swingers' party. Many of my friends have told me how lucky I am to be able to drive around America being creative, but actually, masturbation fantasies make Marquis de Sades and J. K. Rowlings of us all. I halt the dildo motion momentarily to work out what the inside of the spaceship looks like. Shiny? Are there beds? With relief, I suddenly see a bowl of fruit in the middle of the spaceship's dining table. Some fancy knives and forks on the table. Then I'm lying on Nadine. Maybe. Someone faceless with big breasts, in any case, and then the breasts fade out and a pasty, wobbly male belly comes into focus under me. Hairy, a cock. And then suddenly there's the Iranian and Raël and the Brigitte Bardot woman until my head is a carousel of scenes and images glittering unstoppably past. I pull myself up; I breathe a tube of air from my pussy to my heart, just like Barbara Carrellas told me. I struggle to ignore the double bacon cheeseburger being waved at me and strain to wait instead until the tofu stir-fry is properly cooked.

I'm so close now. To the summit. The edge. Fuck the organic stir-fry. The feeling is so intense, the feeling of giving up your kingdom for such a sensation compressed into a few seconds and I can't stop what's coming . . . coming . . . the holy relic, the ro-ro-rope . . . I can't hold back . . .

Twenty seconds later, I feel like crap. Like I've been on a diet and then binged on a load of chocolate at the end of the week. I feel sticky and grubby. Something warm vibrates under my bum. It's a text from Virginia. 'Hey, what's going on? Busy day?'

A SCARLET LOVE SEAT

I'm shocked when I walk into arrivals at Little Rock airport. America's first black Surgeon General isn't the bold pulpit preacher I thought I was going to meet. She is a smiling figure in glasses, wrapped in a bobbly fleece blanket. She beams as she walks slowly over and helps me with my suitcase, and soon she's talking about the turnip greens and the black-eyed peas – which signify good luck – that she had with her family on New Year's Day just a few days ago.

It's an interesting conversation, but I'd half hoped she'd be standing on the luggage-reclaim conveyor belt proselytising about self-pleasure. I worry if this nice lady is going to want to talk about women slithering round in bed, rubbing their genitals to climax.

My plane was delayed and it's now after ten at night. It's very kind that she and her husband, Oliver, have come to pick me up at this late hour. When we get to the car, Oliver says a polite hello and starts the engine. They're both in their eighties, so I decide to stay formal. I've just finished Dr Elders' autobiography, *Joycelyn Elders, M.D.: From Sharecropper's Daughter to Surgeon General of the United States of America.* She is the eldest of eight children born to a poor Arkansas farming family, and I learned that her father used to shoot raccoons, which her mother would turn into stew to feed the family. Joycelyn and her brothers and sisters had to combine work in the cotton fields from the age of five and education in a segregated school thirteen miles from their home in the impoverished farming community of Schaal.

When she was fifteen, Elders won a scholarship to an all-black college, Philander Smith, but the day before she left, her brothers and sisters had to pick cotton all day to help pay for the $3.46 bus fare. I tell her now that one of my favourite parts of the book is about the chewing-gum tree, a tree in Arkansas whose trunk she and her brothers and sisters would extract gum from. 'Oh yes,' the eighty-one-year-old says, as if the memory brings her pleasure. 'My brothers and sisters called that the sweet-gum tree.'

There's a silence, so I fill it with, 'It was freezing when I changed planes in Chicago.'

'I know, how do people survive in that cold?' Dr Elders says, shaking her head.

'You'd get a hat,' I assert, then worry that I sound like a bimbo.

Luckily, Oliver thinks this is a good idea. 'Yes,' he says, slowly. 'You'd get a hat.'

I tell Dr Elders that I'm glad to have caught her before she flies off to Florida the day after tomorrow.

'I'm going for the Trojan conference,' she says.

'Trojan?'

'You know,' she says. 'They do condoms and lubricants. Vibrators. It's one of the best boards I've been on.'

I sit back and watch the night speed past the windows. Clearly there's more to Dr Elders than meets the eye.

They used to say that masturbation kills, and it certainly killed Joycelyn Elders' career. Having struggled to 'get out of the cotton patch,' as she calls it, she fought her way into the University of Arkansas for Medical Sciences. She had been inspired by a talk while still at Philander Smith from African-American physician Edith Irby Jones, the first non-segregated African-American student to attend that educational establishment in 1948. After graduating in 1960 and going on to earn a master's degree in biochemistry, Elders launched herself onto a pioneering career path, combining clinical practice with research in paediatric endocrinology. In 1987, Arkansas Governor Bill Clinton appointed her the director of the Arkansas Department of Public Health. She was so successful, almost doubling childhood immunisation rates, expanding the state's prenatal care programme, increasing home-care options for the chronically and terminally ill and bringing down teenage pregnancy by 15 per cent that in 1993, the by then President Clinton asked her if she would be his Surgeon General.

After only a few months into the job, on 1 December 1994 at a United Nations conference on World AIDS Day, she was asked by a New York psychologist, Dr Rob Clarke, if she thought masturbation could protect young people from riskier activity. This was a time when AIDS was still raging. According to the National Center for Health Statistics, more than 1 million US citizens had become HIV-positive by 1994 and 300,000 had died – 40,000 in that year alone. Dr Elders replied, 'I think that it is something that is part of human sexuality and it is a part of something that perhaps should be taught.'

It's a shame she didn't say taught 'about', because the *New York Times* reported her remark as a suggestion to actually teach children how to masturbate. A few days after the conference, a furious President Clinton demanded her resignation. Little did he realise that masturbation would soon become a central narrative in his own downfall.

The Elders' bungalow is set in a secluded expanse of pine woodland on the outskirts of Little Rock. The house is very long (thirty-two paces from the kitchen to my bedroom) and filled with all manner of knick-knacks. There are ornamental dolls everywhere, as well as various figurines and statuettes: a Hindu goddess here, a Japanese dragon there, a gold Cupid in a basket of plastic flowers, Amadeus Mozart in a powdered wig, a black rag doll in a red gingham dress with 'Prissy' embroidered on its crisp apron.

We gather around the kitchen table and dinner is home-made meat loaf with broccoli, which Dr Elders puts on the table, saying bluntly, 'We all help ourselves here.' She adds, almost sternly, something about how she dislikes serving people and it's one of the few inklings I get of the straight-talking side that Elders was known for during her working life.

Religious conservatives dubbed her the Condom Queen because of her avowed priority to cut Arkansas teen pregnancy rates, at the time some of the highest in the world, by creating sexual-health clinics in schools where condoms would be available. One of her many moments of notoriety came when she accused the pro-life movement of having 'a love affair with the foetus'.

I help myself to a baked potato as the quietly humorous Oliver comments on the basketball game on the kitchen TV. He's famous in these parts for his career as a distinguished basketball coach. 'Can't teach talent, can't teach sass,' he says and then conversation turns back to living with a firebrand wife. 'Oh yes, my wife has opinions,' Oliver says with an ironic raised eyebrow.

Dr Elders elaborates. 'The day I was introducing the idea of the health clinics in schools to my cabinet in Arkansas, everyone was half asleep,' she recalls. 'Someone asked me would I have condoms in these clinics and I said, "Well I'm not going to put them on the kids' lunch plates, but yeah!" And so all of a sudden everyone woke up.'

She looks over to her husband with a smile. 'I told Oliver what I said about the condoms and the lunch plates and he said, "Sug! You didn't say that!"'

Oliver shrugs. 'My line was always, "You know my wife and you know what she feels about young people."' And with that, he turns back to the game on the television.

We arrange to start the interview tomorrow morning at nine and I retire to my bedroom, which is decorated with a collection of Victorian dolls. On one wall is a fantastic pencil drawing of a Buffalo soldier with dreads holding a rifle as he looks slyly askance. A clock that doesn't work is decorated with postage stamps showing different African-American heroes. Some I've heard of, most I haven't: Martin Luther King Jr, Harriet Tubman, Sojourner Truth, Jackie Robinson, Jean Baptiste Point du Sable, Mary McLeod Bethune, Carter G. Woodson and Ida B. Wells.

Back in the kitchen the next morning, I'm greeted by the spectacle of a floral kaftan going up in smoke. It's actually a pan of burning bacon and Dr Elders, clad in an eye-catching robe, is tut-tutting at her clumsiness. She smiles when she sees me. 'My friend Barbara will get on to me about this,' she says. 'She was always better at entertaining than me.' I tell her that I like her colourful kaftan. She does look good in it. She says that Barbara Kilgore, her friend, will be coming round later to drive us to lunch. Barbara is seventy now and a Methodist minister, although they met when they were both medical researchers back in the 1970s. 'We were planning to write a book together, called *The Dreaded "M" Word*,' Dr Elders says. 'It was after I was Surgeon General.'

I sit at the kitchen table and admire the lazy Susan, which holds a huge array of condiments that look as if they've not been used in a while. It's like the rest of the house. On the way to the kitchen this morning, I passed one formal sitting room done out in adventurous colonial style, followed by another in high Victorian decadent, containing the most beautiful object in the house, a button-backed love seat upholstered in scarlet velvet. It's something you might have found in a Parisian bordello frequented by Bertie, the playboy Prince of Wales. You can see that the high life doesn't come naturally to Dr Elders. It's clear nobody ever goes into either of these rooms and certainly, the only person who seems to have ever sat on the scarlet couch is another imperious-looking Victorian doll clad in emerald green. On the walls of this room are framed copies of faded magazines. The *Arkansas Business* from 7 December 1987 shows Elders with shoulder pads and a gauche smile above the headline: 'Joycelyn Elders, the physician of the State Health Department, is girding herself with "a tough skin and a bright outlook".' There's group shot of the fourteenth, fifteenth (Elders), sixteenth and seventeenth US Surgeon Generals in their gold-braided uniforms standing next to Lance Armstrong. A family shot of Dr Elders, Oliver and their sons. Eric has a female partner and Kevin, the younger son, is with a smiling white man in glasses. There's a black-and-white picture of her parents as young beaux. Posed in front of a cotton field in their Sunday best, he stands with his arm draped awkwardly around her, while she looks confident, a half-smile on her lips and a steely look in her eyes.

Dr Elders moves slowly around the kitchen. I haven't seen much evidence of her 'tough skin' so far. There's a definite formality to her, which may be a clever way of keeping people at a distance. But she's keen to give me the low-down about her native state. It's a cross, she says, between the American South (Memphis is only an hour's drive away) and the Midwest. She adds that it's very swampy in the summer (lots of mosquitoes) and cold in the winter. It's home to the recluse, the most poisonous spider in America, and the headquarters of Walmart, and it's the birthplace of Bill Clinton. Little Rock is also the location of the shocking story that became known as 'the Little Rock Nine'.

A pivotal event of the civil rights era, the year was 1957 and nine African-American children demanded their right to be educated alongside their white contemporaries. In 1954, the Supreme Court had ruled that segregated schools were unconstitutional, yet racist business was pretty much carrying on as usual. The children had been specially selected and primed by Daisy Bates, the president of the Arkansas branch of the National Association for the Advancement of Colored People (NAACP) on how to deal with the uproar that was sure to follow the action. And uproar there was. The hullabaloo around the Little Rock Nine kick-started the desegregation of high schools in America.

I ask her if I should call her Joycelyn or Dr Elders, although instinctively I want to call her Dr Elders. 'You call me what you like,' she says. She comes over with the burned bacon and toast. I want to get her relaxed, so I ask her about her mother's raccoon stew. 'Nobody cooked raccoon like my mother,' she says, adding that the meat has a taste between deer and turkey. She says that aside from sharecropping, where you get to work the land in return for giving some of your crops back to the land owner, her father made extra money hunting possum, squirrel, rabbit, deer and raccoon. 'The aim of poor people was to be able to get a fur coat,' she explains.

When I ask what her mother's raccoon recipe was, there's sudden pride in her voice. 'Well, she parboiled it and then she put it in the oven with sweet potatoes and onions and green pepper and she roasted it.'

The raccoon stew has cast a spell. Dr Elders finally comes to sit down at the table. She tells me that her mother made sure that Joycelyn knew her alphabet and her numbers in order that she should, 'get out of the cotton patch'. Her mother had a switch but 'she didn't need to use it often'. Although Elders would rise to become the leading doctor in the land, she didn't meet a physician until she was sixteen years old. She'd heard about them, though. One day as a child, she watched her father set off to a white doctor twelve miles away with her dying little brother strapped to a mule. The hospital wouldn't take him in because he was black, but the doctor sent him back to the farm with a tube in his belly to drain the poison (he had a burst appendix), which saved his life. Elders doesn't speak rancorously about this. 'I was glad the doctor saved my brother's life.' Still, the sex education her mother gave her daughter was non-existent. 'I got my period when I was twelve. I thought I was dying.'

Then, without me asking, she dives in. She says that her first real memory of masturbation was . . . watermelons.

'We grew great big watermelons and I remember really feeling and . . . laying on the watermelons and rubbing up against the watermelons . . .'

'Cut open or still whole?' I don't want to probe too much for details, but still.

'It was still whole. I was around twelve years old. That's the first time I had true masturbation. You know. I won't say I never touched myself prior to that or . . . but . . .'

That's the best masturbation story I've heard yet. In the process of becoming an educated black woman in America, Dr Elders clearly had a lot to rebel against. While she was studying at the University of Arkansas for Medical Sciences, she'd had to eat in the dining room reserved for cleaners. But to rebel in such a taboo way: to champion female sexual liberation when she could have been much more discreet about it. I find her watermelon revelation utterly moving. Where does she think her rebel soul came from?

'I guess I never thought of myself as having a rebel soul,' she says with a smile. 'But I understand the question.'

She thinks for a moment and concludes that her mettle began to form in her thirties, when she worked as a doctor in Arkansas in the late 1960s. Specifically when she started visiting the poor eastern area of Arkansas known as the Delta. The countless young pregnant girls without hope put her in mind of slavery.

'I'd be seeing these teenage girls who had been sexually abused. People were giving them a hard time, but often they'd gotten pregnant by their fathers or grandfathers or uncles. I saw them as poor, ignorant and enslaved for the rest of their lives. I couldn't sleep at night. I was just so upset.'

She pushes the toast plate away. 'I think maybe I got radicalised then.'

Black ministers at her church stopped speaking to her when she set up the condom clinics in Arkansas schools. One refused to shake her hand and talked of condom use being akin to 'black genocide'. But she says she had a 'good working relationship' with Clinton. He knew and appreciated her blunt ways. 'I was always coming out and saying things.'

Her first impressions of Bill Clinton were of a 'young, smart, handsome white man. Very intense. You didn't think he was talking to you and thinking of someone else. That might not have been true, but still.'

Upon her appointment as Surgeon General in December 1993, she caused a stir by suggesting that the legalisation of marijuana should be studied. 'So many young black men were being criminalised forever,' she tells me. 'We were spending billions on prisons and I thought, "You could send them to Harvard."'

Her comments were taken to task when, days later, her son Kevin was arrested for selling cocaine and sentenced to ten years in prison, of which he served four months. 'It was just . . . very devastating.'

And then came the famous United Nations conference on World Aids Day 1994. She gave a talk on what she tells me was, 'The ABCD of AIDS prevention. A is Abstinence, B is Be faithful, C is use a Condom and D is Do other things. I was referring to masturbation.'

Nothing much happened after she'd made her slightly hesitant answer to the psychologist's question about whether masturbation should be promoted as a safe alternative to sex. But the New York journalist who had been writing a story on her warned her at the airport that night that she was going to be a problem for the Democrats. 'He said it was because of my attitudes.'

Sure enough, a week and a half later, she received a summons from Donna Shalala, Clinton's secretary of health. The following year, the Lebanese-American would be described by the AIDS activist and author of *The Normal Heart*, Larry Kramer, as 'evil' for her failure to responsibly address the AIDS crisis. Standing in front of Shalala in her office, Elders was asked if she had talked about masturbation at the UN conference. When a puzzled Elders replied that she had, Shalala went ballistic, repeating the phrase, 'That's a real problem.' The secretary of health had advised Clinton not to appoint Elders in the first place.

'She was giving me her usual lecture,' Elders recalls. 'She goes, "We've been having so many problems with the things you've been saying."'

Shalala passed her on to Leon Panetta, the notoriously scrappy White House chief of staff, who barked at Elders that she needed to resign in writing. Elders said she had no intention of doing that until she'd spoken to the president herself. She still considered what she had said to be 'trivial' and that Clinton would back her up. But in a phone call later that day, President Clinton proved he wasn't the ally she'd hoped.

'He was storming mad. He goes, "Joycelyn, we've just had all the outspoken stuff from you. I need your resignation on Panetta's desk by two-thirty this afternoon."'

She was 'surprised' when Clinton asked her to resign but concedes now, 'You know, I just didn't understand Washington politics.' She tells me I need to remember that, 'Before I got to be Surgeon General, I was a research scientist killing chickens and rats, so I was always thinking science. I was the Surgeon General for the American people and it was my responsibility to make sure they were informed. And if masturbation would protect them from AIDS, then it was my duty to make sure they were prepared.'

She picks up the dirty breakfast dishes from the table, saying she doesn't hold a grudge against Clinton. 'I never felt that Clinton disagreed over anything I was saying. I feel he did what he felt was most politically correct for all of the people. And he felt that the people weren't at that page yet.'

And if she were Surgeon General today?

'If I had it all to do over again, I would say the same thing,' she says emphatically.

She mentions that a few years ago Oliver saw Clinton at a social event in Arkansas and 'he told him, "I thought your wife was right"'.

She doesn't believe she'd have been fired under Obama.

'I think Obama would feel that this is scientific fact and principle. That we aren't going to go round firing Surgeon Generals.'

The good news is that America has got to the masturbation page at last. Elders says it's strange, but at the age of eighty-one, she's suddenly fashionable. After she left the Surgeon

General's office, people wouldn't say anything to her in public 'for four or five years'. And then suddenly it changed. One time, she was in Little Rock putting fuel in her car at a gas station when a woman's voice came over the loudspeaker saying, 'Way to go, Dr Elders!'

Respect for her seems to grow as the years pass. She mentions the new Joycelyn Elders Chair in Human Sexuality at the University of Minnesota, which Barry Komisaruk told me about. She was there just last month. 'It was a summit to educate doctors in human sexuality. Doctors still only get five hours of lectures on all of human sexuality in their four years of medical school.'

She says she was 'very flattered' about the chair because it's the first American university to have a human sexuality course. And she's often being called on to speak at women's conferences. In 2016 she was inducted into the Arkansas Women's Hall of Fame as emeritus professor of paediatrics and distinguished professor of public health for the University of Arkansas for Medical Sciences (UAMS). She's met Barbara Carrellas and Annie Sprinkle. She admits that many of the speakers are 'kind of out there for me' but that they're always 'very nice. I enjoy it very much.'

And then of course there are the Trojan responsibilities. She says she's still sexual, 'Although not as sexual as I was five years ago, even.' Luckily, there are perks to being on the Trojan board. 'Trojan makes good vibrators. They keep you well supplied!'

And how does she feel about her legacy? About being inexorably associated with masturbation?

'I guess it was like when I was known as the Condom Queen. I said at that time that I don't mind being the Condom Queen, and I would put it on my head and sleep in one if everybody who needed to use one used it.'

She's still as unrepentant about masturbation as she is about condoms. 'If people were masturbating then we wouldn't have a lot of the sexual diseases we have, the child abuse, the teenage pregnancies. You can relieve your sexual anxiety in other ways and probably enjoy it even more.'

So there you go. Joycelyn Elders isn't as boring as shit. She may live in a more traditional domestic manner than Betty, but she's just as revolutionary because she had such a high profile in mainstream establishment politics.

'We would have a sexually healthier world if women were taught about their genitals and auto-eroticism,' she goes on. 'I think they'd have a much healthier satisfying life if they realise they're not put here on earth just to be a vessel for the male sperm to hatch a baby. Ninety-nine per cent of healthy sexuality is about pleasure, and women have a right to pleasure.'

There's a knock at the door and her Methodist minister friend Barbara enters. Barbara is a lively white woman who's been married to a black preacher for over forty years and has had a crash course in prejudice from whites and blacks alike. Her high-society mother went spare. Luckily she's got dementia now. 'She's forgotten why she hates me,' Barbara deadpans. She believes that her friend getting fired was 'a good thing for masturbation and reproductive rights because it kind of challenged people to take a position. At the White House they said they'd never received so many calls to complain about a person being removed from office. They just looked silly.'

They both chuckle. And then it's time for lunch. Barbara drives, pointing out sights on the way such as Horace Mann, the school where the gym is named after Oliver. She says she's not sure what the traffic will be like in town, as today is the inauguration of the new Governor of Little Rock. They both apologise for the fact that he's a Republican. They're so depressed about it that they can't even remember what his name is.

I follow Dr Elders' lead at the restaurant we go to and order black-eyed bean soup. Conversation alternates between why 'hog's jaw' is auspicious to eat at New Year ('you mustn't eat chicken because they root backwards, but a pig looks forwards') to the degree the waitress, a friend of Barbara's, has. It's a degree in developmental psychology: 'She knows about babies masturbating in the womb,' Barbara says approvingly.

After lunch, we arrive at the Little Rock Central High School Museum and I learn more about the Little Rock Nine. There are some great pictures: the beautiful Daisy Bates sitting on a lawn surrounded by her young student crusaders, a snarling redneck mob jeering behind one of the young students, Elizabeth Eckford, as she walks towards the school in a crisp, ankle-length gingham dress, wearing shades and clutching her books. She looks like a cool dude, but she must have been terrified. One white woman's face, contorted with venom, looks as if she's about to hiss something foul into Elizabeth's ear.

Barbara is getting passionate, saying how terrible that time was. Yet the one black person in the museum is Joycelyn Elders and she's not talking at all. She walks from picture to picture, nodding almost imperceptibly as she passes by, as if they're well-known photos in a family album she doesn't take out much.

I ask her if she went on any anti-racism marches in 1957. 'I knew a couple of the Little Rock Nine children,' she says. Then she confides, 'You know, I was busy trying to survive medical school at the time.'

This is a clue to the phlegmatic reality behind Joycelyn Elders' intrepid public persona. It reminds me of that phrase attributed to Oliver Cromwell, the controversial seventeenth-century English military and political leader. 'Keep your gunpowder dry,' he urged his army. Meaning, don't use up your resources until you absolutely have to.

One of my favourite parts of the day is when we get back home and I ask Dr Elders if she'll show me what a turnip green is because we don't eat them in England. Barbara has told me that her friend absolutely loves her garden and it soon becomes clear that while Dr Elders is no longer a poor farm girl, the things she observed during that time have helped forge her backbone. 'I'm just like my mother,' she said once in an interview. 'She always had to have enough greens in the garden in case someone needed any.' The day of her mother's funeral, Elders was out in the garden picking greens for the mourners.

And so, in the chilly evening, the two of us walk over to a large plot of vegetables. 'Get that one,' Dr Elders says, pointing with her stick to a patch of straggly leaves. I pull up a radish-sized pink and white turnip that makes me think of the unfamiliar names on the black history clock. Turnip greens are leaves on turnips. They're the bits that most people throw away. Today, you can find them in posh American restaurants, but back in the time when African Americans picked cotton, you'd eat them, like you would raccoons, because you couldn't afford anything else.

In any case, the greens we eat that night are certainly not mere greens. They taste like sour spinach, although the fresh, crunchy heart of the turnip itself is my favourite thing I get to eat in Arkansas. Dr Elders cuts off a small piece for me and herself, and Oliver then puts the rest back in the fridge as if it's a white truffle.

It's a weird teatime. We eat cornbread, white beans and various pieces of pork. Oliver is apologising that there was no catfish to be had today (foolishly I'd mentioned that I'd like to try some) and then an item comes on the TV about a 'Muslim-free rifle range'. A father and son were turned away from a rifle range in Hot Springs, Arkansas, but the father claimed this was unfair because he is actually a Hindu. I almost choke on my cornbread. Jan Morgan, the blonde owner of the range, the Gun Cave, is claiming the pair were exhibiting 'strange behaviour'. She's foxy in an Arkansas sort of way. She makes me think of the photo of the white woman screaming into the ear of Elizabeth Eckford at the Little Rock Central High School Museum. The next item is about the Golden Globes. Celebrities are standing on a red carpet wearing T-shirts that read 'Je Suis Charlie'. The mix of the redneck and the politically correct is mind-boggling. I wonder what the locals are making of it as they tuck into their ham hock and cornbread on the day the right-wing governor got elected into Little Rock.

I ask Oliver about the red velvet couch in the Victorian room. He says it belonged to his father, who spent too much on fine things he couldn't afford. I ask if anyone has ever sat on it. 'Has anyone ever sat on that couch, sug?' Oliver turns to his wife with ironic eyes. Dr Elders doesn't think so. He turns back. 'I don't think they ever have,' he says with a twinkle.

The next morning Oliver is going to drive Dr Elders and me to the Bill and Hillary Clinton National Airport. I'm picking up a hire car to drive to San Francisco and Dr Elders is going to the Trojan conference in Florida. I walk past the high Victorian sitting room on my way to the kitchen and can't resist going in. No. I shouldn't. Should I? I sit on the scarlet love seat that nobody's ever sat on before. The doll with the porcelain face and the green dress gives me the evil eye and I make a quick exit.

Back in the kitchen, I see the book Dr Elders bought at the Little Rock Central High Museum on top of her case: *The*

Mis-Education of the Negro by Carter G. Woodson. 'I thought it was out of print,' she says. She adds that she's looking forward to reading it again. The name rings a bell. It's on the black history clock. It strikes me that I haven't just gained a new insight into masturbation while staying with Dr Elders. Like countless other African Americans, she has spent her life living in a parallel universe, knowing all about people like Mary McLeod Bethune and Ida B. Wells and Carter G. Woodson and Daisy Bates. It's like being able to speak a foreign language, or rather, like being bilingual. Except in most countries, people are impressed if you can speak more than one language.

I found a cream nylon kimono draped over my suitcase this morning. Like one of those electric-shock nightdresses. But how bloody kind. A new magic charm to add to Betty's pink scarf. I thank Dr Elders. 'Well,' she says now, in her gentle voice. 'My sister sends them all the time.' As we drive to the airport, she looks intently out of the window and it turns out that she wants to make sure I see the chewing-gum tree before I leave. The sweet-gum tree. I ask Oliver if he used to chew the sap from this tree too. 'Not a lot I didn't chew,' he says with a smile. He says that his favourite thing was something called a muscadine, which is like 'a cherry crossed with a grape'.

At the airport, he hands me my luggage saying, 'I've enjoyed you.' I'm flattered and tell him I've had an amazing time, which I have. I walk into the airport with Dr Elders and say goodbye. She apologises for not having been able to show me more of Arkansas. I thank her and tell her to take it easy.

'Yes,' she nods. 'I know, I need to slow down.'

And then she's off, the most notorious Surgeon General in modern memory, trundling up the escalator on her way to talk about vibrators in Florida.

OWNING SHIT

I spend that night in Hope, Arkansas, the birthplace of Bill Clinton. There doesn't seem to be much hope in Hope. My motel is called the Village Inn, although there are no garland-festooned maypoles or jaunty hanging baskets of geraniums. Still, the smell inside my room makes me feel at home. I've not been in a cheap American motel ($42 including tax) since I made a road trip across the US with a friend of mine fifteen years ago. The police-station lighting, the whiff that hits you when you walk through the door: high-octane air freshener fighting a battle with something dirty and seedy. And plastic curtains. Are they worried about men ejaculating on the windows?

A particularly heavy Tex Mex meal (the El Caballero Dinner: a tamale, a chicken burrito, a beef burrito and a hard-shell taco for $11.95) just outside Hope has put paid to any thoughts of solo sexual activity tonight. The meal tasted of warm foam and I knew it was my lucky day when the tax on the bill came to $1.11 (more on that later). So I curl up with my bellyache and watch a TV show called *Extended Stay*, a programme about life inside different American prisons. I watch the San Antonio, Texas, episode (mostly Latino criminals and young gay men) and then the episode in the prison in Cleveland, Ohio. This focuses on the all-black Heartless gang also known as 'the Family'. It's great TV. The stress proves too much for one Family member and he goes crazy, smearing himself with his own shit. I finish the night with the TLC channel, which has great shows about fat people, and drop off watching *My 600-lb Life*.

The next morning, I see that my door has been open all night because the lock is broken. Outside is a damp, grey vista: wet concrete, an abandoned swimming pool, the sound of thundering traffic, a few brave trees soldiering on. Still, I'm excited to make porridge in my $14 Sunbeam kettle from Target. I think the kettle is intended for poor Latin Americans who live in crappy city apartments, but it will be perfect for my trip. Inside is a black hotplate you can make toast on. Or heat water or beans or porridge. It's genius. I get very excited by the idea of self-sufficiency. I mix oats and linseed and let it bubble for ten minutes. It's pretty disgusting, but at least it's hot. I eat it, wandering around by the front of the Village Inn, wondering if I should have gone to the Yellow Top Smokery Barbeque with a sign saying 'Breakfast. Dollar Menu. Trucker Special. Be Happy'. There's a green Art Nouveau-style lamp by the derelict swimming pool. It's a replica of one of Hector Guimard's 1920s *réverbères* for the Paris Metro.

Maybe someone apart from Bill Clinton did have hope once in Hope. But then a man throwing junk into a skip starts looking at me like I'm weird. I get in the car and get the hell out of Arkansas.

I make a brief stop-off in the adjacent state of Texas to pick up some weed from a friend of a friend who lives in a self-sufficient rural compound in the middle of nowhere. Christina turns out to be a stoner conspiracy-theorist internet-French teacher and she's a great hostess. I've forgotten how vast America is. I'm exhausted after a five-hour drive and her welcome and her weed make me feel very happy. Plus, when I check my emails I get a magazine commission interviewing Whitney Wolfe, one of the female founders of Tinder, the dating app that took heterosexual cruising to a new level. Weirdly, Whitney Wolfe, who went on to create another dating app, Bumble, is based in Austin, Texas, only a two-and-a-half-hour drive away from Christina's place, according to Google Maps. After some emails exchanged with a humourless New York PR, it is agreed that I will interview Whitney the following day at the Four Seasons Hotel in Austin. This is great news for the masturbation fund. Also, because Tinder is sex-related, I'm sure twenty-five-year-old Whitney will have something interesting to say about masturbation.

The next morning, Christina packs me a picnic of home-made rye bread, home-made mozzarella, a jar of home-made berry jam, three peanut-butter health bars, a Tupperware box of Texan happy weed, a glass pipe and a lighter. On the way back to the main road, I stop at a gas station to buy a map. The man at the till squints at me when I ask if he sells maps. He gestures to a group of truck drivers tucking into doughnuts and coffee. They look like extras from *The Dukes of Hazzard*. When I have been in situations of potential stress before in America, I have found it a good idea to up the *Downton Abbey* quotient of my accent. Surprisingly, this still really helps. So I say loudly, 'Hello. Might you possibly know which road I need to take to get to Austin?'

There's a rumble from the truck drivers. 'Where y'all from?' one of them wants to know and there's an amused murmuring when I tell them I'm from London, England – as if it's moon distance away. Then a trucker sitting on his own says, 'You ain't got no iPhone?'

He's like Quint from *Jaws*, the gnarled fisherman who speaks up from the back of the room and everyone falls silent.

This Quint has missing teeth, faded tattoos and a grey, ratty ponytail. But there's a gravitas to him, even though his iPhone comment does disappoint me slightly. It's the sort of thing a Silicon Valley wage slave would say. Whatever happened to 'Breaker, breaker what's your handle?' Forgetting the *Downton Abbey* bit, I gabble, 'Well, I do have an iPhone but I'm trying to be old-fashioned.'

Quint narrows his eyes. He stares at me for what seems an age. Then he says, 'Turn right and keep going until you hit the 35.'

After just under five hours of driving, I arrive at the Four Seasons. I make a note to burn some CDs for the rest of my trip, because the radio is endless twangy country music and shows about the evils of abortion. Whitney Wolfe is waiting in the lobby like a breath of fresh air. A cross between a young Cate Blanchett and a cool surfer chick, the twenty-five-year-old apologises that she'll have to leave a bit sooner than we'd arranged, but her boyfriend is sending a helicopter to pick her up.

Whitney Wolfe sounds like the name of some gritty Jacqueline Susann heroine determined to make her way to the top, and she is a bit like this. I'm here to talk to her about her new woman-friendly dating app, Bumble. She's with her marketing chief, a quiet twenty-something called Caroline. Whitney kindly offers to put me up for the night in the Four Seasons at her own expense. 'Don't tell the New York PR, she'd kill me!'

It's a sunny Saturday afternoon in late January in Austin, Texas, and Whitney, Caroline and I are soon on the terrace eating steak salad and drinking white wine. Whitney talks a lot about the importance of women 'owning shit'. The idea behind her new dating app is that it's women who have to approach men, in order to avoid the cyberbullying that can happen on Tinder. 'The Bumble message is, "Sorry, girlfriend, you have to make the first move. Have some balls and just do it!"'

Bumble promises to liberate women from the stereotype of the passive creature who shudders at the very thought of sex. Along with talk of 'leveraging friend networks' and 'micro-level marketing', Whitney talks a lot about her role model, a teacher from Southern Methodist University in Dallas, where went to college. 'She was this really beautiful out lesbian. We were all scared of her, she was such a badass. She would pull up in a red Ferrari with her customised cowboy boots and she would own shit.'

By the time we've finished the steak salad, I decide I've got enough material for the magazine story and it's time to move on to unscripted masturbation territory. This is not one of the questions I sent the New York PR in advance. I broach the subject via my old trick of going into whirlwind confessional mode and hoping it will trigger something similar in my interviewee. I tell her about Joycelyn Elders and the watermelon patch. 'My masturbation book has the same rationale as your app,' I go. 'It's about women needing to take control!'

Whitney looks quickly around the hotel terrace. 'You know what?' she says quietly. 'Whatever floats your boat, go for it.'

'Masturbation is very taboo here,' Caroline whispers. 'I would say it's super-taboo.'

'In Texas or America?'

'In America. It's very . . . taboo.'

'Did you ever talk about masturbation with your school friends? If you "owned" it, then surely people would be fine with it?'

'Oh no, that was never a topic,' Whitney says.

'Never discussed,' Caroline confirms.

When I ask Whitney what her angle on masturbation is, a new professional tone suddenly kicks in. 'I really don't have an angle,' she says. 'I know if my New York PR were here she'd tell me not to talk to you about this. If she found out we were talking about anything like this thing, she would literally kill me.'

Poor Whitney looks as if she wishes her boyfriend's helicopter would come right now and take her away. It's interesting how she's shy about masturbation, because she's been talking openly about lesbians. A few years ago, her New York PR would have warned her against that.

I say goodbye to Whitney and wish her success – which turns out to be just around the corner. At the time of writing, Bumble has more than 20 million users and Whitney has added two new female-centric networking services to her company. She has also married the Texan oil heir with the helicopter, Michael Herd, and goes by the name of Whitney Wolfe Herd. I suspect she would have a different answer if I asked her today about the dreaded 'M' word.

I leave the hotel and wander off into a saloon-style live music bar where an Ivana Trump lookalike, out-of-her-mind drunk at seven in the evening, is doing a frenzied ass-waggling dance on a deserted dance floor in Christian Louboutin heels. 'One day baby, ain't gonna worry no more,' croons the lead singer on stage, who looks like the nice man who runs the family hardware store. The woman kind of holds it together, apart from when she falls down on the dance floor. She's clearly with an illicit lover who, touchingly, seems impressed by the show she's giving. It's a great spectacle. I bet *she'd* talk to me about masturbation – if she could talk.

On the way back to the Four Seasons, as I'm looking at a map on my phone a man says, 'Do you need help?' There's a moment when I think of taking him back to my hotel room. And then I remember the great thing about my masturbation project: I don't have to get laid. When I was younger I felt a huge pressure to have loads of sex. One academic girlfriend speculated that I liked the idea of being 'good' at sex because I believed that if you were good at sex then nobody would ever leave you. I think it was more basic than that. On holiday in Jamaica once, I read her diary: 'All Stephanie wants to do is eat and swim and have sex.' *What else is there to do on holiday in Jamaica?* I thought. Sex can sometimes be about everything else apart from sex, but sometimes it's just about sex.

THANKS, GAS ANGELS!

When I hit the road the next morning, I finally experience that 'Woo hoo! I'm driving west!' feeling. The sun's out, I'm down to a T-shirt and Prince is blasting out a tune about a sex fiend called Nikki, who he meets in a motel lobby masturbating with a magazine.

As the immensity of America unrolls before my eyes, I listen to songs on my newly burned CD. By the time I hit the entrance to the 290, the sex fiend from 'Darling Nikki' has captured Prince and taken him to her device-filled castle. Here, the lights go out, and Nikki starts to grind.

Prince came into my life to rescue me from the musical wasteland that Cornwall was when I was a teenager. He also helped flesh out my fledgling fantasy life, which at the time was populated with men like Rowan Atkinson, Barry Manilow and Father Lock from the convent who, weirdly enough, looked a bit like Barry Manilow. I first saw Prince on a televised concert on Channel 4. I was fourteen, and a brown boy-man-girl with rubber hips and naughty eyes was doing thrusting movements with his microphone stand. My fashionable mother with a taste for a new trend came in from the kitchen in her apron and was soon copying his moves with the kitchen broom. We laughed. I secretly couldn't believe they were letting a man act this way. It was 1980 and the following weekend, I went into W. H. Smith's and bought a Prince album they had, called *Dirty Mind*. The man on the cover seemed just the sort of person that Sister Angela had been warning us about in 1 Corinthians. He wore a pair of black bikini briefs under an undone mackintosh. 'Sexual immorality' come to life. *Dirty Mind* was brazen, pumping and pervy. Prince spoke to me much more than that other skinny man, David Bowie singing about space, or that crazy country chick Kate Bush flitting around on the moors. My favourite number on *Dirty Mind* was 'Head', a breathy ode to what seemed like the dirty way of doing sex. The relentless bass, the kinky sound effects, the shocking boasts from the boy with a falsetto voice. I wondered who was on the top? Who was on the bottom? Who was doing what? It would take me a few more years to figure that out.

'Darling Nikki' turns into 'A Little Respect', Erasure's 1988 synth-pop classic, which is by turns elegiac and euphoric. It climbs to a massively high note, which I can never quite reach, but here in the car it doesn't matter if I'm a terrible singer. That's the great thing about a solo drive: you can let yourself go and not care what anyone else thinks. 'To-oo, oo-oo meeeee!' I miss the high note again and laugh as the blue skies and green trees whizz along outside the window. Then 'Yellow' by Coldplay comes on. I know this is the thin end of the wedge of good musical taste, but I don't care, because nobody else can hear it. It's like masturbation. Your dirty thoughts could be the equivalent of Barry Manilow and 'The Birdie Song' rolled into one, but if they hold you spellbound, it doesn't matter.

Soon, I'm singing along to Johnny Cash telling June Carter he's off to Jackson, when a feeling flares up in my belly. There's a sign for the Interstate 10, the southernmost cross-country highway, which takes you from east to west. The 10 was the road my friend and I took when we made our road trip from Orlando, Florida, to Venice Beach, California, in 2000. I can't believe that drive is only coming back to me now. Tutu was a former dominatrix-turned-performance-artist, although she preferred the word 'showgirl'. She was originally from California but moved to London in the late 1980s, where she worked as a nanny before meeting a crew of ne'er-do-well lesbians. She was sometimes seen sporting a tutu, a pair of twelve-hole DMs and a leather jacket with a picture of Jesus painted on the back at some of the many successful club nights she launched in London.

I was trying to write about her at the time. The experience morphed into a novel called *Trix*. Bob Geldof once told me that you're not supposed to sleep with your muses, but I was. She taught me that life is a daring adventure or nothing, and she became one of the big loves of my life.

By 2 p.m. the land has become desert. It's so hot that I stop off in a desolate place called Ozona, where the only sign of life is a gas station. I pump some gas and go inside to pay. It's wonderfully cool and I spend a while perusing the impressive jerky selection: beef jerky, BBQ jerky, green lime jerky, cowboy-style jerky and, Tutu's favourite, teriyaki jerky. At the cash desk, a man with glossy black hair is being short with one of the snowbirds, as they term the old people who drive west for the winter. It's quite unusual to hear rudeness in Texas. When it's my turn, the man narrows his eyes and asks me if I'm on my own. When I was hitch-hiking around France one summer in my early twenties, I would reply '*Je suis mariée*' to the truck drivers who picked me up and invariably asked me this same question. But now I'm nearly fifty, so I tell the man that yes, I am alone. Whereupon, without any trace of humour he says, 'When you drive back this way, stop off and we can have a meal together,' with the brass of some toff back in London saying, 'Darling, shall we do lunch at the Wolseley next Tuesday?'

I get back in the car and don't really enjoy the jerky because of the man with glossy hair. And then as I drive on, the heat turns to really hot heat. This is the part of Texas where things become very arid. I'm soon driving through miles of burned, scrubby land framed by ugly flat mountains and a relentless glassy blue sky. I've got the window open because someone told me that air con uses up petrol, but the outside air feels like hairdryer air and the noise means I can't even hear my music any more. I call Virginia but there's no reply. I call Hadji and he doesn't pick up either. This is the reality of a solo road trip: driving through an arid, repetitive terrain for hours on end and you're all on your own.

When I see a sign for Van Horn, the hairs go up on the back of my neck. It makes me forget to notice how much petrol is left in the car. When I next look, the gauge says that there are only fifty-three miles-worth left. There are still no signs of civilisation, just some trucks parked in the lay-bys, but maybe the truckers will be like the nasty man with glossy black hair. Maybe I could flag down one of the snowbirds. Shit, I don't want to do that either. I was going to have to bite the bullet and call in the angels.

During my New Age of Aquarius period of journalism, I wrote about Transformational Breathing ('feels like someone whizzed MDMA powder into your breakfast smoothie'), goddess workshops ('my other half tells me I look "possessed but in a good way"') and a shamanic Vision Quest ('the Duke of Edinburgh Award with a Carlos Castaneda twist'). I also did a story on angels. They've become big with the high-end hippies because they're all about goodness and light. Once you start tuning into the angels, the numbers 111, 222 and 333 start cropping up. Hence my seeing the $1.11 tax on my

El Caballero meal in Arkansas as a good sign. Clearly, some people are cynical about all this, but frankly, Betty Dodson's magic pink scarf and Joycelyn Elders' nylon nightie aren't coming to the rescue on the gas-station front. Sacred Heart FM, meanwhile, is pumping out the most outrageous things about a man who was nailed to a cross and came back from the dead, so asking angels for gas help doesn't seem that mad.

The thing I learned about the angels is that you have to ask them for help openly, however cringy your request might sound. So I say, 'Please angels, let me find a gas station.' And five anxious minutes later, I do. On the other side of the highway, an Exxon garage on top of a hill. I flip a bitch, as I learned to call a U-turn on the road trip with Tutu, and arrive at the gas station with just 3.33 miles-worth of fuel left in the tank. Just saying. I fill up the tank and the inside of the gas station feels like Tiffany's must have felt to Holly Golightly. The temperature is cool inside and the man behind the till is friendly. In front of the cash register is an array of baseball caps in a glass cabinet like a Jeff Koons exhibit. Some look as if they have wings on. Who knows? Everything gets intensified when you're alone in a car driving across America. The fact is that by the time I drive into Van Horn, a few more miles down the 10, Barry Manilow is singing triumphantly about how he writes the songs that make the whole word sing and I'm yelling, 'Thank you, Gas Angels!' And it's great because there's nobody here to see how naff I'm being. Maybe tonight I'll be jacking off to me and Chris Martin from Coldplay having a candlelit dinner together.

The minute I get out of the car and breathe in the evening air, I remember Van Horn. It's where Central Time becomes Mountain Time. You are literally on the edge of time. I got a shock on seeing the sign for Van Horn earlier today, because

I suddenly remembered that Tutu and I spent the night here all those years ago. It's a name that's hard to forget. I spark up some Texan happy weed in my new motel room at the Desert Inn. It's a no-smoking room, but one joint isn't going to change the lemon-tinged redneck smell. I can't remember if this was where we stayed in 2000, although there are only a handful of cheap motels in Van Horn and one fancy-looking hotel called El Capitan ('Established 1930. Architect Henry Trost'). It looks the sort of place where Miss Kitty with her sass and her plume might be working the front desk. But there's just a stiff Texan guy who says, 'God bless you,' when I start a stoner conversation about Van Horn's beautiful light.

When I go for a sunset wander, the town seems unchanged. Everything is collapsed or crumbled. La Cocina de Maria is boarded up next to a deserted welding shop. A dilapidated sign offers 'Liquor and Beer' to nobody any more, but thanks to the sky, everything man-made can be forgiven. This is the part of America where the desert spell begins. An eerie pink and baby blue light bathes everything at this hour. What a show. It becomes a spectacular finale when there's a long, plaintive wail and an endless freight train rushes across the plains. Railroad trains make America feel like the oldest, most romantic place in the whole world, as if cowboys or brigands might leap on at any minute to hitch a free ride west.

Back in the room, Virginia and her Windex spray bottle cross my mind. I wish I'd brought the scented candle she offered me back in New York. I sit cross-legged on my hoodie on top of the polyester bedcover eating some quinoa with black bits in that I boiled up in the Sunbeam kettle. My back's killing me and my tummy's bloated from my imminent period, but my luxury is that I've come up with the idea of putting a white T-shirt over the nylon pillowcase so my face doesn't get contaminated in the night. I fall asleep but jerk awake a couple of hours later as the room starts to shake. The train. Of course. The track is only twenty metres behind the motel. The train comes distant and faint and then harder and harder until you can feel the vibrations pulsate through your body and the cups rattle on the table and the bed shake under your body.

This *is* my and Tutu's old motel. Tutu loved the train. It comes into you in an eternal moment, a constant rushing through, and it could be like death scraping through your scalp, it could be like falling down a black hole. My body stirs each time the train shoots by three or four times in the night. Memories of flesh and sweat and breath. And yet there is no climax. She's not here. When the rumbling finally passes, there's nothing. The loneliness of the desert at night.

When I wake at six, I'm restless. I feel something like a sting. A pleasure sting. I think back to my pussy pain all those years ago. It has not escaped my attention that the vocabulary I used to describe it: 'stinging', 'tingling', 'throbbing', is the same vocabulary I also use to describe erotic pleasure. A lash of pleasure with a leather belt. As Dr Komisaruk says, there's some fundamental commonality between pleasure and pain.

I'm pre-period horny. I try and forget about the fag burns in the Desert Inn sheet and get down to some homework. I think, *Oh God, I hope it's not going to be the horrible glossy-haired man at the gas station.* But when I close my eyes, there he is, being rude to the friendly snowbird. Then he's in the motel with me, making me suck his dick. Virginia is in the back of my mind in all this. The sucking gets boring so I lie on top of him, but that reminds me of what I do with Hadji. And then something lights up. A red and silver chrome Kenworth truck. Three steps up into the leather passenger seat. Quint sits next to me with his ratty ponytail. A flash of calloused hands and a red velvet curtain. It feels glamorous to be sitting up here, high in a black capsule with a dashboard of glittering lights. There's a blur of gearsticks, a jangle of buckles, the tug of old leather and a cock that feels like velvet as it knocks against my growing clit. Quint pulls me to the mattress behind the cab's red curtains and luckily there's no sense of smell in this trucker dream world. In the Desert Inn motel, I'm lying on my front, head in my white T-shirt over the pillow, the right side of my face drooling onto a sheet whose whiff I'm not aware of any more. My skin is flushed and damp and I'm frigging my clit manically as I realise that it's time to get out the purple bag.

The purple bag contains: a La Perla G-string (a leftover from my affair with the sixty-six-year-old art dealer), a pair of black lace briefs, a pair of tight-fitting Y-fronts with Zap! and Pow! over them from my favourite trashy lingerie shop in Cannes, a bottle of almond oil (a great tip from Betty's workshop), a soft leather harness and a black dildo bought just after I met Virginia. It's hard when you're buying a dildo. You are naturally drawn to the idea of having a big dick, but then you wonder how big your partner will want it. You can't be too selfish, but at the same time you are probably going to fuck yourself with your own dick, so it's a tricky purchase. I regret not having brought my egg-shaped vibrator from England. I can hear a New York octogenarian growling, 'You pack your vibrator like you pack your toothbrush!' I have a vague fear of becoming addicted to vibrators.

The Marquis de Sade had a code word for the sex hardware he used: 'Vanilla and Manilla'. He used vanilla the way gay men now use poppers – as a sexual stimulant helpful for dilating the anus, while 'Manilla' referred to his assortment of fancy dildos. If he was hard on Renée-Pélagie when she brought him wrongly iced biscuits, he was doubly hard about the dildos she brought him in jail. He ordered her to go to the noted Parisian cabinetmaker Abraham to have them carved in the smoothest ebony and rosewood. To distract the attention of the prison guards, Sade tells her to have them double as cases to hold maps or engravings. Renée-Pélagie is clearly a woman who doesn't 'run the fuck', as Betty would call it, but the dildos are the one item on her husband's shopping list that she does baulk at. She complains in a letter to her husband dated 30 September 1783 that the craftsmen laughed in her face, especially when she gave them the specific dimensions the *préstiges* were to be carved in: 20 cm long and 16 cm in circumference. Couldn't get many maps in there. On the edge of a letter she writes on 9 September 1779, she complains that her imagination was 'filling with all sorts of things' because she hadn't heard from her husband. Sade has scrawled on the edge of this letter, 'So is my ass.'

I pull my black silicone dildo from the purple bag and move its length slowly in and out of my cunt. In my fantasy, Quint is a good sexual psychologist. There's pleading and waiting and yielding and the condom-or-no-condom dilemma and then a belt buckle and a zipper on my leg because he hasn't taken his Wrangler's off. He will be wearing Wrangler's and not Levi's. And then, fuck it, I'm going without, I'm going to make him pull out anyway, and then he's on top, even though I'm on my front in the motel bed and I put the black dick inside again and my breath draws in like the door of a house opening to a storm and then suddenly, the glossy black head of hair rises to the surface or rather, it remains as the sediment in the bottom of the cup and I'm drinking sensuality to its last and bitterest dregs. *Fuck me*, I think. *Please fuck me!* And soon I make a shuddering, quick come.

The heart wank crosses my mind, but how can you think about chakras in a place like Van Horn? I suddenly really miss Hadji. I realise I'm going to have to drive 500 miles a day for the next three days to reach San Francisco to hand the car back in time. I'm wondering what the point of all this is. I get up and make porridge. I open the door to eat it and my vest-clad next-door neighbour comes out of his room, coughs up a huge gob of mucus and spits it on the ground. The texture looks like my porridge. Except my porridge always has black bits in it. I think it's metal coming off the bottom of the Sunbeam kettle. I remember Betty's warning back in New York that the path I've set myself on is 'a vocation'. It's like that line from the American writer Joseph Campbell about how you have to 'follow your bliss'. But then later in life he wished he'd urged people to follow their blisters, because things aren't always going to be pretty.

Back on the road, the landscape takes my mind off things. The part of the 10 I'm now driving on tracks closely to the border of Mexico. No longer the faded Edward Hopper of Van Horn, the landscape has become a hot, glaring sprawl, a pinball machine of reds and chromes and blinking neon. Then all of a sudden, I'm at the border of Texas and New Mexico and there are groups of soldiers with guns and a sign that says 'Warning, Canine Presence'. My mouth goes dry as I think about my Tupperware container of pungent Texan happy weed. Tutu, a big fan of the magic plant, always maintained that the pussy is airtight, but it's too late to test out her theory now. The soldier waves two or three cars past a red light, so I assume I should go through too. But there's a scream: 'Stop!' and I realise it's me the soldier is shouting at. The thing with security in America is that it's either very Laurel and Hardy or it's really serious FBI stuff and you never know which it's going to be. Luckily, the Weed Angels must be with me, because no dogs appear and even though I nearly trap the soldier's fingers in the window as I fumble to pass him my passport, he suddenly beams and waves me through the red light too.

I celebrate my good luck by buying my first packet of Cheetos at a gas station and calling Hadji, who is in his office in London, writing a novel about an eighteenth-century Bonnie and Clyde couple. I'm always so excited when I think of calling him and then I call and there's that weird vague politeness thing that we have now. Hadji says he needs to 'do something' when he finishes his book. I'm not sure if he means travel or go shagging. He says that he doesn't want to come across as the boring one in my book. All leek soup and tai chi classes. 'You've done all these things and I haven't done anything.'

Hadji's not boring at all. I have an early photograph of him lying on a bed in a Monaco hotel room, naked but for a bunch of grapes in his crotch. A real butter-wouldn't-melt smile. A satyr with black flashing eyes, mischievous, unstoppable. Like a pretty-boy delinquent who was dirty, sweet and not entirely mine. In the beginning, I'd find scratches on his orchid-petal skin and I knew they weren't from me. One day he lay in bed and said, 'I think I'm still in love with my ex.' His boyfriend of seven years had left him and he still hadn't got over it. We were both crawling from the wreckage of failed love with other people. We floundered around and I fought with jealousy, and then he tied his cock ring on my wrist as a bracelet one day and it felt like the most romantic thing anyone had ever done. Our motto was 'sex, homicide, luxury, battle', which came from an old copy of *Lives of the Saints* he'd bought. We'd added the 'sex' because we added sex to everything back then and our *jouissance* came as much from words as it did from orgasm. He had a line that being with me felt safe and dangerous at the same time. In the beginning, he wanted more danger and I wanted more safety. And now it's the other way round.

He makes a joke about his latest 'kung fu' weekend in London and it feels nice to be cosy for a minute. But then it strikes me that soon I'll be going back to London and the cosiness will start to smother me. Radio 4 and roast dinner all over again. My heart sinks. It's nice to have a Hadji fix though. I tell him I'll call him later.

I drive into New Mexico, towards Albuquerque, listening to a radio preacher talking about how Satan is an evil charmer. I call up Virginia but she says all the wrong things. She says I'm near a place called Socorro where's there's some alien attraction. She's bright and perky and I can hardly keep my eyes open. When it gets too hot, I stop off at a gas station and buy a diet A&W Root Beer and another pack of Cheetos. Christina's healthy mozzarella and brown bread have been good, but when I did this trip with Tutu, we ate Cheetos and root beer because junk food keeps you awake.

At the turnoff at Las Lunas, I pull over on the side of the road, part of the old Route 66. Evening's coming and the clouds look like spaceships. There's a huge rock bathed in the last glow of the setting sun and it gives me such pleasure to gaze at it. It reminds me of Diogenes the Cynic, who lived much of his life in a clay wine urn in the marketplace in Athens around 400 years BC. His life became a scandalous round of public eating, drinking and masturbating. His message was that civilised life is meaningless, that simple pleasures bring the most happiness. Diogenes loved the way masturbation appeased his sexual appetite. He wished eating were as simple. In *Lives and Opinions of Eminent Philosophers* written in the third century AD by another Diogenes, Diogenes Laertius, he quotes the master as saying, 'Would to heaven that it were enough to rub one's stomach in order to allay one's hunger.' Here, looking at the beautiful New Mexican sky, it feels as if beauty is rubbing at my belly, giving me some strange release. I get back in the car. Maybe I've been on my own for too long. Talking to angels? Getting off on sunsets?

I spend the night in a motel in Grants, near the border of Arizona. Grants doesn't have the twisted allure of Van Horn, but my room is only $35 plus tax and it smells of cherry air freshener. It feels great to sit in an OK motel room after nine hours of driving. According to Google Maps, Van Horn to Grants is exactly 444 miles. I'm starving. I wish I could rub my belly and be filled up. Instead, I eat one of Christina's peanut bars, dunking it in the jar of berry jam before putting my clean-ish white T-shirt over the pillow and collapsing into bed. I wonder who I'll see when I close my eyes tonight, but the only view is of endless highway rushing past at sixty-five miles per hour. Being dog-tired is one of the luxuries of the road. Soon everything is black.

THE LOLLIPOP HOUSE

When I wake up, I feel completely refreshed. Like a dry sponge that's been soaked in water overnight. I throw white towels down on the floor and use them like lily pads to avoid having to put bare feet on nylon carpet as I make my way to the bathroom. Then I do a few sun salutations on my yoga mat before eating my healthy breakfast that I'm not sure is so healthy now.

My plan is to go as fast as I can through Arizona and reach California by nightfall. So I drive along, listening to Sacred Heart Radio, with a woman caller saying she felt 'guilt and shame' after she had an abortion. There's an ad for a teeth-whitening product and then a preacher with a voice like Johnny Cash on a show called *Pathway to Victory* is talking about the demonic creatures from Revelation, which will destroy a third of mankind. 'We at *Pathway to Victory* refuse to dodge the tough subjects,' he reassures listeners.

By the time I reach Flagstaff, the location of the Grand Canyon, I'm back to wearing my black thermal top and my Russian fur hat. Tutu once joked that the hat made your head feel like it was having an orgasm. But now I wish I'd appreciated the heat of yesterday a bit more. And then suddenly I'm burying my face in Virginia's huge tits. The moment they get released from her bra at the end of the day, when I make her forget all thoughts of cleaning products. Sucking and slipping, swimming in mounds of warm flesh. My nipples tighten and a ripple of energy passes through my clit. I take a deep intake of breath. I wonder if it's the proximity to the Grand Canyon. The huge rocks. I suddenly see Virginia as an epic goddess, her legs striding the world like the Venus of Willendorf come alive with me underneath, looking up. The Venus of Willendorf is 26,000 years old and it's incredible what a finely detailed vulva she's allowed to have. Because some time around the fourth century BC, Praxiteles created one of the first life-sized female nudes in the history of Western art. The Aphrodite of Knidos is stunning, but she has a hand prudishly placed over her pudenda.

This is depressing, because ancient history is filled with accounts of women using the power of the pussy to avert rain and hailstorms, to ward off evil and to make crops grow better. When the Greek historian Herodotus travelled through ancient Egypt in the fifth century BC, he attended the biggest of Egypt's festivals in Bubastis, the capital of ancient Egypt for a time and the centre of worship for the female cat deity, Bast. She was worshipped as the goddess of warfare, protection and physical pleasure. Herodotus remarks that some of the barges sailing up the Nile are filled with women – many dancing while others 'stand up in the boat and expose their genitals'.

Herodotus termed the genital exposure custom 'ana-suromai', the Greek for 'raising one's clothes.' The custom is also mentioned by Pliny, the first-century historian of the ancient world, who talks of women walking around fields with their cunts exposed to improve the fecundity of the crops. On medieval churches, naked female figures, termed 'Sheela Na Gigs', grab the sides of their outer labia and pull their vulvas open, as if a jet stream of something fearsome is going to shoot out.

When I did my goddess workshop in Wales with one of the UK's most powerful goddess-culture teachers, Anna Ziman, one of the women in the group picked the card of the Japanese sun goddess, Amaterasu. The legend runs that Amaterasu retreats to a cave because of the bullying behaviour of her brother, the storm god. She can only be coaxed out when the shaman jester goddess, Uzume, turns up and performs a puppet show with her genitals on an upturned drum. The watching gods apparently roar with laughter and Amaterasu comes out of her cave to see what the fuss is all about. Some accounts say that Uzume gets lost in the rhythm of the drumbeat and is 'carried away by divine ecstasy'. Which reminds me of *Thérèse the Philosopher* as well as Annie Sprinkle's touring masturbation play.

Meanwhile, I've just crossed the border into California, where Mountain Time becomes Pacific Time. Yesterday at this moment, it was 7 p.m., but now it's only six. I love how the further west you go across America, the lighter it grows and the more minutes you get added to your life. On the East Coast right now, it's nine at night and dark and cold, whereas I'm in the Sunshine State about to check into a palace.

Just as the Village Inn in Hope was pushing it a bit on the title front, the Desert Palace in Barstow doesn't look as though the Windsors will be moving in any time soon. I'm glad I'm in Barstow though. Hunter S. Thompson mentions it on the first page of *Fear and Loathing in Las Vegas*. My room smells not of hookers and squaddies but of one of those Miley Cyrus-type celebrity fragrances you buy these days. The best part is the front desk experience. Below a sign saying 'American Owned' is a girl in her early twenties with snaggle teeth, a cigarette in one hand (unlit) and a heart-shaped ring on her wedding finger with some of the rhinestones missing from the heart. There's a five-year-old girl wandering behind the desk wearing a camouflage onesie, holding a bag of potato chips. Every so often, from around the corner there's a cry of, 'Boo! Stop that, Boo!' as the child runs around.

'Does she belong to you?' I ask the girl behind the desk. I'm feeling slightly delirious by now. I've driven 598 miles on my own in just over ten hours.

'Yes, she does,' the girl says. 'I've got two of my own and three stepchildren.' Rooms are $45 including tax and soon she's struggling to copy the name from my driving licence onto her registration form, saying with unconscious charm, 'I'm not real good at writing.' She generously gives me what she calls a 'deluxe' room on the second storey of the Desert Palace for the regular price of $45 because the microwave is broken. The room has a view of a huge Subway advert on a pole with a shimmering pink mountain range behind. I get into bed and close my eyes, wondering if I'll be able to go to sleep without a railroad track outside.

I sleep deeply and wake at six feeling ready for the day. When I open the door, a rich orange floods onto the blue nylon bedspread and there are birds cheeping in palm trees. When I get into the car, Elton John and Kiki Dee are singing 'Don't Go Breaking My Heart' and before long, I see a big road sign saying 'Los Angeles' and then 'San Francisco'. I utter a huge American 'Woo hoo!' because soon I'll be at the clitoris of America.

I call Jet, my Facebook friend in San Francisco who I've never met, from a gas station outside Bakersfield. She says she has therapy this afternoon but that she can come and pick me up after that at a train station in San Francisco called Glen Park. I drive on towards San Francisco, wondering if Jet is going to be a touchy-feely therapy type and then suddenly, my body starts to tickle. I'm aware of feeling turned on, even more than I was near the Grand Canyon, although I'm just driving along in a car in the crisp blue morning through the golden desert scrub. The Highway 5 to San Francisco is actually quite a boring stretch of road, very straight and lined with neatly laid-out fruit trees. When I turn off onto a smaller road at Gilroy, California suddenly turns into Scotland, only with better weather. There are trees and cows and big hills and curvy mounds of rock covered in green. Sometimes I see faces and forms in the side of the green hills: a laughing African woman's head, the side of a cat. Suddenly I'm breathing properly. 'Darling Nikki' comes back on and I turn up the sound. When Prince signs his name on the dotted line, the lights go out and Nikki starts to grind, I find myself in a pit of warm mud, writhing around with Virginia and then with a lot of sweaty, faceless female bodies of all sizes and shapes. It's strange because there are never any sleazy truck drivers in any of these car fantasies.

Finally, the San Francisco airport sign materialises and I drive the car to the top of a multistorey car park. I return it to Alamo with fourteen miles of petrol left in the tank and 2,563 miles covered in five days. When I open the door and stagger up onto my feet, the smell of San Francisco hits me: sea salt and rusty chains.

Jet turns out to be not touchy-feely at all. She has a serious proper job as an engineer but she seems good at knowing how to have a good time. Over a dinner of kale salad she talks about concepts like 'fuck buddies' and a hairdresser friend who's opening a BDSM beauty parlour. She mentions a book called *The Ethical Slut* by Dossie Easton and Janet Hardy, which is about how you can be non-monogamous and nobody gets pissed off with you if you draw up a set of rules. She says she thinks my book sounds cool. That's one of the good things about Americans – they're still impressed by the idea of a writer.

She's just met a new girlfriend and they're off to Hawaii tomorrow for a holiday. Jet says I'm free to take over her house. She drives me back to her stylish duplex in Presidio, the leafy Hampstead Heath of San Francisco, and goes upstairs to pack. When she comes down later there are two silver packets in her hand. Lollipops. She doesn't ask if I'd like orange or lemon, but rather, would I like Indica or Sativa? It turns out that these lollipops come from the 'edibles' section of Jet's local marijuana store. In California in 2015 you can legally consume 'medical marijuana'. She says that Sativa's the high and Indica's more mellow. *Why wouldn't you want to be up?* I think, and she hands me the Sativa packet. It says: 'Jolly Lolly. Medicated cannabis lolly pop. Raspberry.'

She picks up her bag with a grin and walks to the door, telling me she'll be back in ten days. 'You're going to have so much fun,' she says, handing me a set of keys with a mini bottle-opener attached.

SAILOR 2

That night at Jet's house, the concept of pleasure starts to re-enter my life. The simplest of things feels overwhelmingly sensual: carpets that make your bare feet feel good when you walk on them, pillows that you don't have to cover up with T-shirts before you lie on them. The shock of décor also hits me. A mid-century modern taste in furniture predominates in the apartment and there are carefully thought-out potted plant concepts. By the window in the bedroom is the type of exotic palm tree that looks like an explorer brought it back to Kew Gardens in the 1800s. There are photographs of happy moments in Jet's life as well as a tray holding a glass water bong and a choice of weeds. Jet has hospitably told me to help myself.

I feel like Hansel and Gretel exploring the candy cottage. I check out the airy office next to the bedroom, which doubles as a gym, then go downstairs to marvel at the alphabeticised vinyl collection and a massive drinks cabinet containing things like chocolate angostura bitters. There is a door that opens out onto a porch with a big pine tree ahead and a view of the ocean over the tops of the houses that taper down towards the water. I take a toke from the glass bong and blow the smoke out towards the ocean as a mournful hoot hits the evening air. Foghorns sound nearly as romantic as freight trains in the

desert. Afterwards, I go upstairs and get under the covers of
Jet's bed. With its comfortable mattress and crisp grey sheets,
it feels like sleeping in your mum's bed when you're ill. Safe.
I run my hands over my body and I'm pleased about how
it feels. Lithe, almost. Christina's healthy picnic diet has
done some good. I have an amazing wank and afterwards
I'm surprised to note how soaking wet I am. What did I do
differently? Friendship, maybe. Generosity, hospitality. To feel
loved. I fall into a deep sleep.

I don't wake until eleven the next morning, when I take
a leisurely breakfast on the terrace. I tuck into some of Jet's
fancy granola. It's a luxury not to be eating porridge with
metal bits in. There's a drought in the Bay Area and the late-
January weather feels more like June. There's good news on
the interview front. Nadine Gary, the Raëlian priestess, has
sent me an email saying she's 'tickled' by my book idea and
that she too is fond of Betty Dodson. 'I took a masturbation
seminar with her in 1992. It has literally changed my life and
got me involved in Clitoraid.' She explains that Clitoraid was
launched in 2004 when the Raëlian leader, former French
journalist Claude Vorilhon, returned from West Africa, having
seen the devastating effects of FGM. Nadine suggests meeting
in a couple of weeks on Friday, 13 February at a hotel in
Lake Las Vegas. She signs off by saying, 'The lake view from
the lounge is spectacular; it should be a lovely place for our
conversation.'

This sentence sounds vaguely creepy and Friday the
thirteenth seems a perfect day to meet the aliens, so I confirm.
I decide to have a quiet day and zombie out. If I was back
in London, it would be one of those days I'd make a cake.
But in San Francisco I cycle to Trader Joe's, my favourite
American supermarket, which is like Iceland for healthy food.
I buy avocados, limes, black beans, tomatoes, corn tortillas,

Parmesan cheese, dried seaweed snacks, a pack of Corona beer and a packet of yogurt-covered pretzels. I make jokes with the person at the checkout. It's funny how I feel as if I'm a better version of myself in America. More open, less shy.

I cycle back home, make black-bean stew and revel in the fact that I will be able to live cheaply for the next seven days. That evening, I snuggle up in front of the TV for the latest episode of the *Extended Stay* prison show, eating my black-bean mulch. Actually, I'm only 80 per cent relaxed. At the back of my mind is the idea that I need to be having random sex with someone in spectacular circumstances. I try and smother this anxiety by taking the Jolly Lolly out of its silver packaging. It's a blue heart shape. After a few licks, all my worries float away. I start to think of all the things I'll do with Virginia when we meet up next. There's talk of her coming out to California to stay with me. I'm not sure where yet. Birds are singing outside the window. It's quiet here. I feel between two or three worlds. A strange sort of Stephanie, one taken out of her life and put on a cloud. It's the most peaceful feeling.

The next day, cycling around the city on Jet's bicycle, I come across a street called Valencia. This feels as exciting as stumbling across Sunset Boulevard or Times Square. Valencia is one of the few reference points I have in San Francisco. It's the title of a novel by Michelle Tea, a lesbian writer who chronicled grungy lesbian life in San Francisco in the 1990s. *Valencia* is like *The Swimming Pool Library*, only with more pool tables and roll-your-own cigarettes. It's interesting how the gay male experience in books by Alan Hollinghurst and Edmund White is often portrayed through the prism of cocktails, nights at the opera and aspirational jobs, whereas lesbian life is usually peeling around the edges.

There's a famous shop on Valencia called Good Vibrations. 'Creating a buzz since 1977' it says on the window. They launched national masturbation month in May 1995 specifically in protest against Dr Joycelyn Elders' firing by Bill Clinton. But mainly, I know about this store through the writings of an American writer heroine of mine, Susie Bright. In 1984, in San Francisco, she helped create the world's first lesbian-made porn mag, *On Our Backs*, billed as 'entertainment for the adventurous lesbian'. Think spreads of black dyke cops in leather outfits topping begging-for-it femmes and beach-mermaid photo shoots advertising newly available silicone dildos. The magazine caused a hoo-ha in the days when people thought lesbians preferred eating doughnuts and stroking each other's hair to actually having sex.

Susie Bright was the vibrator expert at Good Vibrations in the 1980s. The number-one concern of most of her women customers was that they couldn't orgasm or that they couldn't control when and how they did. Bright would show them where their clitoris was, how to find their G-spot. She'd explain to lesbians why dildos were not any more heterosexual than kissing.

Today, the store feels pretty much like any other twenty-first-century sex shop. Topshop with more vibrators. In fact, it reinforces my belief that there are way too many vibrators in the world and not enough dildos. A large woman with glasses and tattoos comes up and says, 'Feel free to press all the buttons!' I sense a bat's squeak of doom in her voice, as if she says this many times every day. I tell her that actually I'm looking for books on masturbation. 'No problem,' she says, leading me to the book area. She points to a DVD with a blonde woman in a black lace basque on the front cover. *Nina Hartley's Guide to Masturbation*, it proclaims, informing me that Hartley is yet another 'sex expert'. I notice that Betty Dodson's *Sex For One* is on the shelf. 'Does she sell well?' I ask. The store assistant hesitates. 'Some people give it as a gift. Like, if you have a friend who's pre-orgasmic. It'll tell you about, you know, loving your body and all that.' She says she prefers a book called *Becoming Orgasmic: A sexual and personal growth program for women* by Julia R. Heiman, Joseph LoPiccolo and Leslie LoPiccolo.

'Like, if you're suffering from trauma, this book really tells you what to do.'

This is the first time that I've heard this post-Betty stance. Still, it's good to know that there are now subsections of female masturbation literature. The store assistant apologises for the paucity of BDSM equipment. She blames *Fifty Shades of Grey*. The film comes out next week and she says that Good Vibrations has had a run on steel Ben Wa balls. The assistant sighs. 'Women put Ben Wa balls in their pussy and think they're going to have an orgasm. You need to lie down. You put steel balls in your vagina and you stand up, you're going to break your toe.'

There's a boy in his late twenties at the counter wearing a North Face fleece. He's just bought something in a big brown bag. He says to the woman behind the till, only slightly nervously, 'Does it come with lube?' and then pays with a card. When he leaves, the till girl confides that lots of people buy with cash so they don't get 'Good Vibrations' on their credit card invoice. She shrugs, 'It could be a record store.'

I know what I'm going to buy. There's not a huge section for this product. It's not even mentioned in *Fifty Shades of Grey*. There's a white one for $24 and a black one for $28. When I spot them, I feel that *boi-yoi-yoing* moment like in cartoons when people fall in love. I've turned this item over in my mind for over fifteen years, ever since a friend of mine from Oklahoma showed me hers. 'Cyber skin' she (now a he) told me it was called. It's a dick that's made from a weird goo substance that's meant to feel like a real, flaccid penis. You can 'pack', i.e. go out wearing it to see what it feels like to walk around in the real world with a cock.

I buy the black Sailor 2, because you get one inch more than the white Sailor 1. When I get home and take it out of the box, my first reaction is how realistic it is. It's ugly. Like a slug. But it makes me wet. The prospect of masturbation doesn't feel like homework this time. I get out my tight-fitting Zap! Pow! Y-fronts from Cannes and put Sailor 2 in. Then I go upstairs to the bedroom and get the purple sex-toy bag ready. I'm already wondering if I can penetrate myself and have a dick on at the same time. I don't know what's going to happen. I just lie on my back on the bed and grip my flaccid dick like men do in porn movies. I think of surprising Virginia with it when I see her next. Getting her to feel it and her being surprised and massively turned on. Putting my army boots on and pumping into her with my flaccid dick. I take my T-shirt off and close the blinds slightly. I run my hands over my breasts and look in the mirror. I like the look of me with tits and a dick. I've always wanted to do this and now I'm doing it. Weird how having a fake flaccid dick makes you feel so horny. I think of two imaginary people and we would be playing on the bed with it. How would we be playing? Maybe two girls would be fucking in front of me and I'd be holding my dick and jerking off as I came.

Momentarily I think of penetrating myself with a dildo as I grasp the flaccid cyber-skin cock, but it's too late. I know I'm going to come really quickly. I come 'hard', as they say. Still panting, I pick up the box and read that Sailor 2 'adds realism in gender expression or play', and is 'designed by experienced sex educators'. There seem to be as many sex educators in this country as there are accountants or bus drivers in other countries. I wonder what all this means for my vulva research. It's not that I've deserted Pinky Tuscadero. I'm just branching out. I go downstairs and sit on the porch, still holding Sailor 2 through the Zap! Pow! pants. I get a Diogenes moment as I watch the sky turn a mesmerising purple and orange behind the pine tree. I breathe it in. Is this called a 'natural high'? Then the smell of my dick wafts over in the sunset breeze. Plastic and Play Doh.

A GAME OF TENNIS

The door of a house in north San Francisco opens and a redhead appears who looks as though she might know Miss Kitty, the saloon-keeper from *Gunsmoke*. 'Hi,' she says, chewing on a piece of gum. 'Come on up.'

I follow her up the stairs, wondering how it went at the dentist. She emailed me yesterday about the appointment. 'How did it go?' I ask when we emerge into a sunny kitchen. 'Two thousand dollars-worth of work,' she chews. 'Lucky I sold a bunch of tit prints.'

The masturbation crowd divides into those who used to work in theatre (Mama Gena, Barbara Carrellas) and those who used to work in sex (VV and Annie Sprinkle). Of the two, I really appreciate the porn stars. Born Ellen Steinberg on 23 July 1954 in Philadelphia, Pennsylvania, Annie Sprinkle started life as what she calls a 'nice Jewish girl'. Her father was a social worker and her mother taught English as a second language. From the age of thirteen to seventeen she lived with them in Panama in Central America while her father worked at a new job in international development.

In 1972, she was working as an eighteen-year-old popcorn seller at the snack bar of a porn-movie theatre in Tucson, Arizona, which was showing the buzz movie of the year, *Deep Throat*. The film, which had premiered in New York in June of that year, starred Linda Lovelace and featured a plot and character development, which was unusual for adult films of the time. Lovelace is posited as the quester seeking her truth – in her case, the perfect orgasm. 'There should be more to it than a lot of little tingles,' she asserts to her friend in one scene. To begin with, *Deep Throat* was seen as a glamorous symbol of the burgeoning sexual revolution.

But the backlash wasn't slow in coming. One day, *Deep Throat* was seized by police from Annie's movie theatre. An obscenity trial ensued and she was asked to testify in court. This is when she met the movie's director, Gerard Damiano, a charismatic former hairdresser who, she recalls, had 'the star ranking at the time of a Steven Spielberg'. She asked him if he could teach her deep throat. Given that the film is about a woman who discovers she has a clitoris in her throat, you wonder what he taught her. But Annie says it turned out OK. 'We went to his hotel room together and he showed me.' She followed him to Manhattan, where she became his mistress for just over a year.

Annie says she was partly attracted to porn because 'male genitalia was such a big mystery to me'. But by the mid-1980s, she was bored of 'living everyone else's fantasy' and went into performance art. As a farewell to porn, she wrote and directed her first hardcore feature, *Deep Inside Annie Sprinkle*, a feel-good flick that became the number-two top-grossing porn film of 1982. The 'tit prints' came out of her new career as a sex artist. Some of the works are freestyle – she squirts paint onto her breasts before pressing them onto paper, and some are done with stencils: squares, rectangles and cone shapes, to be topped with multiple scoops of breast ice cream, depending on your budget. You can buy a retro tit print from Christie's for around $1,000. Annie also did 'tits-on-the-head Polaroids' during intermissions from her one-woman shows.

You paid her $10, she put her tits on your head and you took a photograph home. 'The hardest-working tits in showbiz!' she quips.

Today, her impressive DD cleavage is semi-contained behind the plunging neckline of a leopard-print top. She apologises for being a little tired. She was up late last night making stickers and posters for her and her wife Beth Stephens' upcoming ecosex tour ('Ecosexuals Unite!' 'Dirty and Proud!' 'Composting is so hot!'). Beth is an art professor at the University of California, Santa Cruz and a driving force behind the ecosex concept, but Annie says she'll explain more over breakfast. Afterwards, she's going to take me on the 'ecosex tour of the hills with a masturbation twist'.

As we walk through Annie's neighbourhood of Bernal Heights, it strikes me that Annie Sprinkle is a bit like Prince. He was really into sex and then he got into religion. She was a porn star and then she became a hippie. But neither she nor Prince ever really renounced sex. They just decided to come at it from a different angle. *Lovesexy.* Ecosexy. As we walk past colourful houses and lesbians with babies and handwritten signs for poetry slams and climate-change talks, Annie confides that, 'I have a very expanded view of masturbation. I mean, I want an orgasm walking down the street. I want to have orgasmic energy passing through my body without any clitoral stimulation at all. I want to have, you know, that kind of ecstatic release doing all kind of things.'

I nod, thinking, *Fantastic.* And yet when we get to the diner, it's hard to get anything out of her about this amazing orgasm because, unlike my previous interviewees, she keeps asking me about my life. Listening back to the early part of my tape over breakfast is embarrassing. I'm eating bacon and eggs while simultaneously talking a hundred miles an hour about working at *Harper's Bazaar,* and going to Cannes to watch Sharon Stone auction off a trip to space with Leonardo DiCaprio; and getting my first pair of heels, John Richmond by Sergio Rossi, in the Faubourg St-Honoré in Paris with my nightmare-genius big love Tutu; and smoking weed in front of Picassos with my art-dealer married lover, whose father was an establishment figure of his day, and I'd turn up to his boat with my bag of lesbian sex toys and blah, blah, blah.

She keeps saying, 'Wow!' and, 'Oh my God!' and then she wants to know about my Vision Quest in the Pyrenees. Traditionally, this is a Native American right of passage where young men go off alone into nature with no food, no water, no shelter, no clothes and no sleep and came back with a new direction. The experience I do with the shaman, Manex Ibar, lasts four days and involves solitude in the most secret places of the vast Pyrenees. You then return and do 'plant medicine' – ayahuasca or San Pedro – to pin down your vision. When I took San Pedro, I tell her, I talked to ferns and saw that slugs actually wear purple robes and move around like nobles at court.

'Oh wow!' she exclaims, tucking into her eggs. 'That's totally ecosexual.'

I tell her about my love life too because, like most reformed good-time girls, she likes a good gossip. I tell her I'm going out with a gay man who's actually more bisexual and I'm probably bisexual too, although I'd secretly prefer to be what my dyke friend calls a 'platinum lesbian', which means you haven't even kissed a man before. And I can't do the monogamy thing any more and I'm not sure if Hadji's going to carry on being my 'main' or if I'm going to make a thing with the New York chef. Or just be polyamorous, because the thing with Hadji is that the sex wasn't happening but we really love each other so yes, basically . . . that's me.

Annie nods as if she gets what I'm talking about. She doesn't tell me any dirt about her own life, but she does make the most exciting comment about masturbation that I've heard so far.

'In a way,' she says, 'there is no such thing as masturbation.'

I put my knife and fork down. I wait for her to go on. 'Ecosexuality is about making love with everything,' she reflects. 'With clouds, with water, petting your dog, looking at the plant on the windowsill. If you've taken LSD you'll understand that we're all connected. It's like, you know, there's sex and life force everywhere.'

I think about how turned on I was just driving through green hills as I came into San Francisco.

'My view is pretty poetic and experimental,' she admits, crunching on a piece of toast. 'I could be wrong about it. I've done a lot of psychedelics and I guess that kind of inspired me.'

Annie has a naïve-sounding way of talking. Real *idiot savant* Marilyn Monroe stuff. And like Monroe, she's not an idiot by a long shot. She is very polite and solicitous, with a focus on other people's needs, because that's what a lot of her sex work involved. Tutu used to tell me that, like the best waitresses, some working girls can make you feel safe, as if their souls are as old as the hills.

Annie says that the ecosexy thing isn't so different from her days in the mainstream porn industry. The areas she chose to specialise in – gimps, leather, dwarfs; what we'd call today 'fetish' but which didn't exist as a commercial category back in the 1970s – were ahead of the times.

'I was always wanting to push the boundaries. Be more creative.'

Her crash course on meta-masturbation came during her controversial *Post-Porn Modernist* one-woman show that she toured internationally between 1989 and 1994. The show, which chronicles her various careers as sex worker, pro-sex activist and artist, invited audience members to view her cervix with a speculum and thus delve into the mystery of the female body, although she tells me now that actually, 'You can never really demystify it. It's so mystical!'

In 1989, North Carolina senator Jesse Helms denounced Sprinkle's show on the floor of the Senate. He called it a 'sewer of depravity', asserting that federal grants had funded it, although actually, only the theatre she'd performed it in received any money from the National Endowment of the Arts.

If Helms had actually gone to see *Post-Porn Modernist*, he would have been especially poleaxed by the final scene, which Annie calls the 'Legend of the Ancient Sacred Prostitute'. She wanted to reimagine the days when prostitute priestesses were revered in ancient temples. She did some research and found that in Mesopotamia, Sumeria, Egypt and Greece, some women devoted their lives to learning how being in a sexualised, frenzied yet meditative state was the way to connect to the divine. Just like Uzume when she did her genital puppet dance on the upturned drum outside Amaterasu's cave.

'I kind of made up what I thought was the legend,' she admits. 'Then I'd take off my clothes, slather myself in oil and light some candles. Theatre lights added drama, and each member of the audience got a rattle they could shake to this intense music. I'd do a powerful breathing technique and go into a ritual trance.'

She used a vibrator and a dildo, but the key to her heightened state wasn't drugs but breath. 'For me, breath is the ultimate stimulation.' She laughs, dabbing crumbs from the corner of her mouth. 'So weird!'

Post-Porn Modernist has become legendary with the underground sex community. In 2016 in San Francisco, I watched a modern-day adaptation, *Reveal All, Fear Nothing*, created by the woman Annie calls 'my porn-art daughter', Madison Young. The cervix scene was there, although Young, thirty-five, had added some extra anal scenes, as this is her speciality field in porn. At one point, she fists herself on stage and gives herself an enema (with soy milk), although weirdly enough, this was not the highlight of the show. The most intense part was Madison's tribute to Annie's famous masturbation ritual, complete with lights and music and rattlers for the audience and the Hitachi Magic Wand for Young. It was the most incredible piece of theatre I'd seen in years. Young said afterwards, 'Annie first performed *Post-Porn Modernist* twenty-seven years ago and we're still trying to catch up with her twenty-seven years later.'

As with me, it was Betty Dodson's masturbation workshop that triggered a turnaround in Annie's sex life. She attended the Bodysex workshop back in 1981, when she was twenty-seven.

'I met Betty on the first American TV show about sex, *Midnight Blue*. It was produced by Al Goldstein, the publisher of *Screw* magazine. By that time, I'd had sex with a couple thousand people. I'd been round the block. But I was always searching for new information.'

'Did you enjoy the workshop?'

'The masturbation was a piece of cake. What blew my mind was being naked. I always wore a garter belt or something in my movies.'

The experience nevertheless inspired her to make a film in 1990 called *Sluts & Goddesses Video Workshop or How to Be a Sex Goddess in 101 Easy Steps*, where she had what she tells me was a 'beyond-the-physical-body, seven-chakra kundalini orgasm with a lot of throat, a lot of G-spot electricity, as well as multiple clitoral orgasms'.

Annie recalls that her whole vagina was 'completely electric. The two women fucking me with their fingers felt lots of electricity in their hands and going up their arms.' The five-minute-long orgasm was captured in the film, but when she showed it to Betty, Betty informed her that this wasn't an orgasm. She doesn't hold a grudge.

'I love Betty, but she's very clit-centric. I think there's fucking huge amounts more than that. The clit's just . . . the tip of the iceberg!'

When I say I've been told that she christened San Francisco 'the clitoris of America', she points to a narrow street opposite the restaurant.

'That's it,' she says, indicating a thicket of trees on top of a hill. My fork freezes. Am I seriously eating bacon and eggs a few hundred metres away from the clitoris of America? I didn't know I'd find it so soon. I didn't know there were exact geographical coordinates.

'It's called Bernal Park,' she says. And then I can't resist. I ask her if she really could have an orgasm in the street if she wanted. Like, right now.

She raises her eyebrows. 'Well, I could have a kind of energy release,' she says, obligingly. She pushes the toast plate away. 'I could breathe and open up my self to . . . I could make my fingers tingle right now. Which they are. Just thinking about it. It's like when you start to make love, you allow that energy to flow, it's like riding a wave. It's not genital, but it's very sexual.'

She closes her eyes, makes audible breathing sounds and then she's off, doing a *Harry Met Sally* right in front of my eyes. Except Meg Ryan was demonstrating how easy it is for a woman to fake an orgasm while Annie is coming up to climax for real. She's breathing in the way I imagine she did in her 1982 box-office smash, *Deep Inside Annie Sprinkle*.

I'm not sure if I'm feeling the spiritual vibes or if watching Annie with her fabulous rack bobbing up and down as she communes with the clouds and the plants and the dogs is what's making me feel tingly. But I'm starting to feel vaguely high as I copy her breath patterns. After three or four minutes of air masturbation, she opens her eyes. 'Wow. The sky looks bluer . . .'

She says that what she just did was kind of an 'energy orgasm', the practice she developed with Barbara Carrellas back in the 1980s. She qualifies that it's 'better on an empty stomach', and adds that she'll show me how to do it up on Bernal Park hill. She can't speak too clearly at the moment, though. 'You have to amp it down to get back in your head to talk. Right now, I'm just doing it on the sidewalk. But when I did it on stage for *Post-Porn Modernist* with five hundred people out there shaking rattles and lights and music, you can imagine the energy shooting out of me.'

By this time, I'm quite keen to get up onto the clitoris of America and try it all out myself. So off we set on a climb up the hill to Bernal Park and an X-rated nature walk begins. It's not X-rated because Annie's going to take her clothes off. The plants are going to be doing much filthier things. 'Look at that,' she says, stopping in front of a cherry tree in full bloom. 'Flowers are tree genitals. Basically, you're looking at porn.'

We walk on until the siren call of another tree brings Annie to a halt. 'Look at this trunk – it's like a big penis. Isn't it beautiful?'

Hockey-pitch nature walks with Miss Corbett at the convent were never like this. Annie says that I need to find my 'E-spot', her ecosexy take on the G-spot. (She's great at coming up with new words.) I'm drawn to an exuberant hibiscus flower. 'Oh yeah!' she says approvingly in her raunchy porn voice. 'Hibiscus stamens!'

I wonder if David Attenborough shows ever give her that *Deep Throat* feeling. We approach the hibiscus and she says, 'You can smell it casually. Or you can imagine this plant is a lover and it wants to give you a gift.'

She smells her new lover, pulls off one of its genitals and sticks it on her third eye. She sticks one on me too. None of this strikes me as stupid or odd. Cornwall isn't a million miles away from California in terms of country weirdness. My E-spot kicks into action as I notice that a tree we're passing looks a bit droopy.

'Don't you think this tree looks a bit sad?' I say.

'It *is* a little heavy, isn't it?' she nods.

She knows immediately what to do. 'You just need a hug,' she tells the tree, enfolding it in a bosomy embrace. 'Oh, love you.' I participate in the love-in, realising only afterwards that I have just hugged a tree in California. This is the sort of thing that people make fun of back at home, but American Stephanie doesn't care. Annie looks wistfully at the tree, then mumbles something about, 'I may be projecting . . .' She slaps the tree's butt. 'You'll be OK,' she cracks. 'Hang on in there.'

It's fun going on a nature walk with an ex-porn star. She's not great on the names of flora and fauna, but she does things like saying hi to her favourite eucalyptus tree. She plucks a leaf, thrusts it under my nose and chuckles, 'Sniff that pantie!'

The sap must be rising from the ecosexy nature walk, because I soon have a sort of sexual panic attack. I start gabbling about how I want to check out some seedy places in San Francisco and how I really want to get laid and, 'You know that feeling when you want to have sex and you're not having sex and . . .'

'Stay in the moment,' she puffs as we carry on up the steep road. They're magic words and I immediately calm down. I think back to the front of Barbara Carrellas' apartment, when

I became just snow and boots and crunch for a few moments. And then suddenly Annie announces that we've reached 'the urethral sponge': we're in Bernal Park but not quite on the clit. My main feeling is that the clitoris of America has had a bit of a bikini wax. Its green pubic hair is a bit patchy. There's a lot of uncovered soil. Maybe the dog walkers nobbled it. There are a lot of them. Annie says it's the drought. It's been a serious problem in San Francisco. Annie has actually married the main culprit, along with a group of ecosexy friends.

'If you think about it, right now the sun is penetrating your pores,' she says in her incantatory broad-from-the-1950s voice. 'They're fucking your body.'

When I ask her how she knew the sun wanted to get married, she says, 'We can only assume that things respond well to love and appreciation. Like, if you cruise a bunch of girls or guys, you'll get the message who's available.'

She and Beth have also married the mountains, the snow, coal and the ocean. I try and impress her by saying, 'My favourite drugs are sugar and the sun.' She enthuses, 'Oh, I love sugar too,' but adds that she has to lose weight for the filming of her and Beth's upcoming movie, *Water Makes Us Wet – An Ecosexual Adventure*.

'I'm a bad feminist,' she apologises. 'I'm all for fat activism, but personally, I always diet before a shoot.'

By now we're sitting on the very top of the park, a bumpy, grassy area that slopes down with massive views over the city on every side. Looking at the view, it suddenly strikes her that, 'Maybe the earth is the clitoris of the universe.' She laughs. 'Betty would say, "Oh that's bullshit!"' She tells me that we'll do the energy orgasm right here.

She describes the technique as similar to something she used to call 'medabation', meaning a combination of masturbation and meditation. But mainly, she says, it's like learning tennis because, 'It's a technique and at first it's confusing and you're like, "Woah! How do I hit it and how hard?"'

It strikes me that that this 'energy orgasm' is her take on the heart wank that Barbara Carrellas told me about back in New York. Annie explains that the idea came about when she and Carrellas were investigating more spiritual ideas about orgasm during the AIDS years. 'Many of us had lovers who'd got HIV, so we had to figure out how to have safe sex.' They adapted the breath technique from a method taught by sex educator Harley SwiftDeer. He calls it the 'Firebreath orgasm', but Annie doesn't 'because I didn't take the very expensive training that initiates you'.

And so my tennis lesson begins. Annie starts by telling me to, 'Say "yes" to erotic energy. You have to allow it because it's there just for the asking.' She points to the tree in the near distance and says that the ideal would be to, 'Start feeling sexy and then direct your energy to the tree and see what happens.' She tells me to do some kegels (clenching of the vagina, as if you want to stop a stream of pee) and undulating movements of the pelvis. 'That'll stoke the furnace.' After that comes the most important thing of all: the breath.

'You're really sucking the inhale and relaxing the exhale.' She advises to make noises, because that helps shift energy in the body. 'The idea is to bring in energy through the feet and end up shooting it out of the top of the head. Fake it 'til you make it,' she quips, in what she tells me is jargon from the porn world.

It's a great lesson. It reminds me of the Transformational Breathing technique I tried out in my hippie journalism phase with the British teacher Alan Dolan. Basically, you breathe quickly in and out, taking in more than usual amounts of oxygen until a wave of euphoria hits you. And then there I am, lying on a hillside in San Francisco as the woman once dubbed the 'Golden Girl of Porn' makes sounds ranging from deep Witches' Sabbath to mid-range horny-bitch-on-heat to high-pitched damsel-in-distress to glass-shattering Kate Bush on the moors. 'Wooo! Woo!'

Listening to the tape afterwards, I do sound a bit stuck in Witches' Sabbath mode. Clearly I need to work on moving my energy up to more damsel-in-distress mode. Meanwhile, I am in the ludicrous position of lying with my feet towards the top of the hill and my head towards the bottom because I want to face the sun. But something is definitely happening. I get to the state where I forget to worry about what the dog walkers must be thinking of us.

I have a flash of some of the boring-looking dog walkers I've seen in Presidio Heights. I want to unzip them and show them some love. Tell them it's OK. Occasionally I get distracted by the fact that I'm not feeling anything remotely like an orgasm, although Annie is now sobbing. Wailing almost. We get in breathing synch. I try and keep up with her 'Ah! Ah!'s until finally she makes a prolonged, 'Oh yeeeeeeah!' presumably when the energy passes out of the top of her head.

I open my eyes and the sky is indeed bluer. There is also dog shit on the bottom of my right boot. I think I won't say this to Annie. She's clearly having a moment.

'When I masturbate like this, I feel the pain of the world, I really do. The Boko Haram, the *Charlie Hebdo* shootings. The animals, everything. I become a channel sometimes. I just need to release the pain. It's like truly connecting. It sounds really strange.'

'No, it doesn't sound strange . . .' She's right that it's hard to speak after this kind of breathing. Feels as though there's a rubber band around my tongue.

'We can't experience pleasure on a really grand scale unless we clear out suffering first. You have to express your anger and work on emotional blocks. You have to notice your disconnection before you can connect.'

Watching Annie with tears streaming down her face, it strikes me that this is what a modern-day nun looks like. Sending an orgasm to promote peace in Nigeria and Paris isn't that weird. Christians and Buddhists send off distilled thoughts known as 'prayers' to try and alleviate world suffering every day. Yet the kind of energy generated during orgasm is jet fuel compared to the economy petrol that comes from a morning at Mass. And what about His Holiness the Dalai Lama? He edited a French edition of *Vogue* when I was living in Paris, just as Annie was invited to edit a special issue of *Penthouse* in November 1988 (cover line: 'See God and Come'). Mainly, Annie puts me in mind of Amma, the Hindu hugging lady who's been described as a contemporary goddess. Ballrooms in Best Westerns all over the world get packed with people (over 33 million to date) hoping to receive one of Amma's transcendental hugs, which apparently make you feel as if you got blessed by the bosom of eternity.

Annie is a kind of Superwoman too. She swoops in to bring pleasure where everyone else is just seeing pain and downer stuff. Like Dr Komisaruk, her take is: if you want to diminish pain, maybe you should think about heightening pleasure. And just when you're thinking things are getting too Californian for words, Annie has the talent for segueing back into the mundane.

'The trouble with porn,' she drawls, 'is that it uses so much electricity.' She points to the skyline. 'You know how many people out there are watching porn right now on their computers? It's actually eating the mountains where the coal is and destroying the water.'

'I hadn't thought of that.'

'Yeah, I'm like, 'Let's bring back live sex shows. Let's learn how to make dildos out of vegetables.'

She asks how the breathing was for me. Incredible, I tell her, although I didn't feel any energy shooting out the top of my head. 'Don't worry,' she says. 'It took me three years to get the hang of the release feeling.'

As we start the walk back to her house, she reveals that practising energy orgasms has worked as a kind of 'sexual healing' to get over the nastier side of her years in the sex industry. Although in *Post-Porn Modernist* she claims that of her 3,000-plus customers, she only had around a hundred bad experiences, the nastier ones still needed to be dealt with.

'The first year of practising, every time I got the energy up to my heart, I'd cry. I felt a lot of grief. The second year, I choked on the breath, clearing my throat from my one hundred worst blow jobs. You know, guys holding my head down. I even threw up a couple times. I got it all out.'

She says the energy orgasm taught her 'that you can be in a state of ecstasy and simultaneously feel sadness, anger, grief'. She has come to accept what she calls her 'crygasms'. She adds that while a lot of women she knows cry as a form of erotic release in sex, 'I've never seen that scene in a movie.' She confides that a friend of hers died of breast cancer a few days ago. I say I'm sorry. That's a big deal. Then suddenly there's a police car at the entrance to Bernal Park. 'I bet somebody called the police because we were lying down,' she muses.

'Arresting us for masturbating?'

She tells me that masturbation is 'an inadequate word' for what we were just doing. 'It's kind of like, is jogging really about running? Is dancing really about moving your feet? It's just an action, but it's so much more than that.' She narrows her eyes. 'That would be a really cool protest, actually: an eco-erotic breathing ritual protest. Did you hear about the protest in London? Your country has banned female ejaculation and women sitting on men's faces in porn movies. So they did a face-sit sit-in.'

We're soon on our way to visit Annie's 'pro dom' ('professional dominatrix') friend. Annie asked if I'd like to meet her and naturally I said yes. As we sit in a traffic jam, I tell Annie how much I like the ecosexy thing. The nearest I've come to hearing anything like this is when I interviewed the American drag queen RuPaul, who admitted talking to wild flowers during his morning hikes in the hills of LA as if they were the latest bevy of *Drag Race* contestants. 'I stop and say, "Hey you guys, love what you're doing! Welcome! Wow! Gorgeous!"'

Annie says that ecosexuals are trying to make the ecology movement more fun and diverse. They'd like to attract untapped audiences 'like porn stars, drag queens, kinksters, sex workers, people of colour, queers'. And a second crop of flower children isn't looking so silly this time around. The first Age of Aquarius began in San Francisco in a cloud of love and hope and hedonism. In 1967, Allen Ginsberg's Human Be-In in Golden Gate Park welcomed over 20,000 love children, including Timothy Leary, The Grateful Dead, Jefferson Airplane, Janis Joplin and Hells Angels cuddling babies.

There was an incredible amount of 'free love' going on, according to a key sexuality writer of the time, Marco Vassi. But by the end of Vassi's *The Saline Solution*, the hippie vision seems to have boiled down to people high on acid aimlessly butt-fucking strangers in people's gardens. By 1969, the bad vibrations and disillusion had begun with the violence and deaths at the Altamont Speedway Free Festival and the Manson Family murders. The soldiers coming back from Vietnam didn't care about using psychedelics to expand their horizons and envision a positive future. They wanted to stuff their bodies with speed and heroin and forget.

Another problem with the much-trumpeted sexual revolution of the 1960s was that it was tailored to men. The Pill and the miniskirt were invented and endless surveys showed that premarital sex was on the increase. Yet while Lotharios such as Norman Mailer were bragging about their 'apocalyptic' orgasms, nobody seemed interested in what kind of sex women were having. Annie seems a good person to take the lead in the second sexual revolution.

Unfortunately, not all of Annie's friends are into her new direction. This isn't really fair, as Annie has described herself as 'metamorphosexual' for years.

'Kinky people didn't like it when I became tantric, the tantric people didn't like it when I became kinky again. The straight people didn't like it when I went lesbian, the lesbians didn't like it when I went with a trans person.'

She thinks that sex is becoming too complicated. 'You need the right app, you need the right toy. You have to know how to spank and whip perfectly and all that crap. Everything's supposed to look like a porn movie now.'

She says that ecosex puts the gentleness back into sexual pleasure. She has written more about this in her book, *The Explorer's Guide to Planet Orgasm*, where readers are addressed as 'orgasmonauts'. She refers also to a recent trip to Barcelona, when she went to a nudist beach with her class of Spanish ecosex students.

'We went into the sea and made a big anus shape together. Then we went to the shoreline, got on all fours and got slapped by the waves. The waves were butt-fucking us but nobody else on the beach knew! It was very horny and kinky and innocent at the same time.'

I tell her that I love swimming naked in the Med. I tell

her how I took the ashes of Tutu out to sea early one summer morning.

'Your big love died?'

'I poured the ashes into the water and they floated to the bottom like glittery fish food.'

'Oh my God,' she says.

Annie is a good person to volley a ball of suffering to. She doesn't thwack it back hard, say something like, 'Oh, I'm sorry for your loss.' She stops the game for a moment. 'Talk about ecosexy,' she says, shaking her head.

Death changes you. Since I interviewed Barry Komisaruk, I found out that he became the nutty vulva professor because his wife died of breast cancer when she was forty years old. Tutu was forty-five when the disease got her. 'I felt like a dummy standing there, helplessly watching my wife in terrible pain,' Komisaruk said in an interview. 'I felt I should use what I was taught as a scientist: to do something that would be directly useful, and there is a real need to control people's pain.'

I wish I could be as useful. When I took my top off in front of 600 women at Mama Gena's workshop, after the woman showed us her reconstructed breast – that was for Tutu the showgirl. She said once that she was only ever truly comfortable in her body when she was showing off onstage.

I don't have a crygasm, but it's the second time that day that the hairs spring up on the back of my neck in the presence of Annie Sprinkle.

CONFESSIONS IN THE DARK

When we pull up outside the house of the pro dom, I have another sexual panic attack. I've just told Annie that I have an interview this evening with a woman who runs a popular swingers' club. Betty Dodson sent me an email as a follow-up to our talk on orgies-I-mean-sex-parties. The woman I need to speak to is called Polly Superstar. She runs a club called Kinky Salon.

'Oh, they're great people,' Annie says. 'Really cool.'

'Yes,' I go, 'but I like ugly people! You don't always want cool, do you? Sometimes you just want a bit of cheese.'

'I know what you mean,' Annie says, but she doesn't have time to elaborate because at that moment the front door of a house opens and out comes a pale-skinned woman in her late forties, her black hair scraped into a tight knot at the back of her neck. She's wearing black cat-eye glasses and a black cardigan over generic black layers. She makes a small smile and my first impression is of the girl at school who doesn't have many friends but wants to be liked. My second thought is how, like the assistant in Good Vibrations, all the San Francisco sex women look a bit like groovy librarians.

As she walks towards the car, Annie tells me that her pro dom friend has a great eye for décor. The dungeon in her house is apparently magnificent. A respected member of

San Francisco's kink community, she is also admired for her 'erotic domination intensives' as well as being an expert in a type of therapy that Annie describes as, 'spa-treatment-meets-kink. Hot towels, scents, flip-overs, spanking, teasing claws. You know.'

While I'm trying to work out if I do know what Annie is talking about, I get out of the front of the car and go and sit in the back. I've heard about something called 'dom's disease', which means doing dom stuff when you're off duty, so I want to be prepared. The woman gets in, says, 'Hi, I'm Raven,' and makes herself comfortable in the front seat while Annie introduces me as someone who has 'been around the block'. This is the biggest compliment she could pay a back-of-the-bus wannabe like me. I glow in the back of the car while Annie drives us to the unlikely destination of City Hall as she needs to pay some taxes. Because there are long queues when we get there, we pass the time talking about how we masturbated as kids. Even in San Francisco, this seems like a bit of a hardcore conversation to be having in the tax office. So we go and get some fresh air and Annie tells me how she used to get off as a child. 'When I was eight or nine, I'd wake up lying on my back and have to pee really bad. Without moving, a pleasurable sensation would radiate from my pelvis and wash over my whole body. I'm not sure how it happened. But that's why I always connected peeing with erotic pleasure.'

She was eighteen and had been making porn for only a couple of months when her lover, Damiano, presented her with her first vibrator. But it was too weak to give her an orgasm. This changed when she then bought herself a Hitachi Magic Wand.

'I'm so old that when I got into porn in the 1970s there was a debate about if women even had orgasms and if they did, who cares?'

We go back in to join the queue but we're told that the tax office is now closed. 'We're being punished for talking about masturbation,' Annie says, only half-joking.

When she drops Raven back at her house, Raven tells us that there's a spanking party called Lash that she wants to check out this Saturday night. I ask if it'd be OK if I went too and she says, 'Sure.' We exchange numbers and then Annie drives me back to Bernal Heights to pick up my bike.

The day ends with me and Annie sitting in her car as night falls, eating sushi she's bought us from the local supermarket. 'So, what else have you found out about masturbation?' she asks suddenly. I try to think of some wisdom independent from Betty's lines about solo sex being every woman's sexual foundation.

In the darkness of Annie's car, I find myself thinking about pain. My vulva pain when I was about to turn forty. And how it was extra distressing because I was working as an editor at *Harper's Bazaar* and surrounded by beautiful, confident people talking about sex and affairs. I'd go into the editor's office and she'd say things like, 'How's your love life? Oh, and do you have any story ideas?' Most of the stories I had to commission were about high-end sex and pleasure-seeking but I couldn't tell anyone that I was in too much pain to even have sex. What had always come as naturally as falling off a log was now no longer possible. I became very withdrawn.

In 2005, I helped lead a press trip to a six-star resort in the Maldives with a gaggle of fashion celebrities, including Vivienne Westwood and Christian Louboutin. It should have been a gas. In some ways it was. They'd flown in *foie gras* and oysters from Paris, although Christian Louboutin curled his lip at the sight of the oysters, insisting he'd only eat the *foie gras*. Vivienne asked me why he wouldn't eat the oysters and I said,

'It's a long way for an oyster to fly, Vivienne. If I'd flown from Paris to the Maldives, I wouldn't want to eat me.'

I told her that the oysters were all dead and that oysters were supposed to be alive – beautiful and clear as rock pools. The way to see what kind of shape an oyster was in was to squeeze lemon juice on it. So she squirted lemon on her oyster and it didn't move. 'Yes,' she said, gravely. 'It's dead.'

As dead as my own oyster. No longer beautiful or clear. Up until then I'd been able hide things by humour. The high-society people found my fish-and-chip-shop background endlessly hilarious. 'Fish and chips and heroin, that's very aristo!' But some people could tell something was up. The actress Saffron Burrows, who I'd been semi-flirting with prior to this trip, said to the travel editor the night after we all went midnight skinny-dipping, 'Is there something wrong with Steph?' I was impressed she'd noticed. Nobody else did. I wonder if any of the other women on that Maldives trip had thrush or an outbreak of herpes. As Betty Dodson would tell me ten years later, 'We're very seldom honest about what's going on in our little pussies.'

Back in London, I went into hospital for a 'procedure', as they called it. I lay on my back with my legs in the air as the Bupa doctor, courtesy of my magazine health insurance, carved a triangle of skin out of my perineum, the sensitive area between your anus and your vagina, with a scalpel to try and diagnose what was wrong. I cried, not just for the pain but for the sense of defeat. It was a horrible reversal of the Bodysex workshop. Nobody was saying, Ah, what a beautiful pussy, how cute, how adorable. They were cutting a bit out to send to the lab and the doctors didn't seem to know anything anyway.

When this sort of thing happens to you, you realise that your pussy is your heart and this was my heart attack. It felt as though my life had stopped beating. I'd always written about sex, talked about it, bragged. 'Good in bed,' people said about me (because I used to read my girlfriends' diaries). But once I was a sexual adventurer and now I was a sexual cripple.

They wheeled me out to the recovery area after the procedure. Dr Wendy came by later and asked me how I was. I was struggling for something to say when she pronounced, weirdly, 'You have beautiful teeth, you know,' which seemed to emphasise how unbeautiful my cunt was. There's something I didn't mention about the Bodysex workshop. During my turn at genital show-and-tell. It wasn't just about clitoral hoods and Pinky Tuscadero. Betty told me that my vulva looked 'neglected' and she was right. She was neglected for a long time. It's nearly ten years since it all started. The pain only comes at intervals now. Sometimes it's just a burning in my skin. I say to Annie, 'I had this pain in my pussy for a long time. It's why I started doing all the hippie stories.'

Chakras? Vision Quests? Angels? I was open-minded. Dr Wendy had prescribed an anticonvulsant called Gabapentin, which made my body feel like it had been painted over with a layer of varnish, and Bupa didn't seem to have any answers. Nobody at work saw anything weird about my sudden interest in hippie therapies because the A-crowd all have their own personal psychics.

'What was wrong with you?' Annie asks.

What indeed. I'd stolen a Chanel compact from the *Harper's Bazaar* beauty cupboard to do in the mirror what I'd later discover was a version of Betty Dodson's genital show-and-tell. I wanted to see what was wrong. Nothing looked out of the ordinary. In the eighteenth century they might have blamed masturbation for my predicament. In *A Medical Dictionary* published in 1743 by the influential English physician, Robert James, there was a heading, 'Mastupratio', and a warning that the practice was 'productive of the most deplorable and generally incurable disorders' including 'lowness of spirits, hypocondriachal disorders and almost all sorts of chronical distempers.'

I remember talking to Nancy Sinatra on the phone one morning. She was giving me a hard time because I'd used an incorrect past participle in the article about early memories of her father. I said I was sorry. I didn't tell her that I'd just been on the phone to Bupa. I'd got to the supervisor level. I was trying to get money to pay for my latest consultation with Dr Wendy. I was trying to explain what the difference was between irritable bowel syndrome and vulvodynia, which is what Dr Wendy had finally diagnosed me with. The particularly insensitive GP I had at that time scoffed, 'But that just means pain of the vulva.' And it was a good point. They'd identified my chronical distemper but they didn't know what caused it. Stress? Masturbation?

The Bupa woman asked me to spell 'vulvodynia' and describe it. I said 'stabbing pain'. She said, 'But not all the time . . .' I said, 'Yes, all the time. I have a stabbing pain in my vagina.' I hadn't learned then that a vagina was really called a vulva. I cynically registered her shock and ended up getting my £150 consultancy money. I felt low then. In despair, you could say. That wasn't rock-bottom, though. Rock-bottom happened one Sunday morning in bed with Hadji. I girded myself up for the sex I didn't want and when climax time came, I couldn't come properly. I climbed up the orgasm hill and then fizzled out 60 per cent of the way. This wasn't anything new. It had been going on since I'd started taking the varnish pill, Gabapentin, which makes your brain think that pain signals are not really pain signals. And also that pleasure is not really pleasure. I don't know why that particular Sunday got to me. But it did.

I lay on my front after my strangulated orgasm. I felt I couldn't talk to Hadji about what I was feeling. It wasn't his fault. I sank my face into the pillow and wondered if there was any way out of this. A life of no pleasure. Like being locked in a jar with stale air all day long. Dr Komisaruk said that, 'Pleasure plays a crucial role in sustaining life. It ensures that life and species-preserving behaviours get performed.' But what if there was no more pleasure? After I'd tired of trying to get life force from chocolate or cream buns, would the stale air eat away at me so much that I might not want to live any more?

I kept thinking that I'd work my pain out some day, like a piece of algebra. The pussy trouble wasn't the conscious reason I went to Betty's workshop, but it's probably what's brought me to find myself sitting in the car of a former XXX actress in San Francisco. When it was my turn to answer Betty's workshop question, 'What do you feel about your orgasm?' I told the circle that I felt I'd lost it, like you lose a hat. Or like someone palms you off with a woolly bobble hat when you once had a big Russian hat of the finest fur.

After two years, I decided to stop taking the Gabapentin. I wanted to see if my hat would come back. And it did, in a way. It felt as if the varnish was melting away from my body. Life force was coming back and the shooting pain in my legs seemed to have gone, although four years later, my orgasm was still only 80 per cent of what it had been before. Even so, I felt as if I'd been given another chance. I wanted to try my new body out. That's when I pushed myself to have the split-up conversation with Hadji and when I went to New York, met Virginia and realised I'd have to learn about pleasure from scratch. Hadji has given me his blessing for this trip, which can't have been easy. 'You need to heal,' he said, and he's not a hippie at all.

Annie asks what happened to my pain in the end. I say there was no end, really. I tell her that pain in my body seems to come and go. Barry Komisaruk was the first person to suggest that it might be due to damaged nerves in my spine. I know many GPs I spoke to thought it was all in my head. It feels OK to sit in a dark car talking to Annie Sprinkle about this.

'It's good you're writing about that,' she says finally. 'Partly why I went into prostitution was that male genitalia was such a big mystery. But now I'm busy unravelling the female genitalia mystery.'

I tell her that sometimes I think that I'm lucky living in the age I'm living. That if there's scant research on vulval problems in the twenty-first century, how much worse must it have been in other times. In the eighteenth century, Louis XV's *maîtresse en titre* and the big love of his life, Madame de Pompadour, suffered from a gynaecological problem known as leucorrhoea, an inflammatory condition of the vagina or cervix that causes an unpleasant-smelling discharge. Some claim this happened when she gave birth to her daughter, although chances are it was contracted through the sex she had to go through on her way to the top. It was known as 'white flowers' in France, and you can imagine the jokes circulating through the corridors of Versailles. The Comte de Maurepas, a boyhood friend of Louis XV, wrote the following:

> *By your manners noble and frank,*
> *Iris, you enchant our hearts;*
> *On our path you spread flowers,*
> *But they are only flowers of white.*

The condition made it uncomfortable to have sex and the king started to joke that his lover was a 'cold fish'. In the beginning this might have been quite a cute jibe, given that Madame de Pompadour's surname was Poisson. It wasn't ideal though, and who knows if white flowers was all she had. Historians aren't even sure if she died of tuberculosis, pleurisy or lung cancer. And who knows what else childbirth had done to her. Thérèse the Philosopher's mother incurred painful damage to her nether regions after giving birth. This, as well as making Thérèse paranoid about getting pregnant herself (a very modern concern for an eighteenth-century erotica book), made her mother 'swear off forever the joys which had been responsible for my birth'.

Thérèse the Philosopher is an enlightened example of pre-Revolutionary pornography, because it posits the idea that sexual pleasure is vital for female health. When Thérèse is locked in a convent she becomes ill. When she later meets a count who wants to become her lover, she tells him she can't have sex for fear of pregnancy. He makes a bet: if she can contemplate his library of erotic books and paintings for two weeks without masturbating then he won't ask her for her body. By day four, the sight of Mars and Venus coupling sends her thrashing around on her bed, 'my buttocks moving lasciviously'. Luckily, when he comes to claim his prize, the count proves to be a strict practitioner of coitus interruptus.

One hopes Thérèse didn't succumb to Madame de Pompadour's sexual ailments later in life. I wonder if the cold fish used to sink her face into her eighteenth-century pillow and cry. Or sink her pussy into it for a solitary hump to prove she was still a whole woman. Promoting Sèvres porcelain, getting her portrait done by François Boucher and developing an exquisite taste for the arts can have taken her mind off things for only so long.

It must have been hard, having to hide an embarrassing secret. Annie agrees. 'Nobody talks about how radically a woman's sexuality can change over her lifetime,' she says. She tells me how one of her friends, a yoga teacher and the most orgasmic woman she'd ever known, suddenly stopped being able to come when she hit menopause. 'She had to take testosterone to have orgasms again.'

Menopause clearly knocked Annie's sexuality for six too. She last performed her masturbation ritual in Hamburg, Germany, in 2014 with around twenty sex workers from around the world. It was twenty years since she'd last done the show in 1994. Except when she tried using the vibrator this time, 'My clit didn't have the electric charge that it did before.' The ecstasy was mostly coming from her breath, 'which took it down a notch'.

Madame de Pompadour used vanilla as a sexual stimulant, just like the Marquis de Sade, who also used chocolates, truffles and Spanish Fly candy. Sometimes I feel that Western medicine is still on the vanilla and truffles level when it comes to gynaecology. But what I've learned is that you have to adapt. Annie thinks menopause is the reason she's become more experimental with her ideas of what sex and masturbation and orgasm are.

'I used to like hard sex. Fist-fucking. But now playing footsie under the sheets with Beth can do it for me. If you really get into the feeling of the sheets, and your feet on the bed lying horizontal, and rubbing your foot on another foot when you're just waking up . . .'

There's regret in her voice as she talks about vaginal dryness. Something about her pussy drooping these days. She used to masturbate conventionally two or three times a week, but now she does it maybe once a month. 'How much do you need to do it at sixty or seventy?' she drawls.

She says that if things aren't working out, you have to find other ways to get them to work out. 'It's like sitting at the restaurant this morning,' she says. 'If you just let yourself sink into opening up and bliss. It's like, that can be masturbation too.'

I can't see her face, but her breasts are bathed in orange chiaroscuro from the streetlight. There's a chuckle and a jiggle. 'I think we just came full circle,' she says.

MAKE BETTER PORN

The cosmic orgasm on the clitoris of America has taken it out of me. I wake up in Jet's candy cottage the morning after my day with Annie Sprinkle and I feel exhausted. I stagger out of bed and go down for breakfast, getting a flashback to the sex-party woman, Polly Superstar, who Betty recommended I get to know.

After the conversation in Annie's car, I went to meet her in a dark, trendy bar in the Mission. Born Polly Whittaker in London, she moved to San Francisco in 1999 and founded Kinky Salon in 2003. Chapters of Kinky Salon have now started springing up around Europe. I'd been told that her events are sex parties with an artsy twist and that they appeal to the Burning Man crowd, referring to the radical free-expression festival in Black Rock Desert, Nevada, that I've read attracts lots of rich start-up types. In the flesh, she was English and vaguely posh and, rather than swingers, she talked about the seventeenth-century philosopher Thomas Hobbes, 'the Jungian shadow', and how 'the concept of a fully expressive human being that includes sex could shift consciousness'.

I was already spaced-out after the morning in Bernal Park, so I just listened a lot. Polly told me that swinger parties aren't just about sex and fun. Things can get pretty intimate, sometimes painful. 'They bring issues to the surface.' I studied her face as she talked and realised how very intimate it would be to kiss someone, even on the chin. A small brush of flesh. That could be a big deal. So much for my whining on to Betty and Annie about wanting to get laid.

She had an interesting take on jealousy, which strikes me as a key issue to sort out before you enter into an open relationship. Polly said that it's a natural human emotion that comes from feeling unsafe. 'It's how you deal with it that matters,' she insisted. '"Why am I jealous?" is missing the point. It's better to ask, "What am I scared will happen?"'

She admitted it was tough when she found her boyfriend writing poetry to one of his extracurricular lovers. Betty says that jealousy was the hardest thing for her too. Before she came up with the idea of sticking the Bertrand Russell quote on the fridge to quell her jealousy attacks, she admits that she felt physically sick on seeing her big love, Grant Taylor, out with another woman, even though they'd 'agreed to have new primary lovers while we continued to remain sexual friends'.

At the end of our night in the Mission, Polly invited me to a Kinky Salon party on 14 February. That's when I'm supposed to be enjoying the spectacular view from the lounge with the Las Vegas Raëlian priestess. But I've got a couple of weeks to decide.

After breakfast, I set off for an appointment at a place called the Institute for Advanced Study of Human Sexuality. Essentially a private, unaccredited university offering degrees in sexuality. 'The Institute', as it's known in San Francisco, is run by a Methodist minister called Ted McIlvenna. Betty goes as far as to dub him 'an egomaniac sick blubber piece of shit', although she admits that his establishment is an important part of the American sex puzzle. When it opened in 1974 it was one of the few places in the US to disseminate progressive sexual knowledge and it was key in training and shaping generations of sex radicals, activists, teachers and therapists, as well as being influential on the general sex culture of the Bay Area.

McIlvenna claims that the Institute holds more historic sex material than the Kinsey Institute, the British Museum and the Vatican put together. He boasts that his collection includes precious first-edition books, valuable artworks, vintage posters, rare movies and important legal papers. But when I arrive at the Institute, located on the edge of China Town, the place resembles a multistorey church hall in need of a revamp. A cheerful man in his forties called Robert James greets me in a reception area that looks like the set of a 1950s B-movie about an amateur detective agency. He tells me that 'the show' has already started and leads me down a corridor lined with delicate drawings of two 1920s lovers having exuberant sex and emerges into a room filled with erotic art. There are cabinets of ivory Chinese figurines having advanced forms of sexual congress, a huge brass penis and balls, and, on the wall, a metal cast of Debbie Reynolds' naked torso.

Ted, eighty-three, has invited me to a special open day he's having in honour of a delegation of Chinese people who want to set up a chain of sexual wellness spas for women back in China. The room is filled with forty or so Chinese people dressed in fleeces and anoraks. They are facing a large screen, where a middle-aged man and woman are having missionary sex. The woman's big bush, the batik throws and the acoustic guitar backing track make it clear that the film was made in the 1970s. A corpulent old man who looks more like a turtle than a whale sits at the back of the room in suit and tie. Robert whispers that this is Ted. Robert is a film-maker, shooting a movie about Ted called *The Night Minister*, referring to his other life as a Methodist priest. Instructed by his superiors in the early 1960s to investigate why young people in San Francisco weren't going to church, Ted set up what became known as the Night Ministry. He became something of a real-life Kurtz, the character from Conrad's *Heart of Darkness* who was sent to quell a native uprising, but soon went native himself and never came back.

As Betty intimated, Ted has a knack for hyperbole and self-aggrandisement. When we go into his office to talk, he launches into an elaborate story about snatching a famous French actress from the founder of *Penthouse* magazine Bob Guccione one time in Paris when he was young. But Ted does have has some incisive things to say about what he calls 'the second sexual revolution'. This time around, he declares, 'It's going to be all about female sexuality.'

He continues that Wardell Pomeroy, a co-author of Alfred Kinsey's two landmark books, *Sexual Behavior in the Human Male* (1948) and the lesser-known *Sexual Behavior in the Human Female* (1953), was the Institute's first academic dean. 'Every Thursday afternoon he'd sit here and mix his punch and tell me what really happened at the Kinsey Institute. What destroyed Alfred Kinsey was the fact that nobody would take *Sexual Behavior of the Human Female* seriously. Kinsey thought it was going to be the most important book ever written.'

The crux of the book, he says, is the line, 'The female is an orgasm-seeking creature.'

We rejoin the others still watching the 1970s porn film and I note that it's very tender. Very boring. Robert tells me it was filmed by another Methodist minister called Laird Sutton, who worked with Ted at the Night Mission. Sutton got into experimenting with psychedelics when the Haight-Ashbury area of San Francisco became the epicentre of America's hippie Youthquake in the 1960s and he's now living somewhere 'off the grid'. Robert makes the good point that this film isn't actually porn. It's 'erotic *cinéma vérité'*. In an era influenced by the work of Alfred Kinsey, films like these were made to study the sexual patterns of ordinary people. In the room next door, another movie is being screened. Close-ups of a cock in 1970s yellow light and a man smoking a cigarette. It reminds me of *The Joy of Sex*, the 1972 sex manual by Alex Comfort, whose illustrations became famously outdated because of changing hair styles. I doubt this will be running on my secret cinema screen later tonight.

My 'mum friends' in the UK get very agitated about the subject of contemporary porn. One of them goes into a spiral of despair about the anal fissures that twelve-year-old girls are apparently now all getting because they think that buggery is what they must offer up to their boyfriends. And of course the guilty party is porn on the internet. When she calms down, I ask my friend about *her* pleasure. What does she feel about *her* body? She admits that the last time she remembers having private body time was when she was in her twenties and going to a yoga class every Wednesday night.

I'm not denying that porn has changed since my mum friends were young. It's now an expanding global industry with a growing audience and multiple participants, from commercial film companies, to people sharing home-made porn on their phones, to Snapchat. But my thirty-five-minutes-a-day friend, Natasha Salaash, says we don't need to panic. The mother-of-five doesn't have any blocks on her kids' devices: 'I try to have them online in the family room. I talk about it and ask critical questions so that hopefully when they view it they'll see what's wrong with it even if they enjoy it.'

She talks to her children about masturbation too. 'Around twelve, I tell them that it's normal and natural and basically everyone does it. Including me and my friends. So they understand that pleasure is an important part of life at different stages. When they're younger and I see them touching themselves I just acknowledge that it feels nice to touch ourselves. And that it's something to do alone.'

She has a special message for her daughters. 'I tell them that the pleasure that happens when they masturbate should also happen when they're with a partner. This was a missing link for me as a teen.'

Over in the UK, relationship and sex education guidance is being updated for the first time since 2000. It's great that LGBT inclusivity is finally being talked about and that Dr Mary Bousted, the joint general secretary of the National Education Union has insisted that, 'Primary-school children need to be given the correct names of body parts.' Yet when officials talk about this subject, the general starting position is usually doom and gloom: cyberbullying, sexting, anal fissures, how to stop access to the internet.

The new UK guidelines are supposed to come into effect in all schools in 2020, and who knows what other ideas they'll come up with. Some Betty Dodson tricks would be smart: have boys put their fingers slowly up their nostrils so they see what a sensitive matter penetration is. Separate girls from boys and spend quality time explaining why masturbation isn't a second-rate activity. And think about why it's a good idea to start sex education from a position of pleasure.

Anne Philpott runs The Pleasure Project, a UK non-profit promoting safe sex globally. The organisation focuses on the real reasons most people want to have sex: satisfaction, desire and pleasure. 'It's a starting point not usually adopted in most safer sex programmes,' Philpott says. In 2017 The Pleasure Project made three safer-sex porn films and Philpott is currently researching how much more safe sex happens if you watch an erotic film that turns you on with condoms in it.

'My experience to date has been that policymakers think censorship will work,' Phillpott says. 'This is plainly out of date with new free-to-access internet sites now working outside national borders.'

She points out that the most visited webcam site, livejasmin.com, has 300 million visitors a month, which is an incredible 2.5 per cent of all global internet traffic. 'This far outstrips any access conventional sex education has.'

Like Annie Sprinkle said of America's 1986 porn purge, known as the Meese report, 'The answer to bad porn isn't no porn, it's better porn.' The Ronald Reagan-commissioned Meese Report was supposedly a comprehensive investigation into pornography. In fact, it was compiled from a series of non-scientific, Oprah-style hearings in Washington. People like *Deep Throat*'s newly disillusioned Linda Lovelace (shepherded by Gloria Steinem) and anti-porn crusader Andrea Dworkin, came to testify that pornography was only ever about violence towards women.

The Meese Report marked the end of what had become known in the US as the 'golden age of porn'. This was a period from the early 1970s to the early 1980s, when porn was commercially healthy and seen as progressive because it broke the constricting social mores of the time. Some people started to believe that erotica really could be part of the first sexual 'revolution'. 'We were trying to emulate Hollywood films,' Sprinkle says. 'Make films that were good and popular, and had hardcore sex.'

Sexually explicit films such as Gerard Damiano's 1972 *Deep Throat* started receiving wide theatrical release in the US. Stars such as Jack Nicholson, Warren Beatty, Jackie Onassis and Sammy Davis Jr flocked to private screenings. In the US,

The Devil in Miss Jones, Damiano's follow-up movie, became the seventh most successful film of 1973, while in 1974, the French soft porno, *Emmanuelle*, about the adventures of a bored diplomat's wife in Bangkok, was released in the US by Columbia Pictures. It was the first time an X-rated film had been distributed by a major studio. Money was rolling in too. *Deep Throat* had been made with $25,000 but allegedly took $600 million, making it the highest-grossing adult movie in American history.

But President Nixon was on an anti-smut crusade. His predecessor, President Lyndon B. Johnson, had attempted, in 1969, to stymie a Supreme Court decision that people could view whatever they wanted in the privacy of their homes by creating the President's Commission on Obscenity and Pornography. When, in 1970, the scientific methods used by the commission's researchers revealed that obscenity and pornography were not important social problems and that legal restrictions on pornography should actually be loosened, the incoming President Nixon quietly disposed of the report and went on with his scourge anyway.

At the end of 1973, with sexual daring increasingly pushing boundaries, the Supreme Court clamped down with a landmark change in its definition of obscenity from 'utterly without socially redeeming value' to a more restrictive classification. By 1974, courts around America had succeeded in stamping out public showings of *Deep Throat* in the majority of states. The threshold test for obscenity seemed to be increasingly inspired by Supreme Court Judge Potter Stewart's whimsical observation in 1964 that, 'I know it when I see it.'

Methodologically weak research is a problem that continues to hinder proper investigation into the pros and cons of porn. On 21 October 1986, the *New York Times* reported that the Meese Commission claimed to have found a 'causal relationship' between certain kinds of pornography and acts of sexual violence. But Anne Philpott addressed such dubious science in a paper she co-wrote in 2017 for the Institute of Development Studies called *Blurring the Boundaries of Public Health: It's Time to Make Safer Sex Porn and Erotic Sex Education*. She notes that 'the majority of studies rely on self-reporting, a self-selected or volunteer sample and a study design with a negative hypothesis'.

Meanwhile, Donald Trump, US president at the time of writing and pal of now-deceased *Playboy* founder Hugh Hefner, was not an anti-porn man at the beginning of his tenure. Nor were his friends. Jerry Falwell, founder of the now-defunct right-wing Christian organisation Moral Majority, might have told CNN in 1997 that 'pornography hurts anyone who reads it', yet his son Jerry Falwell Jr is one of Donald Trump's biggest supporters. But then porn started to bite Trump's butt. Thwack it, as a matter of fact, in more ways than one.

In early 2018, The *Wall Street Journal* revealed that in October 2016, Trump's lawyer, Michael Cohen, had arranged for $130,000 to be paid to porn actress Stormy Daniels to keep quiet about an affair she'd allegedly had with Trump in 2006, a year into his marriage to Melania. Who knows if *l'affaire Stormy* will topple the government, but stand-out features of the case are that:

a) Post-Lewinski sex scandal women are starting to fight back.
b) TV news presenters are embarrassed by sex.
c) Female sex workers are still treated in an incredibly patronising fashion. As if they don't have brains. As if 'porn star' might be a dirtier job than 'president'.

As fellow adult entertainer Jenna Jameson pointed out about Stormy Daniels, 'The left looks at her as a whore and just uses her to try to discredit the president. The right looks at her like a treacherous rat.'

Meanwhile, every man in America is secretly wishing he could have had the sexual epiphany Donald Trump clearly did when Stormy Daniels spanked him playfully ('a couple swats') with a folded-up copy of *Forbes* magazine when they first met in 2006. In an interview with CBS's *60 Minutes* in March 2018, Stormy Daniels revealed to a po-faced Anderson Cooper how the swats achieved the remarkable feat of making Trump 'quit talking about himself and he asked me things'.

Anderson Cooper looked shocked at this revelation, but for anyone with even a faint knowledge of good sex, such a reaction is akin to not knowing what the capital of France is. Yes, you might be proud to be on the cover of *Forbes* magazine, but pulling down your trousers and being spanked by that same publication is the thing that will really blow your mind. It's about giving up your power for a few moments. It's intoxicating.

I wished someone smart like Annie Sprinkle had been conducting the *60 Minutes* interview. But maybe sexual savvy will be a criterion for getting a TV job in the future, for there are signs that the optimistic ideals from the 'golden age of porn' are returning. Take former advertising executive Cindy Gallop, who has reconceived Ted McIlvenna's idea of 'erotic *cinéma vérité*' by creating a website, makelovenotporn.tv, where real-life couples are encouraged to upload videos of themselves getting intimate so that people can see what everyday sex looks like.

Erika Hallqvist, aka Erika Lust, a Swedish film-maker who makes female-friendly adult movies, proclaims that 'a new world of indie adult cinema is growing'. Lust Films are all crowdfunded, so members (60:40 male-to-female ratio) get to see what they want. 'But we need to start thinking about "Fairtrade" porn,' Lust says. 'When people go to their favourite porn sites, they need to ask, Who are these women? What are their stories? Who is earning the money?'

Annie Sprinkle's porn-art daughter, Madison Young, has a good line on feminist porn. 'On a feminist porn set,' she says, 'you get vegan and gluten-free lunch; on a mainstream porno set you get nothing. On a feminist porn set you get silicone-free lube; on a mainstream set you get spit. On a mainstream porn set, the guy tells you, "Come in two minutes." On a feminist porn set, the actress says, "Give me two minutes and I'll come for real."'

OMGYes is another huge hope. San Francisco-based creators Lydia Daniller and Rob Perkins raised $6 million from mainstream Silicon Valley companies (which wished to remain anonymous) before they launched the interactive orgasm training programme with incredible visuals in 2016. Before omgyes.com, the only funded large-scale sex research was either biological (the physiology of what happens in the body during sex) or behavioural (the percentage of women who, say, masturbate or use vibrators as per Kinsey, and Masters and Johnson). Neither medical nor pornographic, omgyes.com is about the nuts and bolts of how women actually have orgasms. When I interviewed Daniller, thirty-seven, in 2016, she told me that, 'Women need to understand that it's OK to ask for lots of different things sexually.' But British national newspapers wouldn't take my story. One female editor my age told me that she was quite happy not being in touch with her body, thank you very much.

And yet when a celebrity gets involved, everything changes. When Harry Potter actress Emma Watson mentioned omgyes.com in an interview with Gloria Steinem later that year, saying she wished 'it had been around longer,' news about OMGYes went careering around the world.

In London, there's an all-female Sex Tech Collective, which brings businesswomen in the sex-toy business together. Members include Kate Devlin, a senior lecturer in social and cultural AI at King's College London, whose speciality is sex robots with a feminist slant. At the 2018 Veuve Clicquot Business Woman Awards (which used to be a very traditional affair), another member, Stephanie Alys, won the 'New Generation' prize for her smart vibrator. The group's counterpart in New York is Women of Sex Tech led by Polly Rodriguez, thirty, the CEO of Unbound, a sex-toy company that sends subscribers products every quarter.

Polly isn't just about encouraging women to embrace pleasure. As a twenty-one-year-old economics student at Miami University, she was told she had stage-three colon cancer. Her entry into the world of pleasure came from a place of being in extreme pain. When she started to recover, her doctors explained about early menopause and infertility, but it was only thanks to a nurse friend that she realised she needed to think about her sexuality too. 'Chemo had killed my libido and my friend told me to go out and buy lubricant and a vibrator.'

At first she says she was angry at her body 'because I felt it had betrayed me'. But when she started concentrating on her own sexuality, as opposed to defining it for male partners, things started to change. 'I realised that cancer, for me, was my body trying to find equilibrium. I realised how magnificent the human body is. So yeah, masturbation after cancer was a huge part of what healed me.'

Still, it was 2008 and the sleazy, male-centric sex shops of the times pissed her off. Hence the creation of her business. Post-graduation, she worked briefly for Senator Claire McCaskill on Capitol Hill, but the slow pace of legislation made her realise that 'if you want to make a change in the world, then government isn't the way to do it'.

Polly's story reminds me of someone else who wanted to make a big change in the world. Tutu surprised me one day by saying that she had learned to love her cancer. 'It's part of my body and it taught me a lot about my life.' With the photographer Ashley Savage, she created a show called *Punk Cancer*, about the various stages of her illness from a humour-tinged pre-chemo hair-shaving session to a defiant Bettie Page-style pose on a radiation table in a Valkyrie helmet. There were grimmer moments too. 'People don't have to be as out there as me,' she said with a smile. 'But it really helps to let out your emotions about how you feel about it.'

Back at the Institute for Advanced Study of Human Sexuality, a few of the Chinese delegation are paying attention to the dreary sex movie, although most slump in their seats, flicking through their smartphones. Some get up to take pictures of the Asian figures having coitus in the cabinets. It must be strange coming from an ancient civilisation where sex was once so sophisticated and now you end up in Ted's academy watching two unattractive Americans from the 1970s humping away. None of the Chinese speak English, so it's hard to know what they think.

I cast my mind back to Betty's fantasy Rolodex and her insistence that fantasy focuses the mind. 'The dirtier, the filthier the better,' she said. I remember feeling shocked when she reminded the room that you are allowed to think of anything you want in your head. The idea that some thoughts are too unfeminist is absurd and I will stand up for fast-food Xhamster wanks, even though sometimes I do feel grubby afterwards. Back in the 1980s, Catherine MacKinnon and Andrea Dworkin brainwashed women into believing that all porn causes violence against women. This idea is as uninformed as Jean-Jacques Rousseau's eighteenth-century claim that masturbation is a form of rape because you can have your way with any beauty 'without the need of first obtaining her consent'.

Another of the yellow films cranks up and Robert and I watch a wife joyfully stroking her husband's limp cock. 'You know the weird thing about this place?' he whispers. 'It's a sex institute and it feels completely unsexy.'

I decide to search for something a little more titillating. So I walk upstairs and wander through a musty library maze, glancing at original 1960s pulp fiction: *Bitch in Rubber* by Clive Bedford, *Share My Spouse* by Dr Guenter Klow. In a more academic section there are two different editions of Jean Genet's *Our Lady of the Flowers* as well as *The Well of Loneliness* by Radclyffe Hall and a large Freud and Foucault section. I emerge into another chilly room filled with dusty boxes of VHS video cassettes and spools of Super-8 film. A porn magazine from 1992 is stuck in one of the boxes. A naked woman in leg warmers is on the cover. I open it and read, 'His cock was as hard as granite and slick as grease.' I like the fact that Ted McIlvenna takes sex seriously, but I wonder if maybe he shouldn't sort through his collection a bit more selectively.

In another room piled high with overflowing boxes and crates I stumble across a plastic bag filled with a series of beautiful drawings and watercolour paintings. The paintings are mainly of naked green female nymphomaniac aliens with Veronica Lake purple hair. But they're painted as if they're part of an art deco ad for the front window of Tiffany's circa 1932. The lightness of stroke and delicacy of colour contrasts impressively with the explicit sexual poses. I realise these drawings are by Alexander Szekely, the same artist whose frolicking lovers adorn the Institute's hallway. Ted later tells me that the Hungarian artist used to draw otherworldly illustrations for Hans Christian Andersen's fairy tales. He lived in Paris in the 1920s and 1930s when he'd go to whorehouses and return home to recreate what he'd seen. Or wished he'd seen.

It seems a shame that nobody is getting to see the things that actually are sexy in the Institute for Advanced Study of Human Sexuality. And now the situation has worsened. Ted had a heart attack in 2017, which spurred him into selling the rickety but lucrative Institute building and housing its contents in a series of warehouses. His dream, he tells me over the phone in early 2018, is to open educational sex centres all over the globe. He claims he's had interest from India, Russia and China.

Carol Queen, the staff sexologist at Good Vibrations and one of San Francisco's most famous sex educators, says that 'most of this city didn't even know that the Institute was there'. Queen, who also runs the city's Center for Sex and Culture with her partner Robert Lawrence, observes ruefully that the current president has done much more than Ted to place sexuality in the public eye. Everyone knows about 'grab them by the pussy', but don't forget bleeding 'out of her wherever' (Trump's comments on TV newscaster Megyn Kelly) or his so-called 'golden shower dossier'. 'Trump has put sexuality on the table in so many ways,' Queen says, adding that unfortunately many of his policies have proved to be 'anti-women and anti-sexual diversity'.

On the heels of Trump's election came the sexual panic attached to the uncovering of Harvey Weinstein's gross misconduct in October 2017. Queen believes that the fallout from the accompanying #metoo outpourings could lead to 'anti-sex elements' in which the sex act is given as much, or more, emphasis than the lack of consent. She notes also that 'it's important to remember that people can enthusiastically consent to kinky or unusual things and can be harmed by plain vanilla acts'.

The secret to nipping sex-negativity in the bud is, she believes, to go back to the original meaning of that buzzword we hear so often now: 'sex-positive'. 'Sex-positive isn't just about having a lot of sex.' (Which Harvey Weinstein clearly believed was fine and dandy.) 'It's also about social justice: freedom from shame, diversity, access to education and health resources and a focus on consent.'

It's hard to pin down where 'sex-positive' came from. Queen's friend and fellow activist, Gayle Rubin, an Associate Professor of Anthropology and Women's Studies at the University of Michigan, started hearing it in the late 1970s and early 80s when it began circulating in the feminist wars over pornography. 'The people who circulated around the Institute, SFSI, and the leather scene were probably the conduit,' she tells me in an email. (SFSI, or San Francisco Sex Education, was a free community phone service founded in 1973 where people could get accurate information about sex.)

Queen concludes that 'many women haven't been given the opportunity to thrive as sexual beings because of daily breaches of consent'. But all that's starting to change now. 'People are being reminded that if there's not mutual interest and agreement, sex might not be worth the trouble – and that might mean legal trouble.'

She believes that America will emerge more sexually savvy from the sexquake triggered by Trump's term in office. This is because the press is now being forced to cover areas it would previously have dismissed as smut or the norm. 'The mainstream is becoming more "woke" to feminism and LGBT issues than ever before.'

*

I'm tired when I get home. I flop into bed with a Corona thinking, *Too many sex educators and not enough sex.* Raven just texted to say she's feeling ill and she's not sure about the Lash party tomorrow night. I made it clear I wanted to get laid. Although whenever I said something like that yesterday, Annie and Raven went strangely quiet. That's the thing with the sex people: they don't really tell you much about their own sexual selves.

It does feel liberating being in San Francisco, though. I don't feel I have to be lesbian or bi or anything. 'Sex-positive' is the word that everyone uses and in spite of Carol Queen saying that it encompasses loads of right-on stuff, it basically seems to mean that everyone's up for anything. Yet this is my second Friday night in the city and here I am again, alone at Jet's house. Nobby No Mates. I know I should be working on Annie's energy orgasm thing because that will make me a more fulfilled person. But according to Annie, something like playing footsie under the sheets could be seen as masturbation. I break out the Jolly Lolly and start sucking. This is what the life of a masturbator feels like: being a saddo and staying in and making it all up in your head. I'm feeling really horny. Talking to people about solo sex, not to mention all my homework, is spilling over into wanting sex with another person. Like a droplet of water that gets bigger and bigger until inevitably it falls.

Then I see that Annie has sent me an email. She's left San Francisco and gone back to her place in the hills near Santa Cruz. 'Thanks for going with the flow yesterday,' she writes. 'I feel like a country bumpkin in the city these days. If you get to Santa Cruz, do give me a call if you can. Would be lovely to show you around the redwood forest.' So I decide to retire to the bedroom for an intense session with me and

Annie in the trees. Before long, I see the redwoods in a circle with the sunlight streaming through the leaves. There's a hint of English Arcadia. I start skipping around the trees and then I take my top off. Annie's energy soon fills Jet's bedroom like fantastic smog. I'm naked in the redwoods now and she's going to get naked and press me against a tree and what was that thing she said yesterday about 'teasing claws'? Alexander Szekely's green nympho aliens with big tits and Veronica Lake purple hair suddenly appear. They crawl, doggy-style, in the bushes in an art deco Central Park until a dusty photo of Freud from the Institute wraps itself around my mind's eye. I look into Freud's eyes as I imagine two big butch bulldykes pinning me down and fucking me. It's a great orgasm, smelling of patriarchs in Victorian suits that constrict the limbs. But I'm still high as a kite. Jet was right about the Sativa Jolly Lolly being the 'up' one. The masturbation mincing machine demands more food and luckily I remember one of the DVDs Annie gave me before we parted yesterday, *Masturbation Memoirs*.

This public information film, directed by Dori Lane, freaks me out to start with. Different women demonstrate their jack-off techniques. Ugly pussies, bodies I don't fancy. And then one of them squirts. It looks like a clear stream sloshing out, not like pee at all. I'm envious. I want to be able to do that. I'm a bit disgusted too, but that's good. Women need to see this stuff. The anti-female-ejaculation members of the British government need to see this stuff. The best bit is Annie's segment. She's filmed by a pond in sunny woodland. She's talking about her medabation thing, the cross between masturbation and meditation. She's saying that it's 'a way of keeping myself healthy, of releasing emotions, a way of getting into altered states, a preparation for dying'. Dying! She uses the Hitachi Magic Wand to massage her back, going, 'When

I'm by the sea or a waterfall I go into a kind of ecstasy that I don't find in my bed at home.'

Watching the film, I realise that my fantasy about Annie Sprinkle was way out of whack. She would be too much into her ecosexy thing to be interested in me flitting about by the redwoods. She has a very good-looking cunt. Shocking pink in colour and supple in movement. If she'd been in Betty's workshop, her pussy would have been christened Linda Evangelista. Annie makes lots of those, 'Ooh yeah! Ooh yeah!' noises that used to turn me on when I used to imagine having sex with American girls. And then, yes, Annie Sprinkle really does sprinkle. She ejaculates like a waterfall. I come by just looking at the rock pool erupting before my eyes, a *femme fontaine*, as the French call such a gifted woman. Just before I pass out, I imagine the jester goddess Uzume's pussy puppet show, guest starring the Virgin Mary, Linda Evangelista and Pinky Tuscadero ready to start her engine.

SEWGASMS

What a lark! What a plunge! Getting ready for Lash tonight feels like I'm Mrs Dalloway preparing for her high-society party. Late afternoon, I wash my hair, shave my key areas and rinse out the black lace sex pants from my purple bag.

I really like myself at this point. Back in London, when I was secretly monitoring Fab Swingers (the low-rent swingers site compared to Personal Friend Finder, which my desk companion at *Harper's Bazaar* was on), I worried that I wasn't attractive enough to be polyamorous. Looking back, my foray into Fab Swingers was an early attempt to put a spanner in the works of my relationship with Hadji. Yet my first date with Dawn and Terry was cancelled at the last minute when Dawn sent a text saying, 'Terry asks if you're shaved. I am shaved and Terry is nicely trimmed. He also wonders if you could post another couple of pics of your face, as your picture isn't that clear on the site.' This was rich coming from a couple of sixty-year-olds who looked like Fred and Rose West. Hanging out with the sex people in America, I've realised that sex appeal goes way beyond questions of depilation.

Laid out on Jet's bed are my clothes for the evening. Little did I know that I've been carrying my BDSM outfit with me all along. My second-hand army boots, which I only brought to America because I didn't have any waterproof shoes, have become fetish boots. My leather belt with the Flash Gordon buckle I bought in Paris in 1989 has become a portable sex toy. The £35 Yves Saint-Laurent-look blouse from H&M that I used to wear for the swanky parties I used to cover softens the fierceness with a poetic vibe. Its cream colour hides the fact that it's actually filthy.

Raven's text messages suggest she is more dramatic than I took her to be when I met her with Annie. She sends one saying she's feeling 'peevish' and then, mid-afternoon, she sends another, telling me to come round to her place at nine. I've picked up a bottle of pink champagne from Trader Joe's. It's actually a $10 *crémant* de Bourgogne, but she won't notice.

When Virginia calls, I tell her I'm going to a thing called Bawdy Stories, a stand-up porn comedy event. Raven did say she wanted to swing by (although I'm going to dissuade her because it sounds like it will be taking up valuable sex time). I don't mention Lash to Virginia, but I think she figures. There's something in her voice. Then Hadji calls. My heart is always on edge when I speak to him, waiting for him to say, 'I've met someone interesting.' But it turns out he's just doing another tai chi weekend. I kind of wish I could be in the mindset of wanting to do tai chi for the weekend.

I take the compost out to the recycling bin without wearing a bra under my T-shirt. It's sort of a first step. If someone sees me with wobbly forty-eight-year-old breasts, who cares? This is an example of how I've come on since Fab Swingers. I now realise that even thinking about 'wobbly forty-eight-year-old breasts' is a very English Stephanie way of thinking. American Stephanie thinks, *There are a ton of men out there who will see a woman in the street not wearing a bra and have a wank over the memory later in the week.*

It's still a bit early to get changed, so I kill time by sitting on the terrace with the Jolly Lolly and reflecting on a phrase that Raven used the other day: 'Surrender is the gateway to serenity.' I immediately feel calmer and begin to enjoy the light of the late sun shining through the pine tree. I wonder what Jean-Jacques Rousseau would have thought about ecosexy. Rousseau is the big sexuality figure of the eighteenth century, alongside Sade. The philosopher credited with sowing the seeds for the French Revolution is famous for his concept of the 'noble savage'. He never actually used those words, although he clearly had a view of the benevolent and healing powers of nature. At the same time, he had a big downer on masturbation, not just declaring it to be akin to rape but calling it a 'dangerous supplement' in the eighteenth century's most influential work on education, *Emile*.

Behind the scenes, he was clearly a masturbation fiend. He admits in *The Confessions* that as a young man, his thoughts 'were incessantly occupied with girls and women', which kept his senses 'in a perpetual and disagreeable activity' and led to thoughts 'at once tormenting and delicious'. We know what that means.

To try and cure himself of the dangerous supplement, he decides, at the age of forty-three, to leave the bright lights of Paris and lead a reclusive life in the countryside. One of his many sugar mummies, society writer Madame d'Epinay, offers him her cottage to live and work in. It was in the Forest of Montmorency, a few miles north of Paris. Yet, far from dampening his libido, Rousseau discovered that being surrounded by primroses and budding chestnut trees and the song of the nightingale sent him into what he calls a 'rustic delirium'. He was assailed by 'voluptuous imaginings' and erotic 'intoxication'. Annie Sprinkle knows all about how naughty nature can do that.

Rustic delirium served him well, because during his sojourn in the country, he ends up writing the bestselling novel of eighteenth-century France. *La Nouvelle Héloïse*, raved about by Napoleon himself, is filled with longings between a low-born tutor and his high-born pupil. It ends in self-sacrifice for the good of the community, but this is clearly a cop-out. Rousseau himself never became virtuous in his own terms. He believed that, thanks to two very memorable spankings in his childhood over the knees of his governess, Mademoiselle Lambercier, he was condemned to a life of fast-food solo sex sessions. 'I devoured beautiful people with burning eyes. My imagination endlessly recreated them to do with them as I wished, turning them into so many Mademoiselle Lamberciers,' he confesses in *The Confessions*.

Annie should have taken Rousseau on an ecosexy walk in the forest of Montmorency. He had an eye for a great décolletage. He protests that he never had an affair with the flat-chested Madame d'Epinay because 'my senses have never been able to think of one without breasts as a woman'. He could have helped Annie out on some of her plant names (botany was a great passion of his) and she could have given him some calming breathing exercises. Just imagine: the high-voltage vibrator of Jean-Jacques Rousseau and the grounding dildo of Annie Sprinkle.

Rousseau clearly also had the ecosexual gaze. During his first few weeks at Madame d'Epinay's house, he writes of his delight at having left Paris for the rejuvenating joys of the country:

> When I looked out of the corner of my eye at a simple poor thorn bush, a hedge, a barn, a field, when I breathed in the fumes of a good chervil omelette while going through a hamlet, when I heard from afar the rustic refrain of the lace-worker's song, I sent the rouge and flounces and ambergris to the devil.

The reference to the lace-worker's song is more prescient than Rousseau knew. In 1899, the English sexologist Havelock Ellis would unleash the word 'auto-erotic' onto the world in his paper, *Autoeroticism: A study of the spontaneous manifestations of the sexual impulse*. 'Auto-erotic' was a breakthrough in masturbation concepts because it included the Rolodex idea or an 'imagined narrative' going on in the mind as well as what was going on in the hand.

Ellis was an unlikely sexpert, as he was reputedly impotent until he was sixty, although he later reveals that his secret fetish was urolagnia or a delight in the sight of women urinating. (Donald Trump will be glad to know he is in good company.) Ellis's *Autoeroticism* paper is fascinating because it's not just about female masturbation but female masturbation among the working classes. While Madame d'Epinay was waiting for her neurotic house guest to grace her with even a feverish kiss, the 'rustic' lace workers were getting down to some serious pleasure, if Ellis's observations are anything to go by.

Ellis talks of how, by the early nineteenth century, female sewing-machine operators had found an ingenious way of making the working day go quicker. One young brunette is reported to have turned her sewing machine into a pedal-powered Hitachi Magic Wand thirty years before Betty Dodson was born. Ellis reports how she would be stitching away when suddenly, 'Her face became animated, her mouth opened slightly, her nostrils dilated, her feet moved the pedals with constantly increasing rapidity.' Within minutes, she would throw back a pale face and utter a 'suffocated cry, followed by a long sigh'. After casting 'a timid and ashamed glance at her companions' she apparently resumed her work.

Ellis surmises that such pleasure in the workplace was being caused by seamstresses sitting on the edge of the sewing machine's seat instead of in the middle. This was responsible for 'much facilitating friction of the labia', although we know now that friction of the labia wasn't the half of it.

Apparently, the forewomen would try and prevent these . . . what would Annie Sprinkle call them? Sewgasms? Although you wonder why, because presumably the girls were raring to get going on the next pair of trousers. If you were a country girl and didn't happen to be in the vicinity of a sewing machine you were OK, because *Autoeroticism* reveals that bananas and cucumbers were 'especially used by country and factory girls in masturbation'.

Actually, maybe the Marquis de Sade would have made a better playmate than Rousseau for Annie Sprinkle. Ecosexy asks us to think more in terms of 'lover nature' than 'mother nature', but Sade talks of 'whore nature'. The Château de Silling in *120 Days of Sodom* is set in the primitive wilds of the country and peopled with four craven libertines. 'I'm alone here,' hisses one of them. 'I'm at the end of the world, protected from the gaze of all others, no other creature is able to reach me; no more barriers, no more restraints.'

Annie and the Marquis de Sade might have had a kinky meeting of minds. All of Sade's arrests involve flagellation. I can feel myself getting excited. I'll have to leave ecosex for another day. It might be a fabulous sunset and a beautiful tree, but I have a date at a spanking party with a stroppy dominatrix.

STRANGER DANGER

When I arrive at Raven's house, the door is opened by an African-American woman in her forties with a shaved head and piercings on her face. She smiles and says her name is Dill. As I follow her up the stairs, I note that she has a red handkerchief hanging from the back right-hand pocket of her jeans.

I assume Dill is a good friend of Raven's, as she's soon doing the washing-up. Raven calls from behind a door with a rack of high-heeled shoes on the front to say she'll be out shortly. Dill asks me what I'm doing in San Francisco and I say I'm writing a book on masturbation. I tell her that I interviewed Joycelyn Elders back in Arkansas. I'm about to explain who she is when Dill says, 'The Surgeon General. Fired by Clinton, right?' She shrugs. 'A black woman in the White House. You remember those things.' This makes me feel dumb, but she's very gracious about it.

I wander round the flat, licking the Jolly Lolly, starting to feel confident again. *Fifty Shades of Grey* opens in America this weekend but I am not doing research in a library like E. L. James did. On a bookshelf displaying a flying goddess with claws and wings, a wolf head pelt and a wand topped with black feathers are several books including *Susie Bright's Sexwise*, *Slow Sex* by Nicole Daedone and Taschen's *Erotica Universalis*. There's also the 'second sexual revolution' book that Ted McIlvenna was talking about, *Sexual Behavior in the Human Female* by Alfred C. Kinsey, Wardell B. Pomeroy, Clyde E. Martin, and Paul H. Gebhard. I'm about to pick it up when the door with the shoes bursts opens and a creature in a black gown emerges, smoothing down the feathers on her gleaming shoulder wrap.

Raven is much less nerdy than the first time I met her. She reminds me of Estella from *Great Expectations*. Before she pours my champagne, she looks at the label over the top of her glasses and says in a disappointed voice, 'Oh, a *crémant*.' When we clink and drink, she says, 'It tastes like aspirin, don't you think?'

It turns out that Raven had a French lover for years. She speaks French as well as I do. She knows about wine. I change the subject as I try and sound blasé about tonight's entertainment.

'I hope Lash is going to be good,' I say. 'I've yet to be convinced that this town is not all mouth and no trousers.'

'All talk, no action? Please.'

She adjusts the strap of her push-up bra then goes to the sink and pours her *crémant* down it, filling up her glass with red wine from a cardboard box on the worktop. She tops me up with more of the fake champagne. This reminds me of Tutu. Half the skill of a dominatrix is being a good hostess.

'The party's at a well-known dungeon in town,' she informs me. 'It's not very pretty, but there will be play.'

Play. I make another attempt at impressing Raven by saying how nice it was hanging out with Annie. 'I told Annie that my favourite drugs are the sun and sugar.'

Raven raises an eyebrow. 'Mine are sex and wine.' She sits down. She says that she never drinks while working, as it's very looked down on in the BDSM community, then orders Dill to make less noise at the sink. I ask her where she's from originally in America and she says that she grew up in the Midwest in a place that was 'serious, not joking, white trash'.

'The only things to do were get drunk and fuck,' she deadpans, inserting a pin in the stiff black knot of her hair.

She's just finished doing an interview on a podcast show about what it's like to be a dominatrix. 'The media has a very one-dimensional view of us,' she says. She sees herself more as a 'psychic waste manager', because she encourages people to excavate the parts of themselves that society frowns on.

'Which parts?'

'The primal sexual self.'

'Oh.'

'I unearth treasure,' she says. 'And it doesn't always glitter.'

She says that unleashing desire can bring dark things to the surface: jealousy, anger. 'But if we don't accept that we have desire, we can't call ourselves fully evolved human beings.'

She tops up my glass and I feel excited about the prospect of spending the evening with this woman in the black feather wrap and a knowledge that I don't have. When I wrote to Annie that I was going to Lash, she sent me a chatty email advising that, 'Raven is a master spanker. If she offers you a spanking, I'd take her up on it!'

Raven is unnervingly observant. As I'm wandering around her flat, she informs me, 'Mmm, I see you're like me, your belly's where you put your weight on.'

She tells me in a scolding voice that she's only going out tonight for my benefit. Sex parties are work for her. I apologise, telling her that I just 'like the idea of meeting anonymous people in sex clubs'.

'Stranger danger,' she says with a sigh. 'I get it.'

I check it's OK with Raven and then I spark up a pipe filled with the Texan happy weed. She doesn't want any, but when I offer some to Dill, Dill turns to Raven and says, 'May I?'

This is when I first realise something funny might be going on.

Raven speaks abruptly. 'You can have a couple of drags.' Dill comes over from the sink to take some puffs and then Raven says, 'Enough! Your duty's to get your mistress ready.' They both disappear off to the bedroom.

As the evening proceeds, it turns out that the relationship between Raven and Dill is a bit like Scarlett O'Hara and Mammy from *Gone with the Wind*. I sit on the purple velvet couch thanking Annie Sprinkle for my good fortune in helping me fall into such a sticky web on a Saturday night in San Francisco. There's a squeal as some eye make-up drama seems to be taking place in the bedroom. I'm glad that Dill's dealing with that. Dill clearly enjoys playing a submissive role to her mistress. And there is clearly an element of care and concern from Raven although, as she tells me later, she often gets judgemental looks from other BDSM people, who see the racial implications as one fantasy too far.

Finally, Raven emerges from her bedroom. She now has smoky black eyes, a dramatic red mouth and a Paco Rabanne chain-mail bag in her manicured hands. She opens it and offers me a chocolate-covered marijuana coffee bean, her preferred form of 'edible' for a night out. I take one, thinking it can only add to my Jolly Lolly buzz. Raven announces that Dill will take care of our bags all night so there's no danger of losing them.

And then we're in an Uber being driven to Lash. Afterwards, I have no memory of where we were or what the outside of the venue looked like, but thanks to the various forms of marijuana chugging round my system, the interior feels like the dream of going into a chilly church hall on school-disco night. There are a couple of teachers in black macs on the front desk. One of them asks apologetically for the $25 entry fee and then I follow Raven and Dill through to a coat-check area. Again, it is very school disco. But when we turn the next corner, the smirk is wiped right off my face. I am horrified to see a vista of serious U.G.L.Y. open up before me.

In the glare of supermarket lighting I see a sea of big chicks with bad complexions and beefy thighs, skinny women with limp hair and careworn expressions, and the sort of men you see lingering by bus stops late at night. Then an overpowering smell of warm sausages hits me. There is not a BBQ area at Lash; this is the smell of a sex club. It is a hideous dropping off of the veil, the moment you realise that in real life you can't do cut and paste like you can in a fantasy. I realise that I'm going to have to get sexual with someone in this place quite soon and there's no way of wriggling out of it.

There is a dark corridor in front of me, but Raven has stopped at an alcove where a short man in a leather waistcoat and leather trousers is giving an educational talk entitled 'Coming Out Kinky to Those You Date'. I am soon to learn that this is very San Francisco. That you can't have a sex party without a 'sex educator'. It's annoying because I don't want to learn about sex – I want to do it. My eyes are drawn again to the dark corridor where a stream of couples and singles are disappearing. A heart-attack feeling is still happening in my upper chest, but it's starting to calm down. I reason that at some point a spark of desire will flash in me. Won't it? I wonder if it will be a man or a woman to light the touchpaper. As the sex educator drones on about 'respect for personal boundaries', I spot the spark. It's a man with the bearing of an ambitious head waiter from a three-star hotel in the provinces. Mean little eyes. He looks a bit like Ricky Gervais. I hold his gaze when he looks at me. This is what they tell you in those women's magazine articles about flirtation in wine bars. His mouth twitches and then his eyes are off again, hungry for more prey. I'm off too. The pull of the black corridor is too great. I find myself walking towards it, even though a small voice says, *What if you lose Raven and Dill? You're off your head in a San Francisco spanking club and you have no idea where you are.* But that voice is soon drowned out by Hammer House of Horror screams as I walk further into the blackness.

I finally emerge into a huge room that makes me think of a sweaty session in a gym, only the lighting is dimmer and the equipment is different. There are several women tied up to X-shaped crosses, one of whom is making blood-curdling screams. She seems to be over-egging the pudding a bit. The noise she's making doesn't sound like sexual pleasure and pain to me. The school disco has turned into a hammy school play. You expected a villainous 'ha! ha! ha!' laugh to pipe up any minute and someone to come out dressed as a vampire. (Raven loves her city and its scene, and says that she can't comment on the screaming woman 'for professional reasons', but that, 'I know what you mean.')

Salvador Dalí was right when he said that eroticism should always be ugly. Standing here, aware of the gaze of a bus-stop lurker rustling in the shadows, I realise what a find this place is. Like Dalí's *Aphrodisiac Dinner Jacket*, adorned with glasses of crème de menthe with a dead fly lurking at the bottom of each, Lash hits the delight-disgust jackpot. I don't want some sterile *Eyes Wide Shut* orgy, some Sunday-colour-supplement idea of what a sex party should be. Like I said to Annie Sprinkle, I wanted a bit of cheese and here they're serving it in abundance.

People forget that desire is strange. I see Virginia on all fours, writhing, moaning, 'Do whatever you want to me,' begging me to do it, feeling the excitement, seeing the plains of power opening up before me. Weird thoughts, the weirdness of having no thoughts. VV was right about San Francisco being a good city to be sexually frank in. You'd never get a club like

Lash in New York, because they don't understand that that the repugnant can be desirable, faults can be qualities.

There aren't only chubby young women draped over spanking benches as their boyfriends work on them like methodical DIY. A cute young girl in a short frou-frou skirt and with small naked breasts walks past with her nerdy-looking boyfriend. She smiles at me shyly, knowingly, maybe later-ly. And then I see him. Tanned, late fifties, thick head of silver-grey hair. He's chewing gum like an American football coach. Or like Cliff Barnes from *Dallas*, the 1980s soap opera about the feuding Texas oil family. He has that oil-producer ruthlessness and perfectly fits the profile of my 1970s Americana fetish. He looks at me. I look away. I look back. He looks back. He comes over.

'Hi!' He has a voice like Joe Buck from *Midnight Cowboy*. 'Where's your badge?'

At the entrance to Lash, we were offered a choice of three badges: 'Top', 'Bottom' and 'Switch'. At the beginning of the evening, when I was being way too verbal because I was nervous, I had scorned these badges. 'Lame,' I said to Raven. 'How do you know what you want to be? It's not very spontaneous.' I later realised that sex clubs aren't about reading the windows of the soul, they're about, Do you want A, B or C? So I'm not wearing a badge, but he is. It says 'Top'. My hand brushes the sleeve of his jacket. Soft. Cashmere mix. He has a Joe Buck country-boy accent but clearly some taste. I like that he's wearing a sports jacket in a sex club. He grins again as he works the gum.

'I suppose I'm a switch,' I say, adding that I haven't been to a San Francisco sex club before. He says he's a beginner too. (I soon learn that everyone says this.) He talks about how he loves England, how he travelled there when he was younger. The Hammer House screams pipe up again. 'So,' he says, as if we're about to talk oil mergers, 'would you like to see my whip collection?'

I'm chewing gum too. Root beer float flavour. I hope I look casual. 'Sure,' I shrug. He goes to a dark recess and takes out a canvas bag that unravels like a butcher's bag of knives. He has a good collection: big whips, small whips, canes and paddles, leather straps, soft suede floggers.

'This one's real good,' he says, picking up a small whip with leather strands like tangled-up spaghetti. He taps the strands lightly into his hand. He has a joy about his whip collection like some men have about their cars.

'Would you like to choose one?'

I feel nervous, but the mix of kind Joe Buck and mean Cliff Barnes makes him attractive. I pick out a small black whip about ten inches long. It's made up of strips of suede, like the fringing on the original Joe Buck's jacket. It doesn't look too threatening. I try it on the palm of my hand. Then I say, 'Where do we go?' because I'm thinking we don't want to do it out in the open with all these people. He sort of chuckles and pats a table, like the table you lie on at the doctor's. It's covered in yellow leatherette. It reminds me of what VV said about the Hellfire Club and how it was best to wear wipe-down clothes. There's a box of tissues and a spray bottle of Windex on a stand next to the table. I hadn't noticed this table before. But now, looking around the huge room, I see there are several of them, all with tissues and a spray bottle next to them.

'Can't we go somewhere private?' I say.

He smiles again and says, 'People usually do it out in the open.'

I want to do what is normal practice in a sex club so I say, 'OK.' I'm undoing my army boots when Raven suddenly appears and says to Cliff, 'Just to let you know, I am a friend of this woman.' I think this is a bit unnecessary, but maybe Raven is just being protective and San Francisco sex clubs are keen to underline the safety element. Cliff doesn't seem to mind and I am glad to discover that Raven hasn't left the club without me. I wonder if this adventure is going to piss her off, but maybe that's me thinking in terms of the romance-infected world that I've left behind now.

And then she's gone and my boots and jeans are off and I'm getting up on the leatherette table to see what it feels like. I feel like I need my army boots back on. They give me a Sailor 2-type feeling of power. I put them on and climb back up. Cliff Barnes strokes them with a look in his eyes. He's clearly not a man hung up on the 'ladylike' thing, which impresses me. Soon, I'm feeling great in the black lace pants and the fake Yves Saint-Laurent blouse and the bovver-boy footwear. Cliff tells me to get on all fours, so I do. I block out the thought of everyone else around and concentrate on my hands making contact with the cold leatherette. The suede tails of his whip flick all over my bum cheeks, sliding down to tease the crack at the very top of my thighs. I open my legs for more and the cool suede strands hit against my pussy, light as feathers, as he strokes my bum with hands that clearly don't work in an office. I want more of the clumsy roughness, but he takes his hands away and starts to whip my bare cheeks rhythmically. He says, 'Put your ass high in the air,' and I obey him because I want him to touch me some more. He whips gently, then stronger, then gently again. He slaps the inside of my thighs, slaps my pussy, my clit, disrespects my sacred yoni. I start to breathe deeper. Quite sophisticated sexual knowledge from Cliff Barnes. Maybe he's taken some courses from the man in the leather waistcoat. My butt is tingling, my pussy is wet, I want more now, I want him to fuck me and I push my hips towards the leatherette table because I'm desperate for some pressure on my clit, but he commands me to get up. 'Put your ass in the air.' I can tell he's excited by the way he's chewing his gum. I moan and put my ass in the air and he whispers in my ear, 'Good girl,' and it turns me on so much I start to buck like a pony. Writhing now, so excited, and he finally puts a finger in my cunt as he carries on whipping me with the suede strands, then in and out with his finger and sometimes two fingers, maybe haphazard or maybe plain cruel, but it turns me on and I'm pushing back, getting what I can get, anything I can get, a stranger with his big hands in your wet pussy. Is this is allowed? Can you do this? Have an orgasm in public? Shake your hungry ass in a room full of strangers? What if Raven sees? Is he cool enough for her to be impressed? And then that blanks out and I want more fingers, I want a cock, but he strikes harder with the whip and then soft until I want it harder and my clit feels like it's getting bigger and I'm moaning, 'Please!' for release and he's saying, 'Put your ass up high!' and tingling and vibration and pulsation, and suddenly I'm not on a leatherette table, I'm in a field of blackness with no thought, just hole and hot and surrender . . .

Something comes to an end. It takes me a while to come round. Through the corner of my eye, I see Ricky Gervais and a couple of other men lurking. Slowly I sit up and Cliff pushes his groin into the side of the table while my legs swing on either side of him. I'm still wearing my boots. I can feel his hard dick through his tight jeans. I say, 'Can't we fuck?' He looks a bit embarrassed. 'You gotta stick by the rules,' he reasons. 'Spanking's the theme.'

I suppose he's right. The club isn't called Shag. That's the strange thing about dungeon life. Vanilla sex is the ultimate sin. Cock and cunt contact. So there's something almost puritanical about Lash. Cliff Barnes looks me in the eyes and tries to kiss me. I make a game of resisting his mouth. I think that kissing's probably not part of the rules either. He grins and says, 'You want to play again?' This time I lie on my back because I want visuals. He starts slapping my pussy again and that gets me going as much as the whip in his other hand working my inner thighs. I take in the concentration on his face, his uneven breathing, the erratic chewing of gum, this American stranger, an exotic fruit. This could be an erotic reverie of mine – wanking off in the dungeon of a sex club as a man who looks American whips me lightly on my cunt. Except that it is actually happening. I am living a real-life fantasy that I haven't even filed on my Rolodex yet. My right hand goes down to my so-far trusty clit. I start to strum and it feels like jerking off in a fruit machine, just peripheral lights, red and gold, but no people around, just cherries and bananas and the gold bars whizzing faster and faster. And it's daring and bad to jack off in public in a sleazy old dungeon, and I can feel the rough skin on his hand and his grip burning into my leg, I can see his face leer and then the fruit machine speeds out of control until suddenly everything lines up: bang-bang-bang, three everything bagels all in a row. I moan, I writhe in my ripped-open shirt, glistening with sweat.

After a while, my head falls to one side and I see pink buttocks in neat lingerie straining over an adjacent wooden bench. Cliff Barnes is still chewing his gum. 'We had the best show,' he says with a grin, looking over at the performance on the bench. This irks me before I realise that he is right. It is all about the show here at Lash.

Cliff Barnes is ebullient. He's pushing his crotch against the table again. He seems unbothered that he hasn't come. He says I should contact him before I leave San Francisco. He gives me his email. Then he takes the cleaning-spray bottle and the tissues (he has clearly done this more times than he was letting on) and begins to wipe the table, when suddenly Raven appears with Dill. She bids a brief hello and orders Dill to bend over our table. Dill is now naked from the waist down. She bends over, spreads her legs and Raven proceeds to fuck her roughly in the anus with a dildo, calling her a 'dirty fuck-pig' as her black feather cape judders in the air. I wonder why they want to do this right here. Me and Cliff Barnes are having sort-of pillow talk. He's telling me how we could do something called 'red ass' next time, which involves being spanked and then fucked up the arse. 'It's grrrreat!' he says, like Tony the Tiger.

But maybe this is Raven's networking time, like she told me about earlier on. Reminding the BDSM community that she's still in business. Cliff Barnes seems quite blasé about her and Dill's show. This is a moment when I wish this were all masturbation. That I could press the magic button and go back to Jet's house and process all this on my own.

Cliff Barnes tips his Stetson – at least, that's the kind of smile he makes before taking his leave. And then I'm crawling under the leatherette table looking for my black lace knickers. Raven sounds a bit sour. 'Let's get out of this place,' she says. And soon I'm wandering through darkened hallways, past women tied to crosses who are making just moaning noises now. I wish I could stay. I move the word 'Switch' around in my mind as we walk down the street outside. My thoughts are interrupted by Raven saying, 'You go for men who look like one of your dad's friends.' I feel slightly stung, but then she adds, 'I like those kind of guys too.'

I feel like Cinderella who danced with the prince as we walk towards another club, this one for lesbians and trans women. The night's called Rampage, which sounds promising, although Raven says it's going to be 'crap'. She says there'll be nobody there and tells Dill to go inside and check it out before we fork out any money. Dill goes in obediently and I follow her. She tells the glum woman on the front desk that she wants to look for a friend and soon comes back, telling the woman that her friend's not there. We leave. Dill tells Raven that yes, it was dead as a dodo.

Raven, Dill and I walk down the street saying, Typical, another lame lesbian party. I often end up having this conversation. Why are lesbian clubs so hard to pull off? Where are all the women? At home stroking their girlfriends' hair and eating doughnuts? Having babies? Selling out and getting spanked by men at clubs like Lash? I tell Dill and Raven how I'm not sure if I feel like a saddo sellout for sleeping with men or if it's more that I'm being honest about my desires and gay men are just bigoted, only sleeping with the same sex. It's easy to see why they've sectioned themselves off from the rest of the world – they have a fantastic sex Disneyland. But gay men are having babies now, an idea they'd have scoffed at a few years ago. So why can't they be more open to the idea of dabbling a bit with women? Heterosexual men, too, are blinkered for only sleeping with women who, in this world, are automatically assumed to be bisexual or 'bi-curious'.

Oh, but here we are at another club. This one's called Oasis, on Folsom Street, the road famous for its big summer leather party. When we get inside, Raven tells Dill to look after my bag before introducing me to her drag-queen friend, who is looking excitedly at someone on stage who, he tells me, is 'drag-queen royalty', and used to run a club night called Tranny Shack. I wish I could be a bit more enthusiastic about San Francisco transvestite history, but actually, I'm more into the music. I didn't hear any at Lash and it feels great to move round and release some energy. I dance around, oblivious for a while, and when I open my eyes there's a man in a dress dancing opposite me.

He has a big smile like a cut-out piece of apple pie. And a bit of a sticking-out chin, like me. Back in the 1990s I'd have described him as a 'trucker tranny', a term meaning bad hair and make-up, weird lumpy tits and a demeanour that wouldn't pass as 'female' as most people read it. There's something very friendly about him. He smiles and I smile back. He seems to be copying my dance style and I keep catching him looking at me. I think, *Surely he doesn't fancy me.* There is something sexy about him. The longer we dance, the more it strikes me that he looks like Marc Bolan. Maleness and femaleness jump out at unexpected moments. He asks me if I want to go outside for some marijuana and I think, *Wow, these kind of cool circumstances haven't cropped up in years.* So I do go outside with him. But then Raven comes out in a strop, saying she wants to leave and so the guy, who says his name is Roxanne, gets worried. When Raven's stomped off, I say, 'Fuck it, let's have the smoke anyway.' And it's fine because as we're puffing away, Dill suddenly appears to tell me that Raven is waiting for us out front.

I tell Roxanne to come with us. Raven's been saying all night that the party's back at her place. Roxanne has a car and offers to drive us back to Raven's. As we walk along the road, he tells us how it's a shame that 'tranny' has become such a politically incorrect word now that it's been banned by the transgender community.

'I'm basically a guy who likes to dress up on the weekend,' he explains, telling us that his other name is Ralph. Roxanne/ Ralph clearly sees himself as a 'she' this Saturday night and I alternate between thinking of him as both 'she' and 'he' at different points of the night, depending on what I'm projecting.

Roxanne has trouble remembering where he parked the car, and Raven starts saying that he's 'useless' and 'hopeless' and I'm thinking, *Enough of the dom's disease, we need a lift home*. Besides, I like Roxanne/Ralph. She's got a good sense of humour. He doesn't seem to mind Raven getting on his case, and eventually she finds her car and drives us back to the dungeon.

CHICKEN DINNER IN THE DUNGEON

When we get back to Raven's place, Raven starts doing her being-a-good-hostess thing with Roxanne as she simultaneously orders Dill about. It seems like a lot of work having a slave. I'm wide awake, marching around as if I own the place. I've really grown into my sex outfit – the stompy army boots and my even dirtier now H&M shirt slashed open to my waist as if I'm Britt Ekland.

I suspected that my masturbation homework would eventually spill over into a desire for sex for two. But I didn't realise that when the droplet of water finally exploded it would make such a splash. I'm now thinking in terms of sex for three or four. Things are looking good. I know the night's not nearly over yet. I see a black spiral staircase in one corner of the sitting room and realise this must be the entrance to the dungeon. I ask Raven's permission to go down and then I'm off.

At the bottom of the stairs everything is dark and glittery and the air smells of fresh leather. So this is Raven's lair. No wonder Annie wanted me to see it – it's like having a fantastically mad theatre in your house. Chains hang from the ceiling, a black leather sling sways and a bondage suit on a table awaits a body to zip itself up into oblivion. On the walls are arrays of whips and ropes, and everywhere are mirrors and cabinets containing shiny metal probing instruments.

There's the sound of heels on metal as Roxanne descends the staircase. And then a rich, demonic chuckle. 'It's like Christmas!' she says with a sigh of relief. Then Raven comes down. This is the happy part of the night. We're all new to each other. Still vaguely polite. Excited to see what will be revealed when sexual abandon kicks in. Roxanne and I wander round, touching chains and leather, feeling the strength of rope. Nothing has happened yet. It could all be innocent. I sit in the black leather sling, which is like a leather hammock. I lie back and put my feet in the stirrups and then I realise I don't want to make light of this. Waste it by turning it to humour. Raven says, 'Try these on,' and hands me a pair of leather thigh boots. They're like boots you see in nightmares, spindly heels and a truncated toe so you're hobbled. This is another good bit: when I am the centre of attention for at least thirty minutes.

I get out of the sling and take my jeans off. Then I bend over, knowing my bum looks great in the black lace knickers. I want to keep my see-through shirt on, but Raven says to take it off, so I do, but I keep on my fancy black balcony bra from the trashy lingerie shop in Marble Arch. I get back into the sling and pull the boots on. 'Great legs,' she says admiringly as I spread them and put my feet into the silver stirrups. The leg thing I also know, although that's about the end of my bodily trump cards. Then suddenly her mouth's on my pussy and she's sucking me, saying to Roxanne, 'Oh yeah, she tastes good,' as if they're doctors doing an operation. Roxanne comes to sample my taste and croons, 'Yes, she's good.'

Then Roxanne moves higher up the sling to start fondling my breasts while Raven sucks my clit a bit too hard, but I'm distracted by Roxanne's hands on my nipples. She's stroking them hard then pinching them and it's making me moan, which is surprising, as I'm normally squeamish around my nipples. The chains of the sling start clanking as I writhe around. This is what they call 'discovering your limits' in the SM world. In the darkness of a dungeon you can zip off your old life like an old snakeskin. How long would it be before I started getting off on some mistress cutting my inner thighs with a razor blade? Then Roxanne starts kissing me, which isn't great. But I don't mind because I'm concentrating on his Marc Bolan aspect. And I love his up-for-anything smile. I wish he'd get out of that ridiculous dress. Raven is exciting too, but she's the treat that I'm saving for later.

I start to feel Roxanne's tits. I've always wanted to have sex with a biological boy with tits and a dick, but I realise, as she takes the top of her dress down, that they're strap-on breasts. Still, this revelation has its charms. Raven, proving her expertise in this domain, doesn't fail to notice that there's some kind of chemistry going on between me and Roxanne and she says with a smile, 'I think you two have unfinished business,' before exiting the dungeon up the spiral stairs.

Then the chains of the sling really start to clank as I suck Roxanne's limp Sailor 2 cock. She's pushing it insistently into my mouth (just like a man) and at one point I'm thinking, *Yuk, yeasty, testosterony, spunk, salt, limp sock in my mouth.* But the situation is also mad and absurd, and having sex with a Marc Bolan hermaphrodite is a turn-on. I start to look around the room to see if there's such a thing as a bed so I can lie on it and rub my clit on something. A sling's pretty hopeless for that. But there isn't a bed, so I drag Roxanne to the floor and he says, half-amused, 'What kind of thing are we going to do?' Luckily, I am high enough on marijuana lollipop to carry on sucking his dick, although at the back of my mind I'm sure he'd rather I was sucking his nipples, going, 'I love your double-D rack.' But soon his cock gets hard and I'm going, 'Spunk on my tits! Spunk on my tits!' because that's the sort of thing they say in porn films, and I've noticed that my Marble Arch bra was worth spending £20 on because it gives my small cleavage a level of Annie Sprinkle gravitas. Roxanne shoots over my tits like a warm milky sea.

And then suddenly there's a pale hand and it's thrusting something warm and oily into our mouths. 'Spring rolls!' Raven says, with almost maternal glee. 'Are you guys OK?'

Roxanne starts laughing. Maybe the spring roll is optimising her post-orgasm glow. For me, a mouthful of greasy bean sprouts does not hit the spot like a mattress on a clit would. Once again, I worry that I might have the wrong end of the stick about dungeon culture. About what you're allowed and not allowed to do. I'm not frustrated for long, though. Tonight everything, even waiting, feels like pleasure.

Upstairs, Raven and Roxanne are on the couch drinking vodka. Dill is doing more washing-up. I'd forgotten about her. I know I'm being a brat, but I also know I'll get away with it. I announce to Raven, 'I'm going to sleep in your bed,' and I prance off past the velvet couch, through the door with the display of shoes on. I hear Raven say to Roxanne, 'Where did I find *her*?' But with affection and latent lust in her voice. And then she comes into the bedroom and closes the door behind her. In brat mode, I say, 'Bring Roxanne in.' Then, 'And Dill too.'

The minute they come in, I realise I should have stuck with just me and Raven. When Raven says, 'Stephanie wants a foursome,' Dill starts acting really stroppy for a slave. So Raven takes her aside, puts her hand on her shoulder and cajoles, 'Come on Dilly Dill,' in a secret affectionate voice. So Dill reluctantly takes her clothes off and gets into bed. Roxanne is already naked and willing.

This where things get scrambled. All types of vibrators are wielded and there's the snap of condoms being attached to heads of dildos. There's the revelation of Raven's beautiful firm breasts, like white apples with silver bars through each nipple. They're alluring and she doesn't always let me have them. And then Dill, on all fours, shoves a dildo in my hand, saying, in a submissive-with-attitude manner, 'Help me out, can you?' She raises her bum in the air ready to be fucked just like at Lash. The aromas from her arsehole make me suddenly aware that this is real life rather than fantasy, although I eventually get interested in her breasts. They're sort of spongy, like a cake filled with that delicious, foamy spray-on cream. And then the bed becomes a production line of insatiable bodies and big cock dildos and relentless coming and coming. There's so much flesh, an endless banquet and the great thing is that I finally stop thinking. I get out of my head. I am absent. Just a body. I only come round as Raven is giving Roxanne a tetchy lesson on how to fist a woman. It's like the spanking theory lesson at the club. She's going, 'Twist and enter. No, not like that!' It's not very spontaneous.

I decide some fresh air would be good, so I get up and go and lie on the velvet couch in the other room. I flick through Raven's copy of *Erotica Universalis* until I get to the familiar images accompanying the 1797 Dutch edition of Sade's *La Nouvelle Justine, or the Misfortunes of Virtue*.

There's a big-bellied naked lady suspended by rope from a neoclassical ceiling at pelvis height. She's being fucked by a woman who is being sodomised by a man who is oblivious to the forlorn young girl behind him, all left out. A podgy Cupid, garlanded in acanthus leaves, surveys the scene from a wall.

By now, I don't see these people as weird, old-fashioned cartoon types having comedy sex. I see them as kindred spirits. There are lots of flagellation scenes in the *Nouvelle Justine* engravings. As the Marquis de Sade's arrest record and Rousseau's stories of his governess prove, spanking was meat and potatoes in the eighteenth century. In 1757,

Inspector Louis Marais was appointed the head of the Paris Libertinage division. His job was to compile detailed reports on debauched priests, Parisian brothel depravity and gossip from the city's top whores and courtesans. These documents went directly to King Louis XV, who'd become notorious for his love of salacious gossip. He and Madame de Pompadour would read them together as a substitute for their defunct carnal relations.

Marais writes that on one occasion, two prostitutes used up two whole brooms on a librarian. 'After which, having run out of cane, they were forced to take straw from a doormat. When I came in, his entire body was dripping blood.'

Venus in the Cloister, a flagellation blockbuster in Sade's uncle's library, was translated into English in 1725. It gave rise to the English take on flagellation erotica in works such as *Exhibition of Female Flagellants* (1777) and *Venus School Mistress* (1808). If virginal pudendas and peachy breasts had been the hotspots of seventeenth-century porn, by the late eighteenth century, thanks to spanking fiction, buttocks, thighs and plump upper forearms had become erotica's favoured zones. The backdrop for English spanking was not the Church, because we were anti-Catholic already, but the home, and especially the boarding school. The favoured spanking practitioner was not a nun but a governess – a strong, forceful type who wore an elegant costume and had delicate manners.

As a child, I never found my own personal Mademoiselle Lambercier, but I did find Enid Blyton. She created a boarding school-based despot who was not a governess but, in the same ballpark, a school prefect. Nora was the monitor of the dorm in *The Naughtiest Girl in the School* and an influential character in my early masturbatory forays. She was always threatening to spank Elizabeth, the wayward heroine, with her hairbrush.

Elizabeth 'couldn't bear to be spanked by Nora', but I could. Lying on Raven's couch, I realise now that my first experience of intense genital pleasure was not actually with Jemima, my stuffed doll, but with my own hairbrush. Back in my bed when I was ten, I'd worked out there was some holy trinity revolving around wanting to pee, lying on my front and pressing on the bristles of my yellow plastic hairbrush and getting a type of pleasure way beyond anything my space hopper offered.

A howl comes from the bedroom. It's Raven. She sounds like what Popeye looks like when he eats spinach. Roxanne's fisting lesson must be going well. Meanwhile, I haven't come in at least twenty minutes. I start to jack off as if my clit were a dick. I'm getting quite good at this technique. As I do it, I look at the black feather wand on the bookshelf and I think of chewing gum and cold leatherette against my cheek. It's not a big explosion, but it does the job, like a cup of tea and Marmite on toast in the early hours after a big night out. It's starting to get light. The birds are starting to sing.

When I wake up, the light's brighter and I've had enough of being on my own. I get up from the couch and go back into the bedroom. Raven is facing the wall and Roxanne is facing her back. Both are asleep. When I climb into the middle of them, Raven yields and then moves away from my touch. When I push my bum back into Roxanne's crotch, there's a barely audible sigh of pleasure and he languidly starts to spoon me. I rock against his Sailor 2, which is nice, although I realise we're not going to get anywhere. I fall asleep again then get woken up by the sound of a deep male voice whispering in my ear, 'A Stephanie sandwich.' Roxanne is pressing his groin against my bum and caressing my body like soft feathers while Raven turns towards me, saying that I look like I'm at the beach with my tan and my hair. She says she was impressed with me last night at Lash. 'You knew immediately what you wanted and you went for it.' I'm not sure I did know what I wanted, but I blush with pride at the compliment from Raven.

Soon I'm whipping Roxanne's pale buttocks with my Flash Gordon belt as she moans into Raven's pussy and Raven takes phone pictures for her Twitter feed. When we get up, we wander semi-dressed around the flat in a post-sex afterglow, touching a cock here, a pierced tit there. We feel totally relaxed with each other. I lie on the velvet couch and when Raven passes, I brush my hand confidently over her shaved, studded vulva like some big pasha swiping up a handful of pomegranate seeds from a silver platter.

It's Super Bowl Sunday, the Queen's Silver Jubilee of American patriotism. It's the most macho day of the sporting year, when two teams of men put on helmets and comedy padding and spend a couple of hours charging into each other. This time last year I was in London, probably having roast dinner and listening to Radio 4 with Hadji. And now I'm in a dungeon in San Francisco with a sadistic dominatrix and a horny cross-dresser.

Raven takes Roxanne aside to give her helpful tips on how to put her make-up on better and she lets Roxanne try on some of her own dresses. As I walk past them on my way to the bathroom, I see Roxanne take her feet out of her 'lady' boots and there are blokey socks on her feet. She definitely needs some lessons in how to be one of those ladylike women she's so impressed by. I check out my bum in the bathroom mirror. Red and bruised. I'm delighted. Proof that I *did* go to the ball.

I take a photo and send it to Cliff Barnes. I come out of the bathroom thinking that it's sweet, all this BDSM lark. In the midst of the sleaze, there is something very honest and healthy about it. It's just sex and sensation. None of the romance drug. Since yesterday evening, I have been in charge of my own orgasms, as Betty Dodson would put it. It's actually been quite like a glorified masturbation session. The idea of actual penetrative sex, in other words a man's cock going in a woman's cunt, seems the thing that would get you in the most trouble. Raven says she doesn't think of what she does in terms of sex. She thinks of it in terms of masturbation: 'getting myself off' or 'getting someone else off'.

For me, coming fifteen or twenty times last night was more like aided wanking. I can't say I had sex with Cliff Barnes exactly, although I did lose it with him at one point on the leatherette table. I wonder what happens if you keep yourself off the romance drug for too long, though. Do you become an expert dominatrix, like Raven? Do you worry about if you can ever just fall in love and forget about all the SM classes and the stipulations and the rules on how to do spanking properly?

Raven and Roxanne have started giggling on the velvet couch. I guess it's logical they'd get more intimate after the fisting session. I can hear Roxanne saying things like, 'Wow, it was the most beautiful experience!' I feel a bit boring in comparison and then suddenly paranoid about that picture I just sent. What if Cliff Barnes posts it on the internet? Can you see it's my face? I'm aware that my ego is starting to flag. I go into the bedroom for a lie down, but I can't sleep. I hear Roxanne say, 'Where's Stephanie?' which makes me feel a bit better. Egos can get fragile if you play at this sex game for a lot of hours, so comments like that are important. I feel better and there's something like the smell of roasting chicken in the air. I spring out of bed and go into the sitting room, where I see Raven with her head resting on Roxanne's shoulder watching the Super Bowl. It's one of those catching-your-boyfriend-writing-poetry-to-his-lover moments and it makes you feel much more jealous than watching two people have sex with each other. I realise that what they call 'the power dynamics' are changing between Raven, Roxanne and me.

My confidence drops like a ton of bricks. Clearly this wasn't just glorified masturbation, because you don't feel jealous if your clitoris isn't feeling horny tonight. Or maybe sex is just masturbation with more ego. I think back to Raven's warning about how unleashing desire doesn't always bring pleasant things to the surface. I wonder if my insecurity means that I'm a fully evolved human being at last. Raven looks annoyed to see me. 'I'm making a chicken dinner,' she says, which is funny in a way, because I associate chicken dinner with being buried alive back in England. I nod and force a smile and do my see-through shirt up by two buttons. Then Dill comes back with some vodka that Raven sent her out for. It's Absolut Pear, which is very appropriate, because things now start to go pear-shaped. I offer to make cocktails for everyone but Raven erupts on tasting hers, declaring it to be 'disgusting'. She comes over to the kitchen area and pushes me aside, saying, 'You're such a pest!'

Luckily, at that moment, I get an email from Cliff Barnes. I just read the subject box: 'Hey pretty horse rider!' I decide not to open it yet. I may need compliment reinforcements if Raven starts getting really mean. Her web's a tricky one. You never know when it's going to be soft and yielding, and when it's going to snare you. Naturally, it's very exciting hanging out with Raven.

And then she starts yelling at Roxanne. Roxanne has gone to make new cocktails and she hasn't washed up the old glasses. 'Oh, so you think someone else is going to do that, do you?' she bellows. I think both Roxanne and I assumed that Dill was here to do the washing-up, but we don't say anything. Raven strides over to the sink, takes a metal egg flipper and spanks Roxanne's bare buttocks with it. Hard. It looks painful and not in a good way. A look of anger flushes over Roxanne's face and I make a joke about dom's disease. But Roxanne doesn't seem to mind being bossed around and spoken to meanly.

Suddenly, the San Francisco sex sparkle is gone, like dust from the wings of a butterfly. A murder of crows. An unkindness of ravens. I feel self-conscious about brushing Roxanne's ass in his new black dress. He doesn't seem to want to come over and touch me as much and Raven has become crotchety and mad. I can't wait any more. I need to mainline some flattery. I go to the bathroom and open Cliff's email. It says: *Hi Sweety, you a dream come true girl! I had so much fun with you! I do hope we can keep in touch young lady. Have fun Hottie!* He adds a PS about checking out his profile on FetLife, the social network for the kink community.

I emerge from the bathroom feeling ten miles high. My ego is boosted and the fact that he can't write very well turns me on even more. Then Raven says, 'Dinner is served.' It's funny, the three of us are soon grunting like animals, but this time over roast potatoes and chicken bones (it turns out we all like the dark meat). Still, I also feel like the kid who's done something wrong, but she's not quite sure what, as she watches Mum and Dad sitting next to each other on the velvet couch watching the Super Bowl while she sits at the table behind. Except I want Mum or Dad to touch my bum in an entirely inappropriate way. Still, it's a nice way to close our time together. And it makes me realise that a chicken dinner is what you make of it.

We do messy washing-up during which I get my turn with the metal egg flipper from Raven. There's no build-up and it hurts a lot without being sexy. I push her away in the end and she runs off giggling like a kid. The atmosphere turns momentarily ugly towards the end of the evening when Roxanne starts asking Raven if she has any coke. When Raven says no, Roxanne says she'd better be getting home, mentioning something about kids. One is twenty and one, Roxanne grimaces, 'is three and a half'. Raven mutters a comment about the ex-wife 'stitching him up on that one'.

Then Roxanne pulls out a small weekend bag and transforms back into Ralph. She looks good in male drag. He has to drive back to his home in the suburbs and Raven tells him that he'll give me a lift. We leave at 7.25 p.m., almost exactly twenty-four hours since I arrived. Raven opens the door. She says a perfunctory goodbye to Roxanne and when it's my turn, she says sternly, 'You slapped my tits last night. I did not ask you to slap my tits.' There's a sly smile on her face as she says it, so I think she didn't mind that much. Then I experience the most mind-blowing sensation I have felt in the past twenty-four hours. A small kiss from the warm, lipsticked, pillowy lips of Raven as I say goodbye. Suddenly all my candles get lit up again, whereas they have long gone out with Roxanne. I kiss Raven on the lips and I realise what could have been. But then I have to go.

I float out to Roxanne's car, which looks like a battered old pumpkin. Now it's his turn to be grumpy. He's clearly feeling the weight of imminent Monday morning and babysitting three-year-olds. 'Where do you live then?' he grunts. It's strange how strong the male odour is. I was naked and alone in the bedroom with Raven and then we let him in and immediately his scent was headier; it was as if we had to bow down to him. In a very subtle manner, but it was still the case. Girl-and-girl action is so much more intense when you finally allow yourself to throw off men.

When we arrive at the Presidio, more pixie dust blows away when Roxanne asks me if I'd like his card and he passes me a cheap thing advertising an office cleaning business. He flashes a shadow of his piece-of-pie smile and we kiss briefly on the lips. I run inside, slam the door and make a big sigh of relief.

But I'm soon to discover that promiscuity is not like a roast-chicken dinner at all. It's more like Chinese food.

SEXUAL DEMENTIA

I'm lying on Jet's porch the day after the Raven weekend, not sure if I'm sunbathing, having sex with the sun or taking part in some advanced form of masturbation recently taught to me by a retired porn star. I think I might have a case of *démence libertine* or 'sexual dementia'. It was what Napoleon finally put the Marquis de Sade away for back in 1803, confining him to the lunatic asylum of Charenton, where he died eleven years later. I've not yet got to hollowing out cunts with red-hot irons or eating a piping hot omelette from a girl's buttocks with a very sharp fork, as Sade imagined in *120 Days of Sodom*, but I'm getting there.

My body feels as though it's vibrating with a kind of perma-tingle. Everything I look at reminds me of sex. Even Jet's flat reminds me of a 1970s porn movie set with all the potted plants. But here on the porch is something that really revs up the tingle: the beautiful pine tree ahead. I feel as if I want to shimmy up its trunk and melt into it as I have an insane orgasm. I feel as if I am part of the sky and the trees and the grass and all the 'what ifs' that hang in the air. Actually, maybe this is more Rousseau's rustic delirium than Sade's sexual dementia.

Or maybe I'm transforming into one of Annie's ecosexuals. Last night I had sex with the moon, something that not even

Caligula managed. I woke up feverishly horny and plucked Barry Komisaruk, the New York neuroscientist, from the air. I lay in his MRI machine jerking off as he watched. Then he's in bed with me, his hairy body glinting in the moonlight like a docile werewolf. And then he disappears and Cliff Barnes arrives. Tonight's tennis practice is endless. Set after set until it becomes desperate. Nothing is enough. And then I see her. The light of an incredible full moon pouring in through the bedroom window, pouring all over my belly. When the moon shone full and bright, Caligula always invited the moon goddess to his bed. And now the moon is swirling in the sky with the black clouds and the mournful hoot of the foghorns and the crash of the waves and when I come, it doesn't stop there.

A new desire has woken me up. During the day, everyone seems asleep, but I am constantly euphoric. I now know what gay men must feel like. Those young men I used to see slumped against the wall smoking beatific fags outside the sauna in Waterloo. Or walking on a cushion of warm air down Old Compton Street on a Sunday night, all passion spent. Annie says that once you become a member of the eco-masturbation club, you look at sex in a different way. You find some sort of peace with your body, the big bucking bronco that you sometimes have such a hard time with. Your legs get steel girders running down through the clay. I still haven't got the breathing down properly. The proper tennis game is with breathing. But maybe it's good to aim for something.

Except the bucking bronco often rebels. I'm beginning to realise that there's a dangerous side to this *démence libertine*. 'The appetite comes in eating,' Sade wrote in *120 Days of Sodom*, implying that debauchery is a doomed quest and ultimately unsatisfying. The fantasies of the four libertines in the Château de Silling become increasingly awful until, in the final months of the experiment, narration ceases. There are just lists of increasingly appalling fantasies and acts which culminate in what one of the libertines calls 'the Hell Passion'.

Sometimes I feel as if things are becoming more *Heart of Darkness* than *The Wizard of Oz*. It's hard to concentrate on the purity of Annie's energy orgasm here in San Francisco. Sexual energy glugs through the streets, making you constantly frustrated because you're panicking about where the next sex is coming from. I think back to the weekend: the Cliff Barnes moment when it all turned off, when I collapsed down on my front and left the room, left San Francisco and the world. I only came back slowly. An itchy, polyester-mix blouse, a wipe-down surface on my cheek, the first flickers of anxiety. I wonder if I will see Cliff Barnes again. I still have my bum bruises. And my see-through blouse smells of Roxanne's body. His salty spunk smell in spite of wanting to be a woman for the weekend. Also, a subtle BO under the arms and lots of grime on the cuffs and the neck. Something sweet, too. Tacky, sweet cologne, like the room in the Desert Palace in Barstow with the Miley Cyrus fragrance. Strange – for a few moments on Saturday night, I felt as if I could be falling in love with Roxanne the tranny. The glittering slice-of-pie smile. The eye contact. It's so easy to trip up, think your life would be solved if only you fell in love.

I keep waking up early with that flame feeling. Like the Sappho poem, 'under my skin a fire runs'. Like a horrible Ready-Brek glow. I wake up and something falls into my stomach, like a stone to the bottom of a well: the knowledge that I haven't had sex with another person for a while. The sun is out right now and I feel I have so much energy. But my energy feels like flat beer or a glass of water that's been left out for days. Why can't I think of good things, like how I can breathe, how I didn't drown in the bath at the age of twenty-four, how I can walk, how there's no pain in my body right now? But I keep thinking of how I haven't had enough sexual encounters with strangers today.

At night, I turn on the TV and I'm convinced that people in bedrooms around America are having more sex, better sex than me. A shopping channel selling sex toys has two women talking like CNN newscasters about a 'jelly vagina with suction pads' and 'the Couples' Enhancer Ring – you can be in any position and her clitoris never gets ignored!' The dilemma of whether to have sex or whether just to masturbate bothers me. When I'm doing one, I usually wish for the other. I'm starting to rebel against masturbation, which D. H. Lawrence termed 'the dead sex of the mind'. I want to stop thinking about sex, but what would the opposite of sex be? I once met a member of the Scouse Mafia, a Hells Angel in charge of security at the Royal Court Theatre in Liverpool, a city known as much for its Artful Dodger underbelly as for the Beatles or football. When I asked him how he relaxed – did he read? Listen to music? – he looked incredulous and said, 'I stare at the fooking wall.'

And then I'm saved by a journalistic commission. A magazine wants me to write a travel feature on Palm Springs. I also get an email from my writer heroine, Susie Bright. She says she'd be pleased to talk to me for my book and would I like to appear on her radio show? She lives in Santa Cruz, a two-hour drive south of San Francisco. I decide to hire a car, visit Bright, then drive further south to Palm Springs. Getting out of San Francisco will clear my head. I'll be back in time for the Kinky Salon sex party on 14 February. I'll invite Virginia. It's a Valentine's date nobody could turn down.

I pack a small bag and take a $5 Uber carpool cab to the hotel where I'm going to pick up the hire car. The Uber driver is wearing sunglasses at 8 a.m. on a foggy San Francisco morning and quite soon, concepts such as taking acid enter the conversation. He says that there are too many tech people in San Francisco. 'The hippies brought love and peace, the techs will just buy you out.' He asks what I'm doing in San Francisco and I decide to tell him. 'I'm writing a book on masturbation,' I say. His reaction is interesting and it gives the lie to all those books with comedy bananas on the front that currently cater to the male masturbation market. 'Guys could learn from watching women masturbate,' he says. 'Men like to jerk off hard but with a lot of women you realise you can't do it like that.'

I come out with the line about how a female clitoris has 8,000 nerve endings while the end of a penis only has 4,000. He passes me a crumpled card that says he is also a scriptwriter. I'm not sure what he expects me to do with this. Write a screenplay about masturbation? Or does he really want to have sex for two?

'We'd better change the subject,' he says, getting out of the car to open the door for the new passenger. She is a woman in her early thirties, wearing a navy-blue business suit and smelling like she's just washed her hair.

'Good morning, how are you?' I say

'I'm good,' she twangs back like a taut rubber band.

EROTIC KIDNAP

Susie Bright says, 'I'm not trying to be sexy or anything, but you're welcome to join me in the hot tub.'

I'm in Santa Cruz watching a naked giantess descend into the swirling blue as I think, a) dirty bathwater, b) pruney fingers, c) I'll look like a prude if I say no. So I get in and it is actually quite sexy. She has blue veins in her breasts and those pink-cherry nipples that François Boucher painted on his lusty models.

Susie Bright came as a revelation to me when I was living in boring Paris in the late 1980s. Her essays covered subjects such as vibrators, female ejaculation and lesbian SM sex. Lesbian SM sex? In Paris I was still struggling to find a woman who wanted to go to bed with me. Often when you did pull a Frenchwoman, she'd start sobbing into her pillow about how she was still in love with her ex-girlfriend. It used to piss me off when gay boys would say, 'Oh, but you lesbians are so lucky. At least you can fall in love.'

'And so can you!' I'd rant in *mal baisée* despair. 'Only you have such a Disneyland of no-strings-attached sexual possibility that you don't want to put in the groundwork.'

Water splashes over the side of Susie's hot tub as I tell her about the 'lesbian SM debate' I kept hearing about when I went to visit London. From what I could tell, the debate seemed to mean something about dykes wearing leather jackets being refused entry to mainstream lesbian nightclubs because they were somehow 'offensive to women'.

Susie Bright says, 'Don't you know about Samois?'

I look blank.

'Their book, *Coming to Power*?'

I shake my head. 'You should be ashamed of yourself,' she says and explains that Samois took its name from Samois-sur-Seine, the location of the chateau belonging to the lesbian dominatrix in *Story of O* by Pauline Réage. Samois became the first lesbian feminist SM group in the world. Based in San Francisco, it admitted members who liked not just adventurous sex, but the ideas and social life implicit in lesbian-feminist BDSM. The Samois collective, which existed between 1978 and 1983, included members such as Carol Queen's friend, the feminist academic from the University of Michigan Gayle Rubin, and the brilliant dirty-story writer and sex radical Pat Califia (check out 'Jessie' in Califia's *Macho Sluts* collection), who was to become Patrick Califia. They often came under fire from anti-porn feminists who considered their sexual practices to be violence against women.

Bright believes they were just being honest about their desire. 'Samois asked, "What would it be like if women expressed their erotic imaginations as far as they wanted to?"' She closes her eyes and throws her head back into the sun. 'I mean, I have really insane fantasies. Most of them are physically impossible and morally repugnant. But they're in my head, so it's like criticising me for pretending I'm a princess or riding a dragon. Samois made me realise that we needed a more nuanced psychological understanding of this. I mean, I don't actually want to be ravaged by nuns and priests on the altar, but in my imagination it can make perfect sense.'

Flaubert said you shouldn't touch your idols because the gold paint comes off on your hands, but Susie Bright in the flesh doesn't disappoint. I've completely forgotten about pruney fingers. I've been excited to meet my first real writer of the trip, and she passes the Princess and the Pea writer's test with flying colours.

When I arrive, her partner, Jon, who has the chilled amphibious vibe of a diver, lets me into the house. It's a handsome Victorian pile on the outskirts of Santa Cruz with a tree house – and the hot tub in the backyard. We walk past a bedroom where she's sitting cross-legged on the bed, hunched over a computer. She turns round when Jon announces me and snaps, with barely disguised irritation, 'Oh hi. I'll be with you in a bit.'

I breathe a sigh of relief. I can relate to that 'fuck off, I'm writing' state too. I wonder what Susie will be like when I get to speak to her. She is the woman Hollywood hires when it wants to know what lesbians do in bed. She was an adviser on the dyke sex scenes for *Bound*, the 1996 lesbian mobster movie by the former Wachowski brothers, both of whom are now sisters. In her books, such as *Susie Sexpert's Lesbian Sex World* and *Sexwise*, she was writing about stuff I thought only me and my first-ever girlfriend, Sam, talked about secretly in Brixton pubs when I came over from Paris for my London visits. Sam was the one who first told me about the 'lesbian SM debate', because she worked in Sister Write in the late 1980s, when there were still such things in London as women's bookshops.

You always got a transgressive extra with Bright. She didn't only have sex with women, for instance. In *Sexwise* (1995) there's an essay called 'Dan Quayle's Dick' where Bright, a member of the International Socialists in her teens, imagines having sex with the Republican vice president to George

Bush, Dan Quayle. In the essay, Bright imagines a night of passion between her and 'Danny', who she admits she has some sympathy for, ever since he avowed on live TV, much to his wife's wrath, that he would support his daughter if she wanted to have an abortion.

> Of course, he's cut and his erections fly straight up, not curving or bowing. The head looks like a polished marble doorknob – only it feels, of course, like purple velvet. In fact, his hard-on turns more rosy violet the longer he moves in and out me . . .

As an out lesbian in my mid-twenties, I wasn't yet admitting that I had fantasies about sex with men, let alone ones who were on the wrong political team. I was writing about lesbian matters for the *Guardian* women's page, usually ranting about how lame the lesbian-sex world was compared to the gay male equivalent, which was true. Meanwhile, on the weekends, I was flicking through the free gay-boy magazines. The back sections were filled with rent-boy ads: 'Enzo, fit Eastern European, 35', 'Ricardo, Italian, 10.5 inches'. The dicks often made their way into my fantasies. In my diary, on Thursday, 18 June 1998, when I was thirty-two, I wrote:

> My fantasy when I brought myself off on Diane's bum just now was me pretending to be Jeremy Paxman, fucking one of his guests on a couch in the green room. This was about having power. A big crown of warm, concentric circles that throb round your head. The trouble with this fantasy is that Jeremy Paxman isn't sexy. I can just see his stringy legs and Marks & Spencer's Y-fronts. And who would the chick be that I was shagging?

I never used to write about these fantasies in the *Guardian* because, like Michael J. Fox says in *Back to the Future* when he starts playing heavy-metal riffs at the 1950s school prom, 'I guess you guys aren't ready for that yet. But your kids are going to love it.'

Thanks to Susie Bright, I knew what 'vanilla sex' and 'safe words' meant back in 1990 when my straight friends had no clue. Little did they know that this sort of fare would be dished up in newspapers on Sunday-morning breakfast tables twenty years later when a publishing phenomenon called *Fifty Shades of Grey* hit the mainstream.

Susie tells me about the time that the lesbian photographer and film-maker, Honey Lee Cottrell, went over to London in the 1970s to show a masturbation-consciousness-raising movie (funded by Ted McIlvenna's Institute for Advanced Study of Human Sexuality) at a women-only squat.

'It was a girl getting off in a bathroom using a showerhead. The London women started complaining about all the hot water that was being used. They said it'd be untenable in their cold-water flats.' She makes one of those 'woman are so hard to please' shrugs. 'Water was one of my early masturbatory discoveries. It can be so soft yet so powerful. I've rented whole apartments on the basis of water pressure in the bathroom.'

The water roars as she stands up. Even though she finds masturbation an ugly word, 'like something in a legal procedure', she doesn't understand why women wouldn't want to masturbate. 'It's an exceptional consciousness that happens in one's private moments,' she says. 'Just like you have a bath on your own or a wonderful idea when you're all by yourself. Why would I want to get rid of that? I think any writer would understand that.'

I climb out of the tub first and it's only when I'm putting my clothes back on that I remember about my Cliff Barnes marks. Maybe she noticed, because before we leave the house, she points to a high-backed armchair with a pile of soft toy birds all over the seat. 'Sit there,' she says. So I sit on the birds and they all make a big 'Eeeek' sound. Susie thinks this is hilarious. She's already sitting on the armchair opposite, squashing another load of birds until the room is reverberating with Eeek! Eeek! noises.

'You're very cruel' I say, hoping she's going to treat me like one of the birds after we've finished recording the radio show. I'm feeling pretty cocky at this point in my trip. Why shouldn't I rock into town and get my sex heroine into bed within three hours?

While Susie goes to get ready, I spy a copy of *Coming to Power* by Samois on her bookshelf. I flick past a chapter entitled 'How I Learned to Stop Worrying and Love My Dildo', then come to a section on handkerchief codes. A red handkerchief in the right-hand back pocket means 'fist fuckee' (as opposed to 'fist fucker', if it's on the left) which makes me think of Dill. A white lace handkerchief signifies something called 'Victorian scenes'.

And then we're in the car driving to the studio and there's a welcome return to the being-ravaged-by-nuns-and-priests conversation. Like VV and Barbara Carrellas, Susie is another Catholic. She went to a convent school for three years from age eight to eleven and declares her childhood to have been 'heavy on the smoke and mirrors, and deeply sexual in a completely repressed way'.

She had an orgasm the first time she ever masturbated at the age of eight. Afterwards, as she groped guiltily down her flannel pyjama bottoms, she detected something that 'felt like a wart'. She would later discover that this was her clitoris, but at the time she thought, *I don't think that was there before. The devil must have put it there to punish me.*

She considered going to confession but, 'I couldn't imagine explaining what the hell I just did to the priest.' The next day, when she took the communion host at Mass ('that whole thing is so fucking kinky anyway – taking Christ's body in your mouth?') she had a 'little talk' with Jesus. She promised him she wouldn't touch herself down there ever again. But she did. In fact, August 1966 turned out to be a pretty big month for Susie Bright. In the same week that she'd experienced this incredible sensation in her groin, it was reported in America that John Lennon had declared the Beatles to be more popular than Christ. When her parish church decided to throw a Beatles book-burning party except with records, she realised she'd have to call it a day with the Catholics.

'I had spent my precious babysitting dollars on my first Beatles album. I was president of the school fan club. I was not burning my Beatles album.'

She convinced herself that Jesus would have liked the Beatles and even if he didn't, 'I just had this sense of, like, "I guess I'm going to hell. Well, that's a relief. At least I don't have to wonder any more."'

With convent-girl perversity, she regrets the end of the Catholic hegemony in America. The popular new arm of Christianity, evangelical Protestantism, is distinctly lacking in sexual frisson. On the rare occasions she goes to Mass these days, she says she finds herself sounding like her mother.

'I'll be like, "This isn't a Mass. This is a post-office meeting! You've drained it of everything that was dark and mysterious."'

I used to have priest fantasies too, although probably because Father Lock from the convent was the only man I was in regular contact with. Although he was skinny and resembled a cross between Barry Manilow and Rowan Atkinson, I was jealous the day I heard my friend was driving alone with him to Cardiff to see Pope John Paul II appearing at the National

Youth Rally. On the way, a cat jumped in front of the car and Father Lock slammed on the brakes. Too late. He was quite traumatised, apparently.

My friend and I giggled about this story, but the cat drama was to become huge inspiration in the silence of my lonely bedroom. It would be just me and Father Lock in the car. The cat would get run over, and then, after trying to help him get over his sadness, we'd start sort of rubbing. There was never any penetration. No venerable rope. In fact, Father Lock would have no noticeable genitals and the rubbing would be facilitated by liberal quantities of baby oil. Maybe the oil obviated the need for me to know what sexual beings actually did, and I played this film in my head well into my teens.

When we arrive at the studio, Susie's show is fun. She bills it as 'Stephanie Theobald – Dirty Truck Drivers and the Ultimate Jill-Off Trip'. I talk about Joycelyn Elders and Annie Sprinkle's breathing techniques and Betty Dodson's workshop and the massive orgasm she gave me with her Hitachi Magic Wand. When I say that I'm not always up for really intense orgasms, Susie says, 'Why not? To me that's like asking, "Does one always want a nice, creamy ice-cream cone?"'

'Yes,' I say. 'But I was raised a Catholic and not being allowed stuff always turns me on.'

When we leave the studio, she takes me to a former Wild West bordello in Santa Cruz, where she orders us Lady Greys (gin mixed with Earl Grey tea). 'Clits up!' she toasts, and soon we're back to her days as head vibrator saleswoman at Good Vibrations. She had blanket advice for all the women who came in hating themselves because they couldn't have an orgasm.

'I told them, it's a gender issue. We have more hidden plumbing and we've been kept as chattel and that's a deadly combination.'

I came to vibrators late. Maybe it was a rare case of anti-American prejudice. Typical Yanks with their Coca-Cola and their high water pressure and their plug-in sex aids. My art dealer gave me one when I was thirty-eight. The Rabbit. It was 2004 and they'd just started taking off as a topic for heterosexual London dinner party conversations. At the Serpentine Summer Party, an annual event held by the gallery in Kensington Gardens, I remember talking to an editor from the London *Vanity Fair* office about it. She sounded guilty. 'It's so quick. I didn't use to masturbate.'

Susie agrees. 'You hear men complain about premature ejaculation but when you've never been able to come fast, you have the opposite yearning. You're like, "What would it be like to just get hard immediately?"'

The other great thing about a vibrator, she says, is that it can circumvent all the problems keeping you from getting a hard-on: inhibition, lack of education, not knowing your anatomy, not knowing what triggers your mind. 'A vibrator straps you into the jet pack whether you like it or not.'

Occasionally a shadow comes over her and she gets mad about how her country is more reactionary about sex than it was in the 1980s. She declares anti-masturbation activism to be 'the lingerie of fascism', meaning that religious fundamentalists use sex 'to destroy democratic discourse and egalitarianism. Oh my God, I could get so extreme about this . . .'

She has lectured in universities around America for the past thirty years and she always asks students if they masturbate. 'I remember one guy of nineteen said, "No I haven't and I've never come." I thought he was having me on. But that was the beginning of a trend. Nowadays I'll always have up to five per cent of young men in an audience having not experienced orgasm.'

The regression in sexual experience started, she says, after the AIDS epidemic 'and the morality panic that went through everything'. Twenty per cent of women used to tell her they'd never come. 'Now it's twenty-five to thirty per cent. Abstinence education, monogamy mania and slut-bating have taken their toll.'

She asks if it's OK to invite Jon along for a drink. I say, 'Sure,' thinking, *Drat*. She orders us another drink and says that she enjoyed the Samois SM scene in a playful way.

'Everyone has their different Ground Zero of what makes them tick sexually. But it's nice if you can lend out your body and imagination just to see what it's like to be in someone else's skin.'

She looks at me. 'That's what you've been doing on your Grand Orgasm Tour of America, right?'

I wonder if she's right and then suddenly she's going down the Annie Sprinkle road, saying how women's bodies and sexuality change all the time. That you can never afford to get too smug about what a great sexual being you are because you'll never know how you might change.

'Touch my neck,' she says. 'It's different from your neck. You have younger skin.'

She started menopause a few months ago, although she'd had perimenopause for years, which made her go 'haywire'. She's recently experienced the revelation of an oestrogen patch. Her litmus test of where her libido is at is 'how often it occurs to me to jill off'. The minute the oestrogen patch was on she noticed she had the urge 'to stick my hands down my pants. I thought, "Wow, That's real." Because I'm not responding to any outward influence, a lover going, "Do you love me? Do you care? Are we still together?"'

The waiter brings us another round of Lady Greys. The drinks are potent and I'm convinced by now that she's coming back to the motel with me. She's started grabbing at my notebook. She must know that's a really outrageous thing to do to a fellow writer. She asks me if I have a 'sweetheart'. I listen to this on the tape afterwards because at the time it feels very intimate. I'm stuttering and spluttering all over the place.

'I understand that he's like family to you,' she says of Hadji. 'But do you still yearn for him sexually?' I flinch at the strong word, 'yearn'. 'Do you and your guy feel like, "Let's be a classical gay couple and just fuck who we please but we're each other's primary?" Is that where you're at?'

The first time I had sex with Hadji was extraordinary. It felt as though we were not human beings but creatures. I was a wood nymph and he was a young Pan, the goat-legged man-god. A bucking bronco crescent moon curving into me and I didn't have to think of a fantasy. We played, we fucked and afterwards I fried up some raw steak and we ate it bloody like triumphant partners in crime: sex, homicide, luxury, battle. I felt arrogant about our love. That it was more exciting than other people's love.

After a while I realised that my head was rarely turned off when we were having sex, although that could have been more about being two neurotic writers together. Still, I never felt that Hadji truly yearned for my body. And it was the same on my side. I loved his body. Loved him. But the dirty thing was never there. I started to think of the older woman in *Birds of a Feather*, the MILF in self-consciously elaborate lingerie who picks up the apprentice plumber from the local caff. They all know that she's on heat and that each night one of them will be chosen. And then everything was complicated by my vulvodynia. My pain. You might say our sex life never really got off the ground. But it doesn't make the idea of separation any easier, and I wonder if we will have to separate.

Havelock Ellis's lesbian wife Edith told him that the beauty and intimacy of their relationship was founded on 'independence and the frequent separations'. Which is very like us. Ellis described their relationship as 'a union of affectionate comradeship'. But he didn't always feel like that. In 1892, when Edith develops a passionate friendship with an old school friend called Claire, Havelock Ellis pinpoints the trouble with 'free love'. He writes that 'this new absorption in another person was leading unconsciously to a diminution in the signs in her tenderness in her love towards me'.

Creating new rules about sex is never going to be easy. Sometimes I want steak and sometimes I want to grow lettuce. It's a bewildering spectrum. Yet what's known today as polyamory does make sense.

The chances are, you're going to want to have monogamous periods, but you're also going to want to have sex with more than one person over a period of, say, thirty or forty years. Ideally you need to talk about this with your partner. Polly Superstar's relationship with the boyfriend who wrote poetry to another woman lasted ten years, which seems pretty good going, as monogamous couples who don't write poetry to other people often don't last that long. It's about having the courage to untether yourself from the familiar. To suffer the pain of jealousy in order to escape the claustrophobia of exclusivity. It looks good on paper.

Susie takes me to a good motel she knows. It seems that Jon isn't coming for a drink after all and I'm soon chatting to the girls on the reception desk. My tipsy conversation comes round to horoscopes and I tell them that I'm a Virgo – 29 August. Susie pipes up that this is the same date as Jon's birthday. We're laughing as we walk out of the office and it's twilight and there is Jon sitting in a car wearing earphones and looking meditative as he waits to pick his partner up. Susie says to him, 'Guess what, Stephanie's birthday's on the twenty-ninth of August too!' He looks about as interested as you would when the chick who shares your birthday clearly has the hots for your wife. Then she turns to me and says, 'I'll come by tomorrow for breakfast,' before enveloping me in an embrace that seems to last for about eleven seconds and I'm thinking, *Wey-hey! She's totally coming back for me later!*

But thirty minutes later, there's no knock on my door and, with horror, I realise that Susie Bright is condemning me to a night of solitary homework. I pick up my Kindle and read the introduction to her book, *Sexwise*, where she says that in sex matters, the first time is always the best: first time with a man, first time with a woman, first anal sex, first spanking, etc. Maybe she's already done a first secret assignation in a motel room with a drunk out-of-town writer. I pull out my sex-toy bag, hoping she's back at home doing a Dan Quayle on me.

In the old days, when I'd find myself alone in a hotel room, I'd eat the free plate of macaroons, check out the products in the bathroom and then take to the high-cotton-count sheets to flick through the TV channels. Since I hit the masturbation trail, my routine is very different. I still take to the bed, but now I bring my purple bag with me. I can't really settle down until I've done my solo sex homework. It's like suddenly remembering I've got half a bar of chocolate left in the fridge. Except of course, auto-eroticism is much better for you than chocolate. Someone should do a magazine story: 'Now *you* can masturbate yourself down to a size ten.' Diogenes wished you could rub your stomach to allay your hunger, but actually it's amazing how masturbation makes you forget your appetite.

I'm still high from the drinks and I've just sparked up some Texan happy weed to work out how me and Susie B are going to have sex tonight, when my phone rings. It's Virginia. Even as I'm pressing the green 'accept' button, I know this isn't a great idea.

'Hi.' Virginia's voice sounds formal. I sense imminent drama. I know she wants to talk about 14 February and I haven't said where we'll meet yet because I don't know where I'm going to be. But now the solution comes to me in a flash. 'Come to San Francisco!' I say. 'I'm sure Jet will lend us her flat. And there's this sex party I've been invited to!'

Virginia just says, 'That won't work for me.' In fact, she keeps saying it throughout the phone call, like the Vicomte de Valmont in *Dangerous Liaisons* going, 'It's beyond my control.' I know she thinks I've been stringing her along and she needs to regain some ground. I know she's been taking advice from that bitter pastry chef at her restaurant who's already on her third marriage.

'Come on,' I urge, 'we'll have a great time!'

'I'm sorry, that won't work for me.'

I sigh, thinking that a) if she doesn't come to the party then I can go with Raven and that will be more fun, and b) I'm gagging to get going on my Susie Bright masturbation fantasy and this phone call is killing it. I say something useless like, 'OK then. Well, let me know if you change your mind,' before pressing the red disconnect button and disappearing under the covers with a sigh of relief. I put my hands over my crotch and immediately I feel safe. For a while now, this has become an automatic way of relaxing. I remember something Hadji said about male masturbation. How when you're a young man, you worry about getting on a bus and the wind blowing the wrong way in case you get a hard-on. And how it gets more difficult as you get older. But sometimes, something inexplicable happens. A real visitation. 'The urge rises up and you feel you have your hand on the tiller. You can go wherever you like.'

Last year, my pussy was in a bad way, but now Pinky Tuscadero is growing in confidence. She feels wet, plump, slightly hungry. She pulls me in, impatient. My session in the Santa Cruz motel room is not really a creamy ice-cream cone of a wank. It's more like some weird trendy ice cream that the chef from El Bulli would come up with: strawberries and liquorice and roast quail and rusty nail flavour. Rousseau might have called it rape, but I don't think Susie will mind. I toss and turn with her in a sea of weird chronology and disjointed plot and wake up the next morning feeling like a cartoon character who's been bludgeoned over the head with a steel bar.

It's 9.30 a.m. and I shower under a pitiful trickle of water (for America). I wander around the room in a state of carefully arranged semi-undress in readiness for the sudden knock on the door. But then I check my email. Susie says she hopes I had a restful night followed by news that she's been 'slammed' into meetings first thing this morning and so won't be able to have breakfast.

The cold sweat of paranoia comes upon me. Has hanging out on the San Francisco kink scene made me delusional? Was Susie just being hospitable and taking me for a drink? Maybe sex wasn't in the air at all. I think back to Barry Komisaruk warning that 'inhibition is as essential as the brakes in a car'. Luckily, these doubts are soon smothered by the transcendent quality of the DIY waffles in the pink motel breakfast room. I pour batter into an iron and the waffle comes out salty and crisp on the outside, and soft on the inside. I pour maple syrup all over it and the taste shoots me off to some sugar rush pleasure zone I haven't been to yet on my trip. The waffle machine also gives rise to kinship in the anonymous breakfast room. A mousy woman says to me, 'They're the best darn waffles my husband and I have ever eaten,' and everything feels safe and warm and lettuce-like again.

But it seems that when there's an abundance of lettuce, my taste for steak always returns. I go back to my room and send Susie an email. 'Waffle maker amazing but the water pressure in the shower wouldn't give anyone an orgasm.' I sign off *mille tendresses*, which is a cop-out, because Hadji used to use it on me. Susie says to let her know when I'm back in town. She signs off, 'We'll see!' which I now decide is filled with coquetry and intrigue.

I leave Santa Cruz feeling like David Banner at the end of *The Incredible Hulk*, when he's forced to leave town to the backdrop of a schmaltzy piano motif signifying loneliness.

But by the time I'm back on the road, I'm thinking of Oscar Wilde's quote about a cigarette being the 'perfect type of a perfect pleasure' because it leaves you unsatisfied.

The creamy ice-cream cone hangs in the air.

SEAL ORGY INTERLUDE

America is an amazing country, when you think about it. This is the place where you have the death penalty and also people who make a living from teaching you how to have an orgasm with a tree. As I drive south down Highway 1, I'm very excited to see my first sightings of redwoods. Real redwoods and not those involved in an Annie Sprinkle fantasy. I'm quite shocked when I finally see one. Redwoods helped build America. The pioneers used them for railway cars, schoolhouses, cradles, desks and posts. Being a slow wood to burn was one of their strong points but also, as I see now, they don't have many branches, so they're basically ready-made telegraph poles. Poor mighty redwoods. If you saw one at Lash it would be wearing a badge that said 'Bottom'.

The stretch of coast I'm driving down is known as Big Sur and has been described as one of the wonders of the world. There are some breathtaking sights – massive viaducts straddling impossible ravines, huge waves smashing onto vicious rocks, but my gin hangover is kicking in again. So about three hours out of Santa Cruz, I decide to spend the night at a campsite in a place called Kirk Creek. I do the clichéd thing: I sit on the edge of a cliff and watch the sunset. I'm just a stone's throw from Esalen, where all the high-end hippies went in the 1960s to get in touch with themselves and to do what I'm doing now: try and find some sort of deeper meaning in their life. Looking out onto the huge ocean, watching the Sun Angels tap dancing on the water, I can see why people traditionally came to California to seek enlightenment. Yet all I can think of is a) is sex really important? If my Cannes friend were here, she'd probably be happy painting a picture of the sunset, and b) what will it be like spending a night in a car? The answer to the second question is easy. It's a nightmare spending a night in a car. After dining in my $25 a night camping patch on an amazing avocado (five of them for $1 at a Latin American warehouse just outside Santa Cruz), Trader Joe's corn tortillas, fake Parmesan cheese and a squeeze of lime juice, I get into the back seat of the car and prepare for sleep. I'm feeling optimistic. It's a cheapest-of-the-line car-hire car, but it feels almost spacious as I curl up on the back seat using my sex-party leather coat as a blanket. I get my Kindle out and start Jack Kerouac's *On the Road*. I read it years ago, but it now strikes me as appallingly sexist. The women are all stupid blondes, nagging wives or 'whores'. I open *The Function of the Orgasm* by Betty's hero, Wilhelm Reich. A renegade psychoanalyst and a contemporary of Sigmund Freud, Reich was the ultimate nutty professor who believed that good orgasms could bring good health, combat fascism and 'ultimately determine the happiness of the human race'. In 1939, he fled to America, where the FBI spent $2 million trying to incarcerate him. They succeeded in 1957. His books were burned and he died of a heart attack in November of that same year, aged sixty.

Reich is probably best remembered today for his famous orgone machine, a telephone-box-sized device that you sat in and were bathed with mystical currents or 'life-force energy'. William Burroughs and Norman Mailer swore by them, especially Mailer, who declared in *The White Negro* in 1957 that the key to self-liberation was the ability to come up with an 'orgasm more apocalyptic than the last one'. (He admitted at the end of his life that he'd never actually had an 'apocalyptic' orgasm because 'intellectuals never have good orgasms'.)

Speak for yourself, Norman, I think, switching to Marco Vassi, Annie Sprinkle's one-time lover and friend, who used to work at *Penthouse Variations*, the short-story spin-off mag filled with tales of bondage, water sports and sadomasochism. His masterpiece, *The Stoned Apocalypse*, is a much more readable and sexually honest version of *On the Road*. 'Are you . . . searching?' a colleague asks him one day in his office, and so his voyage through 1960s counterculture begins. He travels to Mexico, Arizona and LA, where he meeting an array of Scientologists, Communists and macrobiotic freaks. He has a lot of group sex, takes lots of hallucinogenics, visits Esalen, finds himself taken for a guru, sees through 'the West Coast philosophy of euphoria-at-all-costs', and concludes his journey by working in an experimental psychiatric hospital, where he ends up as a patient which – no surprise – he finds really mind-expanding. The hardest part seems to be his return to the 'real world'. In the familiar setting of a New York apartment, trying to describe the visions of his trip to friends, the whole experience 'took on the cosiness of an adventurer's story told by the fire at a comfortable club'.

I've soon dropped off into my customary instant darkness but I wake an hour later with a seat-belt attachment digging into my hip. I realise that the back seat of a car is really not cut out for sleep. I lie awake thinking about Tutu, the first person I ever met who'd spent the night in a car. She slept in one in Venice Beach, California, many times as a rebellious teenager, before taking a plane and getting that nanny job in London. It's very quiet in a car at night. Rousseau once warned that 'the imagination lights up and whets its appetite in the silence of the study' and it does in a car too. I wish I'd bought a vibrator in Good Vibrations because I'm feeling lazy about being manual. But instead I decide to be like Thérèse the Philosopher locked up in the count's erotic library. I pick up the Kindle and look for *Fair Chloris* by the Earl of Rochester, the rakish seventeenth-century poet. It's about a swine herdess who has to 'rub one out', as Raven would put it, when she wakes one afternoon from a sexy dream in a barn with her pigs:

> *Frighted she wakes, and waking frigs,*
> *Nature thus kindly eased,*
> *In dreams raised by her murmuring pigs,*
> *And her own thumb between her legs,*
> *She's innocent and pleased.*

It was still OK to masturbate in the seventeenth century. Samuel Pepys was always at it. On Christmas Eve of December 1667 he performs *la cosa* at midnight Mass in Queen's Chapel, next to St James's Palace.

> Lord, what an odde thing it was for me to be in a crowd of people, here a footman, there a beggar, here a fine lady, there a zealous poor papist, and here a Protestant, two or three together, come to see the show. I was afeared of my pocket being picked very much. But here I did make myself to do *la cosa* by mere imagination, *mirando a jolie mosa* and with my eyes open, which I never did before – and God forgive me for it, it being in the chapel . . .

He'd have felt much worse if he'd been born a century later, because in the eighteenth century, masturbation becomes officially notorious. For the philosophers of the Enlightenment, masturbation suggested a dark side to their ideals of autonomy, independence and rationality. The fear that there might be recesses of the mind that the civilising process couldn't control meant that solitude became something to be shunned at all costs. The rot set in around 1715 with the publication in London of an anonymous pamphlet called *Onania: or the Heinous Sin of Self-Pollution, and All its Frightful Consequences (in Both Sexes)*. Offering 'physical and spiritual advice to those who have already injured themselves by this abominable practice', it slams masturbation on moral, religious and medical counts. The author warns that indulgers will develop 'meager jaws and pale looks, with feeble hams and legs without calves, their generative faculties weaken'd, if not destroyed in the prime of their years'. A lucrative industry soon sprang up selling quack medicines to cure the eighteenth-century young from the iniquity that one pseudo-doctor likened to being trapped 'in th'embrace of a phantom'.

By 1760, the celebrated Swiss physician, Samuel-Auguste Tissot, respected for his successful work treating smallpox, had picked up the anti-solo-sex baton and published *L'Onanisme*. Tissot categorised the six illnesses caused by masturbation as: memory loss, stunted bodily growth, sharp pains and intestinal pain, pimples, foetid gonorrhoea and constipation. The book became a sensation and from 1765 to 1782 it was re-edited almost yearly. *L'Onanisme* influenced Kant and Voltaire's damning views of masturbation as selfish and a dangerous addiction to a secret, interior life.

By the end of the eighteenth century, thanks to Rousseau and Tissot, masturbation had gone from being a harmless *je ne sais quoi* that a swine herdess might indulge in during her siesta, to a fully fledged scourge of 'self-pollution'. In 1792, Mary Wollstonecraft talks of the 'indelicate tricks' that girls in single-sex schools get up to in *A Vindication of the Rights of Woman*. Meanwhile, on the other side of the Channel, one of the charges brought against Marie Antoinette in 1793 was that the Widow Capet, as she was called after Louis XVI's execution, had taught her son, the nine-year-old dauphin, 'pollutions that were both indecent and harmful for his temperament'. It was a low but clever attack: the secretive, dishonest act of self-pollution was fostered in the dark bosom of the *ancien régime*, which only the cleansing light of revolution could remedy.

By the nineteenth century, when developments in medical science began to demonstrate that masturbation didn't actually cause feeble hams and all the rest of it, the witch-hunt eased a little. The practice was still frowned upon though. The main problem was that, unlike coitus, it was a form of sexual activity that didn't produce anything. In an industrialised world of factory-line production, masturbation was the unacceptable cottage industry of sex. By the twentieth century, Freud was mooting that the urge for solitary sex was not fostered by a corrupt society, as Rousseau had suggested, but rather that it came inexorably from within. From the early twentieth century, masturbation was deemed by the father of psychoanalysis to be OK-ish (although until 1896, Freud still believed it was the cause of bed-wetting). His final position was that it was an immature sexual stage that a woman had to go through. And then Betty Dodson, the hick from Wichita, Kansas, came along and insisted that far from being an aberration, masturbation was the cornerstone of every woman's sexuality.

In the most authoritative of Latin dictionaries, first published by Lewis and Short in 1879, the entry for the verb to masturbate reads: '*Masturbor*, perhaps from *manus-stupro*.' *Manus* means 'hand' and *stupro* comes from *stuprare*, a verb meaning 'to defile' or 'violate'. So if you masturbate, you rape yourself with your hand. The entry then refers readers to the Greek word *dephei*, which is translated in the Greek dictionary as 'to soften by working with the hand', or 'to mould like wax', and the phrase *depho seauton* ('to soften oneself'). The Victorian Lewis and Short dictionary tends to obfuscate the meaning of anything sexual. Softening seems the opposite of what men do during masturbation, but sort of on point for what women do. The meaning could also come from *mas*, meaning 'male' and *turbor*, meaning to excite; to stir up one's manhood.

The Swedes threw this whole raft of Victorian prudery out of the window in 2014 when their Swedish Association for Sexuality Education (RFSU) held a competition looking for a female-specific word for masturbation. The winner was *klittra*, chosen because, said the RFSU, 'It highlights the importance of the clitoris for pleasure.'

Solo-sex history works better than counting sheep. I finally drop off, although I wake up every half hour until first light, when I drive off again down the coast feeling cold and sticky and like I've won my hobo spurs. The road is deserted at this hour. The sky is bruised black and silver, birds screech and shards of light dazzle through the clouds. I have to admit, there is something amazing about Big Sur. I stop the car and walk down a track towards a beach where I suddenly see something incredible. I can hear Betty say, 'It's not an orgy, it's a sex party.' But this one looks more like an orgy because there's very little consensual intercourse going on. One gigantic hook-nosed male manoeuvres his way along the sand in blubbery lollops and then hurls himself on a female. Seals! My heart's pumping. There must be a hundred excited furry animals in front of me and I'm the only human being. It's a weird feeling. The wind wails and the seals' passion comes out as desperate fart noises. Rousseau claimed in *Emile* that 'A solitary raised in a desert, without books, without instruction, and without women, would die a virgin however long he lived.' Sorry Rousseau, but if you were a noble savage and you saw this, it would definitely give you some ideas.

An information board says that these are elephant seals and February is the peak mating season. During this time, some of the young ones fight each other instead of mating, but lots of the young ones look like they're having a love-in. A couple of babies near their mother nuzzle each other's noses. The third sibling sits on its own doing something weird with a flipper. Is he or she . . . ? This was supposed to be my break from masturbation. But maybe, like Annie Sprinkle says, you never can escape it.

Five hours later, I'm on the outskirts of Barstow, looking for the Desert Palace motel and my snaggle-toothed friend. But I can't find it and I end up at a place called the Rodeway Inn. I get offered a good deal from the Asian Indian woman who runs the place. Only $40. 'It is a very good room,' she keeps saying. When she shows me room 123, the décor and the furniture are terrible, but there's a sense of someone trying to make things better. There's a piece of ruched nylon hanging over the shower curtain and, on the bed, a towel has been twisted into the shape of an animal like they do on cruise ships. The creature has thick legs suggestive of an elephant but no discernable head, like one of those pea-brained dinosaurs. Before she goes, she tells me her name is Nikki. Like 'Darling Nikki' by Prince. I think this must be my lucky room and wish her good night, trying not to imagine her masturbating with a magazine.

When she's gone, I sit on the bed, looking through the open door at the pink mountains beyond the glittering lights of Family Dollar and Vons. I peel another of the Santa Cruz avocados. It's a strange experience, eating Michelin-quality food in a motel with cheap carpets and police-state lighting. When I've finished, I take the dinosaur elephant off the bed and slide under a nylon blanket with a wolf pattern on it. I think about Hadji's thing about healing being the reason for this trip. And this morning, Virginia said to me, 'How's your body?' She often asks that.

The wolf blanket lights up green in the night.

PALM SPRINGS WEEKEND

I'm grinning the next morning when I hit the road for Palm Springs. I'm thinking of pools, cocktails and Frank Sinatra, and I carry on trying to reach top C on the Erasure song: 'A little respect too-oo-oo-oo me!' It's a great drive. There's no traffic, just scrub and shimmering forms in the distance because it's so hot. I feel incredibly relaxed and limber, as if I could whack off in the car and then turn a somersault behind the steering wheel while simultaneously coming.

When I arrive in Palm Springs, I check in for a free night at the Viceroy Hotel. The place is all hummingbirds and topiary alcoves and a sense that you might get a sighting of Greta Garbo at any moment. Down by the pool, where I'm waiting to meet Jerry the PR, I breathe in the warm Valium air and contemplate the huge grapefruit breasts that hang heavy on a branch above my head. When Jerry arrives, he is very friendly and has a manner like Liberace: warm and soft and slightly lizard. He orders brightly coloured drinks and tells me that Greta Garbo actually did live for a while in the Spanish revival villa I'm staying at. Then another round of drinks arrives and the amazing dry heat and the grapefruit breasts and Jerry's revelation about the 'pink moment' (the seconds of uncanny light on the mountains just before the sun rises) make me feel even more relaxed. When he asks me what other journalistic stories I'm working on, I say, 'Actually, I'm writing a book about masturbation.' For a few seconds it seems as if a lizard tongue is going to whip out and lasso me into a deep dark place where I'll never be seen again. But then his face lights up. 'Oh boy!' he says. 'You should meet Grace Robbins!'

When he tells me that Grace is the wife of the 1970s bestselling trashy novelist Harold Robbins, my heart starts pumping like the seal orgy all over again.

'Grace is a friend of mine,' Jerry says. 'She's just written a book about all the orgies and the sex in the 1970s. I'm sure masturbation would be right up her alley.'

Robbins' novels evoked a world of super-rich, highly sexed excess before *Dallas* or *Dynasty* had even been thought of. Until books like Robbins' *The Carpetbaggers* and, later, Jacqueline Susann's *Valley of the Dolls* hit bookshops and drugstores, you could only read smut in America via literature smuggled in from Paris: the Marquis de Sade, Henry Miller, Pauline Réage's *Story of* O. Both Robbins and Susann shone a light onto a world of fur coats, cocktails at Sardi's, abortion, lesbian sex and suicide. Robbins spent the last years of his life in Palm Springs, married to the nurse who'd been looking after him when he had his stroke and contracted aphasia, the most shocking condition for a writer – the inability to put thoughts into words. But it was glamorous Grace who he was with for twenty-eight years during the Acapulco/Beverly Hills/ South of France years.

Jerry gives me Grace Robbins' number and, back in Greta Garbo's bedroom, I call her. The perky voice on the answering machine is very Beverly Hills mansion, circa 1973. 'Hi, this is Grace. I'm not around right now but leave me a message and I'll get back toot sweet!' I can see her at the door in a velvet pantsuit, brandishing a tray of Quaaludes, telling me to slip off my clothes and go join Jane Asher, Michael York and Sammy Davis Jr in the bedroom with the mirrored ceiling.

My phone buzzes and it's a text from Raven. 'Just finished a five-hour kidnap scene,' it says. 'Exhausted and happy. How's Palm Springs?' I make a snap decision about Valentine's Day. If Virginia's going to give me grief, I'll spend it with Raven at Polly Superstar's Kinky Salon. As I write Raven a text, I get a flash of our voluptuous kiss goodbye after the weekend with Roxanne. I wonder if I'll end up in bed alone with her. She sends back a message saying, 'You're on for February 14th! Send a dirty pic by the pool if you can ;).'

I decide that I'm going to ask Grace Robbins for her take on orgies of the 1970s when I meet her. The only Harold Robbins' sex scenes I recall from the books on my mother's bookshelf involved rape or uncomfortable anal sex. But I do remember a great psychedelic orgy in Robbins' rival Jacqueline Susann's *Once Is Not Enough*. I read it one rainy afternoon as a twelve-year-old, lying on my front in my bedroom. Jemima was at the ready and I was half waiting to be called in for the usual fraught Sunday-evening roast. The book's sex-party scene set the template in my mind for what an orgy was. January, our innocent heroine, goes to a party in New York peopled with underground movie stars smoking 'skinny cigarettes', drinking acid-laced sangria and wearing velvet pantsuits, saying things like, 'Drink the wine . . . you'll blow your mind.' There were poppers, naked dancing, group chanting, an orgasm that lasted 'forever and ever' and finally everyone passed out.

Masturbating to Jacqueline Susann on the head of your childhood doll sums up all the frustrations of adolescence. But I was grateful. There might have been cows outside my bedroom window but before Jacqueline Susann, the only place you could find any decent stuff about lesbians was in the Bible. When January comes round from the group orgy of the night before, someone gives her a funny sugar cube and soon she's watching two girls embracing. One of them comes to slip her lips over January's breasts as the other unzips her jeans. January feels one of the soft hands, 'touching her . . . no . . . that was wrong . . . only a penis should do that . . . or a man. She pulled away . . .'

'Tea's ready!'

My pelvis froze. Tea was ready *and* January was such a wimp? I was furious. What did January mean it was 'wrong'? And what about those sugar cubes? I sat at the table, glaring at my roast-beef dinner, wondering how many more thousand years were left until I could attend one of these parties myself.

The next evening I meet up with my friend Richard Dupont at a restaurant called Tropical. He's going to give me some insider tips about Palm Springs for my magazine story. I met Richard years ago on Long Island at the imposing house of C. Z. Guest, one of Truman Capote's 'swans', as he called the circle of glamorous women who adored him. I was there to interview her daughter, Cornelia, who refused to have me in the house while she was being attended to by the hair and make-up team. She smiled and thrust a horrible baggy swimming costume at me. saying, 'You're like me: long body, short legs!' and sent me to the swimming pool.

I was soon doing laps in the pool that Salvador Dalí, Bianca Jagger and Wallace Simpson had once swam in, wondering when I was allowed out. When the pool-cleaner guys arrived, I finally escaped, only to jump in shock on bumping into two identical men sitting in a greenhouse. I thought they were gardeners, but it turned out they were Richard and Robert Dupont, Cornelia's resident court jester identical twins who appear in *The Andy Warhol Diaries*. Richard, born in 1959, was soon telling me tales of how he'd once gone up to Truman Capote in Studio 54 and called him a 'tired old queen' following a dare from a friend.

The twin brothers were teen runaways from Connecticut. They hung out with the second-wave Andy Warhol crowd in the New York of the 1970s. Andy loved identical twins so he paid them in Quaaludes and drawings and got them to sleep with rich guys at Studio 54 to persuade them to get portraits done.

Richard still can't speak without uttering some anecdote about Truman Capote (who befriended him) or Freddie Mercury (who dated him) or Salvador Dalí (who painted him). He prefaces many of his sentences with 'Wait 'til you hear this!' and describes many of the inhabitants of Palm Springs as 'wack-o-doos'. He came to live here ten years ago because the Valium heat makes everything disappear from your head, giving you what he calls 'guacamole brain'. When Truman Capote came to Palm Springs in 1968 to finish *Answered Prayers*, guacamole brain got to him too. He famously never finished the book, although falling in love with the air-conditioning repairman can't have helped.

Tammy, our waitress at Tropical, twirls our plates of Green Goddess Lobster Salad like a demented Harlem Globetrotter. 'You can't just be a waitress,' she informs us. 'You got to give people entertainment!'

When the plates finally land, I start telling Richard about Grace Robbins. When I say that Jerry thinks she might have a great masturbation story, he curls his lip. 'Wait 'til you hear this,' he says.

Andy wasn't trying to be funny when he said that 'sex is the biggest nothing of all time'. Richard learned early on that masturbation was more to the artist's taste. Or, rather, watching other people masturbate. The seventeen-year-old had already earned his spurs with Andy by jacking off over the balcony at Studio 54. Andy, then in his late forties, was soon inviting Richard to the Factory at 860 Broadway on

Saturday mornings. 'We'd go out back and he'd sit there and go, "Oh yeah, oh Richard, you're wonderful. You're going to be famous."'

And he was, in a way. In 2014, a unique Warhol Polaroid print of Richard Dupont's bottom (*Nude Male Model*) was sold by Christie's for $5,000. The Polaroid was taken in 1977, after one of the Saturday morning auto-erotic sessions. Richard only remembered about it when Christie's contacted him.

'I was very impressionable,' he reflects, taking another Diet Coke from Tammy. 'I thought, "Adults ask you to do stuff, so you do it."'

Yet his ultimate solo-sex performance occurred in the late 1970s in the back of a New York limousine. Inside were Andy Warhol, Salvador Dalí, Dalí's Russian wife Gala, a Dominican drag queen called Potassa and Richard Dupont. The drag queen was swigging champagne and spilling it all over her Oscar de la Renta gown, when Andy suddenly grabbed Richard. 'He said, "Hey, bring it out!"'

Richard speculates that Andy was trying to show off to Dalí or get the artist aroused, but he admits he was 'terrified'. But everyone was staring at him and Potassa was making suggestive gestures with the champagne bottle, so he knew a show was expected. 'Dalí started chanting this special word he had for "orgasm" I don't recall now, and Andy's grabbing me, going, "Come on!" So I had to do it.'

Richard ejaculated all over the black leather upholstery to screeches of horror and delight from the four spectators, including two of the most significant artists from the end of the twentieth century.

If you ask art critics about an important piece of masturbation artwork of the twentieth century, they might cite Vito Acconci's 1972 performance piece, *Seedbed*. For three weeks, Acconci lay under the floor of the Sonnabend Gallery in

New York City and masturbated over a loudspeaker, apparently inspired by dirty fantasies about the gallery visitors above. Not only is the limo jack-off more pure than Acconci's piece because Richard didn't have any fantasy in his head ('Now I have to think of something dirty, but back then I could just do it'), but there was no seed to see in Acconci's *Seedbed*, whereas there was plenty in the back of the limo by the time the moving bacchanal had arrived back at 860 Broadway.

The good thing about Richard is that he doesn't get too deep. 'You needed to keep them amused,' he shrugs. 'They were all, like, "Drama! Drama!"'

He takes a sip of his Diet Coke as we look over at Tammy, doing her hoopla with the plates.

When I finally meet Grace Robbins two days later, she tells me that she doesn't consider herself a sexual adventurer in the way that VV and Annie Sprinkle do. She only attended 'four, maybe five' orgies in her life, all of them 'with Harold as the ringmaster'. Born to strict Sicilian parents, she thought she'd found her Prince Charming in Harold Robbins, who wooed her in the early 1960s with jewellery, lobster and Dom Pérignon. She eventually quit her job as the casting director of a New York advertising company to take up with the man who was to become one of the bestselling authors of all time.

Born in 1932, the kittenish eighty-three-year-old answers my masturbation questions slightly warily. She never used to do it, she says, because Harold was a 'magical' lover, although two years into married life he announced that he wanted an open arrangement. 'It hit me very hard,' she admits.

'But at least he was honest,' I say, finding myself sticking up for Harold Robbins.

'Yes,' she nods, 'I realised it was the way he had to work.'

Ah, that delightful 'but I'm a writer' get-out clause. Harold

Robbins, raised in a Catholic orphanage until he was twelve, did set up some rules for their open relationship. 'He didn't want me to have an affair with anyone in the social group. And he didn't want me to have an affair with any celebs. But he broke rules and I broke rules.' Grace adds that she didn't feel the need to have as much extramarital sex as Harold did.

In her memoir, *Dreams Do Come True*, there's a picture of Harold on his eighty-five-foot yacht in Cannes in the mid-1970s. He has a deep tan and a restless grin. He's wearing a gold medallion and a white lace shirt open one too many buttons at the neck.

'What were the four or five orgies like?' I ask Grace. 'A huddle?'

'Oh no, not at all,' she says, topping up my glass. 'There were never a lot of people. It was just so . . . smooth and so . . . flowing and right.'

She's more graphic when she talks about the mid-years of their marriage, when Harold decided their sex life needed to be spiced up even more.

'Harold brought out the sex toys. Vibrators. They were quite exotic then.' It was at this time that she learned the rudiments of masturbation. 'He would also pop cocaine on my nipples and he'd put it on my clitoris. And then of course there were the poppers.'

She beams. 'Oh,' she says, in the tone of one who has just had a lovely day by the pool. 'How we loved poppers! And the one who really, really, really loved poppers was Sammy Davis Jr!'

Grace had a brief affair with Sammy but it fizzled out when he asked if he could come to one of Harold's orgies with his wife, Altovise. He'd never been to an orgy before. There were only three other people there and Grace makes the point in her book, 'I realised that night that orgies only work if you don't know the other guests very well.'

After twenty-eight years of marriage came an acrimonious divorce when Harold began an affair with his personal assistant Jann Stapp. They married in 1992 when he was seventy-six and she was thirty-nine. He went down the aisle in a wheelchair because seven years previously he'd had a coke-induced seizure in the shower, smashing his hips and pelvis and forcing him to relocate to tranquil Palm Springs. He never walked again.

But Grace doesn't regret her life with Harold. When I ask her for her most glamorous moment, she plumps for the 1965 party at the Four Seasons in New York to celebrate the film of *The Carpetbaggers*. There was more lobster and Dom Pérignon and, 'Harold had these beautiful women in mink coats with nothing underneath sitting at tables with a writer on each.' She describes how the timid (and gay) author James Baldwin, a good friend of Harold's, was sitting, 'slightly bewildered' at one of the tables.

Opening the next bottle of wine, she wants to know more about my book. When I tell her it's about female masturbation, she exclaims, 'I think that's marvellous!' She leaps up, explaining that she has a vibrator, 'But it's a very old-fashioned one. I'm not sure of the name . . .'

There's a husky laugh and she dashes off to fetch it. I follow her to the bedroom and for a minute I wonder if this is a ruse and she's going to push an ejector button and a waterbed is going to appear from under the floor and we'll both topple onto it. But after a while of searching under her bed, she gives up. 'Obviously I haven't used it in a while,' she says cutely.

She's really warmed up by now and admits that she is masturbating 'more now than I ever have in my life'. It's not that she particularly likes masturbation, it's more that the men in Palm Springs are so desperate. 'The older ones, I guess they feel their time is shortened, so immediately they want to get into bed with you. There's no courting, no romancing. That's not for me.'

The new man in her life is Luke. 'My very own Skywalker! Isn't he incredible?' She pats a Shih Tzu-Yorkie mix sitting on the couch next to her.

ORGASM ANGEL

The next morning, in a Bel Air mansion in LA, one of California's biggest sex gurus is telling me why she doesn't like masturbation either. The house looks like a bit of a Jacqueline Susann orgy pad, all white marble and reproduction chandeliers.

'We've been using orgasm to blow off steam,' a blonde woman in a white blazer has been telling a room of spellbound listeners. 'But imagine if we could harness its energy – like harnessing the rays of the sun! It would be limitless, sustainable and truly transformative!'

The trouble with self-pleasure, Nicole Daedone tells me now, is that, 'You can't take yourself out of control. Like, you can't tickle yourself. You always know what you're going to be doing.'

It's great having a spanner put in the masturbation works so late in the day and in such an intriguing way. Daedone is one of the few American sex women who is making serious money out of the second sexual revolution. Although in 2017 she would step down from her role as CEO of the multimillion-dollar orgasm business, One Taste, she is still very active behind the scenes. One Taste grossed $20 million in 2016 and is based on the belief that the clitoris has the power of the third eye. Gwyneth Paltrow is a fan of the forgotten yogic practice, which

Daedone has termed Orgasmic Meditation (OM for short). Specifically what happens is that a man strokes 'the upper left-hand quadrant' of a woman's clitoris for fifteen minutes and leads them both into a state of nirvana.

Daedone says she hasn't masturbated in years but don't get her wrong. She was a huge masturbator in her time. 'Three, four times a day,' she tells me. 'I loved it. Vibrators, dildos. I lived in San Francisco, remember. I shopped at Good Vibrations. I did it all.'

She seems to have a more detailed understanding of the clitoris than anyone I have yet talked to. It's strange listening to someone who talks like a Wall Street analyst, not about money but about the clitoris. During that morning's 'intensive' she talked to a group of people about the 'ten different areas of the clitoris', each one offering nuanced emotions, from 'relaxation' to 'reverence'.

Daedone's liberating message is that a real tip-top orgasm is more than a split second of physical climax. Rather than experience a brief high followed by nothing and then, possibly, a feeling of sadness, Daedone's method promises you a reliable fifteen minutes of hovering in out-of-body free-fall bliss. The cumulative energy that both men and women gain from these alphagasms is said to transform everything from your love life and career life to your sense of fulfilment. As one of Nicole's staff tells me, 'You can use OM in your sex life as one of your tools, along with BDSM and fluffy handcuffs, or you can take it further – you can awaken something deeper.'

It's a very aspirational club. She attracts high-end professionals and Silicon Valley executives. Daedone's 2011 TED talk, 'Orgasm: The Cure for Hunger in The Western Woman', is one of the site's most-viewed talks. Before she plunged into her journey of self-discovery, she ran an art gallery in San Francisco. When I ask what number and street it was, she says, '111 Minna Street,' and I go, 'Oh, that's the number of the angels.'

It works like a Freemason's handshake. 'You got it!' she exclaims. 'Oh no! Ah!'

In spite of the executive white blazer, Nicole is clearly a bit of a hippie too. Her inner crystal child now emerges as we talk about 111, 222 and 333 and she tells me that the number 11:11 is the 'portal to infinity'. She sounds relieved. 'I can talk to you in LSD,' she says, and soon she's giving me the low-down on her story: the curious child from northern California who wanted to be a Buddhist nun, the degree in semantics, the art gallery, the getting-bored-of-the-art-gallery-people, the moving into the acid house in San Francisco and seeing what that threw up.

She says she wants the word 'orgasm' to trip off people's lips 'as easily as "yoga" and "meditation" do now'; that she wants "spiritual sex" to develop like the American health-food industry has developed since the 1970s. 'The OM movement will soon have reached the level of Whole Foods Market,' she says.

At the end of the afternoon, she asks me where I'm staying. 'Venice Beach. With the dad of an old friend of mine. An ex lover, actually.' I hesitate. 'She died of breast cancer. Funny, he lives on 222 Pacific Avenue.' I feel as though there are about a hundred hearts pumping in my body as I say all this. I don't know why I blurted it out. Nicole just looks me in the eyes. 'Did it feel intense to say that?'

I nod. She asks me if I'd like a lift and I say, 'Yes please.' I'm wondering if it's the Free Transport Angels helping me out when suddenly a big black spaceship lands in front of us. The doors open and there's a cool black chick with a quiff working the bridge. Inside, everything is black with red and green flashing lights and wafts of fresh leather.

'I love murdered-out cars,' Nicole says, belting up in the passenger seat of the box-fresh SUV Porsche with 'Beverly Hills' on the number plates. 'Murdered out,' she explains, 'means matte black paint and super-dark windows like rappers have.'

There's the rumble of an expensive engine and then we're off. I try and get her back to masturbation. 'But do you never want the dirty truck-driver fantasy?' I ask.

'I wouldn't mind the dirty truck-driver reality,' she says. She likens orgasms to pit bulls because 'people demonise them'. Whereas if you look at orgasms in the right way, 'They're your best ally, they take you where you want to go, which is to a state of connection.'

This strikes me as real *Brave New World* stuff. Back in 1931, Huxley imagined future human beings taking a recreational drug called Soma so that they'd feel loving about each other. When you read the book now, you think, *Oh, that must be ecstasy then*. But what if orgasm were to be the new love drug? It's not even something you have to take: you have it in you, right there in your barn. What if you could make something of your orgasm, use it as energy, fuel, drugs to make your day more loved-up. 'Powered by orgasm' is One Taste's motto. When Nicole drops me off at 222 Pacific Avenue, I promise to try out OM in London and wonder if I've just been brainwashed out of believing in masturbation by a weird clit-stroking multinational.

That night Tutu's father takes me out for Mexican dinner at a great family-run restaurant in a perfectly unfashionable part of Santa Monica. He's an old-school gentleman. He opens the doors and treats me to margaritas. He was a handsome, laconic figure when I first met him fifteen years ago at the end of my road trip with Tutu. She idolised him. When we finally arrived in Venice Beach, she tracked down some rare tickets for a special Los Angeles Lakers game, his beloved basketball team. They were one of the hottest teams in America. Then I remember him as the tired old man in her London flat in the final days, shaking his head at the inexplicably un-Californian pizza the local takeaway had delivered with no 'bay-zil' on it. Interestingly, he was unfazed by the range of trans cabaret stars, rowdy lesbians and odd-looking friends who streamed in on a regular basis like extras in a demented David LaChapelle shoot to pay their last respects.

In the middle of the spiced pork and rice and the explanation of American basketball rules, he suddenly puts his fork down. I'm glad he mentions it at last. Slowly, he talks of his gratitude for how Tutu's friends cared for her with such love when she was dying and I get another flash of the scene around her bed that day. He was one of the five. A surprise ticket to the grand finale. The woman at the humanist service said she'd died peacefully, but she didn't die peacefully. I watched her being born into death, choking and heaving her way into it. At the end it was the three breaths. One breath in. One breath out. An age before the next. And that was when I knew what death means. This mass of flesh just needed to fill up with air again. Just breathe in a lung of air, that's all she needed to do. And if she didn't, it would mean she didn't exist any more. Part of me was excited. I was witnessing death, the most extreme thing she'd ever done and she was showing me. But now I think that VIP seat was a mixed blessing. Like some massive tattoo you have that you'll never be able to get off.

There's a roar from the basketball game on the TV. 'Lakers,' he says quietly, picking up his fork. 'A real shame what happened to them. Kobe Bryant left. He was the glue.'

The next morning I wake up early. I'm lying in Tutu's old bed and looking round her wood-panelled room, which hasn't been done up since the 1970s. I get out of bed and pick up one of her books. An old Girl Scouts guide from 1961. Rule number ten says, 'A girl scout is clean in thought, word and deed.' It makes me smile.

THE SKY CHILDREN

Now that I've digested Nicole Daedone's belief that the clitoris is the third eye, my next interviewee's belief – that the aliens want us to masturbate – doesn't seem so strange. Besides, my mind's wandering. Tomorrow is Valentine's Day and I have a date with Raven in San Francisco at a sophisticated swingers' club.

I've also just received a text from Cliff Barnes: 'Dear pretty horse rider,' it reads. 'I hope you're enjoying Southern Cal. Would love to take you for dinner when you're back in San Francisco. Still thinkin bout ya!' I'm quite excited about this, yet Richard Dupont seems more interested in Nadine Gary, the French teacher who is a high priestess of an alien sex organisation in the Las Vegas desert. Back in Palm Springs, when I told him I was meeting her, he said, 'Oh, how fabulous!' And it does feel quite fabulous when I first meet her. She is the most beautiful creature. Her heels tip-tap across the immense stone patio of the Westin Lake Las Vegas Resort & Spa like Stéphane Audran as Frédérique, the cruel Parisian housewife from Claude Chabrol's *Les Biches*.

She has almond-shaped eyes, dark hair tumbling down her back and she's wearing a short but chic animal-print shift dress. Around her neck on fine chains hang two modest pendants: a heart and something that looks like a Star of

David. As she reaches out to shake my hand, a beam lights up her features. 'So lovely to meet you,' she says with a Central Casting French accent.

Soon we're chatting. She's not cruel like Frédérique at all. She's very smiley. 'They have sex on their planet and they love it, you know. And they have robots. Yes! Because sometimes you want to have sex in all different kinds of ways and maybe sometimes someone doesn't feel like it, but with a robot . . .'

It doesn't feel as if Nadine is saying anything out of the ordinary. She could be a French teacher explaining the imperfect subjunctive. This might be because I'm exhausted after a six-hour drive from LA or it might be because Lake Las Vegas feels like being on the set of a 1960s episode of *Star Trek*. The hotel is situated in a gated community in the middle of the Nevada desert and while huge stone turtles spew water into a fake lake in front of us, real mountains glow an ominous salmon-pink and gold in the background. When Nadine starts talking about how the Raëlians want to build an embassy to welcome the Sky People when they come back to earth, all I can do is nod and wait for Lieutenant Uhura to jump out from behind a rock in her red minidress.

Nadine, fifty-two, who is originally from Lyon in France, tells me that the Raëlians don't think in terms of 'aliens'. They call the people who created planet earth 'Elohim', which is a word from the Hebrew Bible and means 'those who came from the sky'. They look just like us because they created us in their image. They are scientific whizzes like us but just a bit brighter.

I don't think the Raëlians sound nearly weird enough. They don't have any equivalent of swallowing a bit of bread and it turning into the flesh of a man born over 2,000 years ago. The Raëlians sound a bit Swedish, as a matter of fact. They're almost boringly open-minded about sex.

'In order for a society to be balanced, it has to be balanced with its sexuality,' Nadine explains. 'Taboos make you aggressive. The Elohim created us as sexual beings. But sensual meditation is what we teach, not sexual meditation.'

My heart sinks. Is this all going to turn into the Annie Sprinkle and the bedsheets thing? I'm glad I decided not to stay for the Raëlians' sensual meditation class on Valentine's Day and that I'm going to Kinky Salon instead. I cut to the chase. 'So how much sex do the Elohim want us to have?

'It's never a case of "should",' she says gently. 'Some people have a very active sexuality – three times a day. It's whatever feels comfortable to you.' I tell her about my imminent trip to Kinky Salon and she smiles and says, 'I'm not so big on swingers' clubs. I went to a club called the Green Door in Las Vegas but I didn't feel good. People go there to have sex, but I like to have more of a connection . . .'

Nadine prefers to share sex with one person. 'Or maybe another additional person – the three of us together.' She is married to a French man and uses masturbation to get up her pleasure quotient. 'I masturbate maybe once every couple of days.'

The waiter arrives with a Bloody Mary for her and a glass of water for me. She picks up the glass and stirs the red liquid with a celery stick.

'Sensuality is about enhancing all your senses: touch, taste, smell. Sexuality is all of these senses together.'

She takes a bite of the celery and flinches. She touches the Star of David pendant around her neck. I now see that it has the swastika sign woven into it, the Sanskrit symbol of infinity. The Raëlians give it the same meaning.

'You know what I mean by infinity? You're made of little cells. And maybe inside these little cells there are little universes with little people inside.'

'Little people?'

'And around us – we are sitting in this space and maybe we are inside this person who is talking to someone else now.'

Now she's starting to mess with my head. Are me and Nadine sitting in the Nevada desert in a cell in some giant person's leg?

'So when you are making love it's like two universes meeting together and with orgasm it's like, wow!'

Whatever you think of the philosophy of the Raëlians, they do have an undisputed trump card held by no other so-called cult. Thanks to their belief in the importance of sensual pleasure, they have created a humanitarian organisation called Clitoraid, which surgically reconstructs the clitorises of women who have been victims of female genital mutilation. As well as waiting for the Sky People to come back to earth, much of Nadine's extracurricular time is taken up with being a masturbation coach. She conducts a kind of genital physio session by Skype after the operation has been performed, often by Dr Marci Bowers, an American transgender surgeon who works with Clitoraid on a voluntary basis. Bowers has just started working with FGM victims in Nairobi, Kenya, alongside the clitoral restorative surgery she already performs in Burkina Faso, West Africa, and San Francisco.

Nadine explains her role in all of this.

'Once you do the surgery, the clitoris takes three months to heal. Then you start to recover sensation. It's like when you have surgery on your hands: you have physio after the operation to get your hands moving. The clitoris is the same thing. You have to use it. It's better to masturbate than have your husband try it first.'

She says it's vital to keep the post-op women motivated. 'Sometimes they get discouraged, but the coach is there to entice. I say, "Where do you feel something?" Sometimes there's more sensation, say, to the right or to the left.'

Clitoraid refers European patients to Pierre Foldès, the French doctor from Médecins Sans Frontières, who came across FGM when he worked in Africa. He realised that a new clitoris could be reconstructed since, as Nadine says, 'Ninety-nine per cent of the clitoris lies under the surface of the vulva.'

The Australian urologist Helen O'Connell has been credited with 'discovering' how big the clitoris really is, thanks to the study she published on the subject in 1998. Actually, a 1970s art student got there before her. At the masturbation weekend, Betty showed us her female anatomy bible, *A New View of a Woman's Body* by the Federation of Feminist Women's Health Centers. The book was published by Simon & Schuster in 1981. It followed years of research by a team of women in LA, including the book's illustrator, art student Suzann Gage, who were passionate about taking back knowledge from a male-dominated medical profession.

When I tracked Gage down on the phone, she explained that she was attending Black Hawk Community College in Moline, Illinois, when she saw a notice about a meeting involving 'vaginal self-examination'. It was 1971, Gage was nineteen years old and it was the dawning of what was known at the time as the Women's Liberation Movement.

She arrived an hour late at the meeting because 'it was pouring with rain and my windscreen wipers weren't working'. Still in the uniform she wore to her part-time waitressing job and reeking of meat loaf and cigarette smoke, she entered a room where eight women were watching an instructor examining her cervix with the aid of a torch and a mirror.

I thought immediately, *This is the greatest thing!*

The instructor was mother-of-four-turned-health-activist Carol Downer, who later retrained as a feminist lawyer. Her assistant was Lorraine Rothman, a schoolteacher who co-founded the Feminist Women's Health Center. Both women were travelling across the US in a bus with boxes of plastic speculums teaching women how to look at their own cervix (the entrance to the uterus at the back of the vagina).

The concept of a feminist health movement evolved from the 1960s human rights and anti-war movements. The radical idea of examining your own cervix is a good one, since you can learn to distinguish between natural secretions and unhealthy discharges (a useful thing if you don't have a National Health Service to pay for trips to the doctor). The experience of women sharing information about their bodies, their periods, their vaginal infections and their birth control was empowering in the days when even superstars like Jacqueline Susann were too embarrassed to go public with awkward health stories. Fearing for her glamorous image, she'd had a secret mastectomy in 1962 and in 1974, just over a year after *Once Is Not Enough* came out, she was dead from what was believed to be metastatic breast cancer.

When Gage first saw her cervix with the aid of a torch, she had a reaction similar to mine after the Betty Dodson weekend. 'It was the most amazing moment,' she tells me. 'I felt as though I'd gained a part of my body.'

In 1973, she dropped out of higher education and moved to LA because Downer and Rothman were starting an internship programme. She began work on a small book about DIY cervical exams. Except it became a very big book called *A New View of a Woman's Body* because Gage, hired as the book's illustrator, discovered with the other team members that most of the medical books of the time were 'cartoonish' in their depiction of the female anatomy. Some of her best sources came from medical reference books written in the 1800s with images based on cadaver dissections.

She recalls how she and her fellow researchers spent a lot of time trying to 'piece together' information about the female genitalia, as though this were some kind of crazy Nancy Drew mystery. One light-bulb moment occurred in 1975 when she started reading about genital development in foetuses and learned how the cells that form the genital tissue in males and females look, up until around seven weeks, identical. 'As the foetus grows, the genital tissue rearranges itself to form a shape of a penis or a shape of a clitoris, but it's basically the same mass of cells.'

Gage also recalls a 'spectacular mechanical drawing' in one older German textbook showing the inner workings of the penis. Although there was no equivalent female drawing, 'the author kept saying, "and by the way, the clitoris is very similar"'.

A new world started to open up for Gage and her fellow researchers. The only difference between a clitoris and a penis was that most of the female erectile tissue (the corpus cavernosum and corpus spongiosum) is inside the body, beneath the labia and adjacent to the vaginal opening. The (mainly external) male erectile tissue is shaped like a dolphin, whereas ours looks more like an inflatable wishbone or a bird with wings and an external head that rises when we're turned on.

The chapter 'The Clitoris: A Feminist Perspective' in *A New View of a Woman's Body* is such a milestone in the history of sex-positivity because, for the first time, the knowledge that the penis could equally be referred to as a male clitoris had been liberated from dusty medical tomes and openly announced to thousands of women around America. And while older medical tomes might have talked about the female corpus cavernosum and corpus spongiosum, Gage believes that this was the first time that 'the clitoris' had been referred to as something encompassing the whole large organ – both internal and external.

'It was very exciting,' says Gage. 'And it helped women. It helped explain their sexual experiences.'

Gage went on to retrain as a nurse practitioner specialising in women's health and now runs a clinic in San Diego called Progressive Health Services, which offers both traditional and more alternative healthcare. She decided to turn in a more alternative direction when she began to encounter women with severe and chronic vaginal infections who were unable to get any relief from mainstream Western medicine. 'It can be devastating for women. The alternative health community has often been the only real hope for these types of situations.' She adds that this type of medicine also tends to be more self-help orientated, which goes back to her roots.

As a kid in the 1960s, Gage was fascinated by 3-D art. So it's fitting that one woman taking on her baton is a French researcher who had a breakthrough with a piece of 3-D technology. In May 2016, independently of the work done by Clitoraid and Pierre Foldès, Odile Fillod created the world's first open-source, anatomically correct, printable 3-D clitoris for use in sex-education classes. It's great that Gage's insights finally got to be depicted in a truly modern way, and yet there is still uncertainty about how long the average clitoris actually is. As of 2018, according to scientific literature, the average size is probably about 10 cm, with around 0.5 per cent of that visible. The penis, including its internal tissue, measures an average of about 19 cm.

Fillod has some bad news about the 8,000 vs 4,000 nerve endings theory. 'It's not backed by scientific literature,' she tells me. Unless you're a sheep. It turns out that the magic 8,000 number came originally from Natalie Angier's 1999 book *Woman: An Intimate Geography* where research was done on rams and ewes. In the 2014 updated version of Angier's book, the author revises her original estimate of clitoral nerves in human women to a mere 'thousands and thousands'. She then refers to a 2013 study led by Cheryl Shih at the University of Washington School of Medicine. Shih discovered that the average nerve density was 3.5 times greater in the clitoris than in the penis, although the sample size was small (she analysed the genital tissue from the dead bodies of five women and four men). Still, given the size of the clitoris head to that of the penis, Fillod agrees that the former is clearly 'more densely innervated and with a likely higher sensitivity potential'. Unfortunately, that doesn't look as good on a T-shirt as '8,000 nerve endings'.

At the height of my vulval pain, when the friction of my underwear on my clitoris could feel like a knife, it felt as though I had 10 million nerve endings in my female dick. And I still do on occasion and I don't know why. Actually I do. According to the online medical search engine PubMed, there are five times as many clinical trials on male sexual pleasure as there are on female sexual pain. On dyspareunia, a blanket term referring to the severe pain some women experience during sex, there are 393 clinical trials (of which a mere forty-three are looking at vulvodynia). On male erectile dysfunction, a toughie but not usually painful, there are a massive 1,954 studies. And while a man can often pick up a packet of Viagra these days with more ease that he can a packet of cigarettes, a woman will suffer on average for 9.28 years before she is diagnosed with the crippling illness of dyspareunia (source: the North American Endometriosis Association). Debby Herbenick, a professor at the Indiana University School of Public Health, observes that,

'When it comes to "good sex", women often mean without pain; men often mean they had orgasms.'

The good news is that women are coming to the end of their rope about all this nonsense – at least a growing wave of pissed-off pioneers are. Take New York artist Sophia Wallace, whose ongoing multimedia project '100 Laws of Cliteracy', begun in 2013, promotes discussion around the ignorance and shame surrounding the clitoris. Other women making some noise include artist Alli Sebastian Wolf, who paraded round the Sydney Opera House in January 2017 brandishing a huge gold 'glitoris' on a stick.

Odile Fillod of 3-D wishbone fame is not the only French clitoris activist. In 2016 a 'crop clitoris' appeared shaved into a farmer's field in the village of Montferrier-sur-Lez by sexologists Marie-Noëlle Lanuit and Jean-Claude Piquard. The pair were protesting against 'the female taboo of sexual pleasure'. Parisian academic and jeweller Anne Larue has created a popular yet discreet line of clitoris pendants in gold or bronze ('For the uninitiated, it looks like an octopus or a Neolithic goddess') and Nice librarian Amandine Brûlée is creating fanzines with animated clitoris characters. Her latest work is a series of joyfully grotesque cartoon vulvas illustrating the myth of Baubo, the old woman from Greek mythology who (like Uzume) flashes her pussy at Demeter, the harvest goddess, who is mourning her kidnapped daughter Persephone, and cheers her up no end. Clit jokes are so much more sophisticated than dick ones.

Newcastle-based Nicola Hunter's Raising the Skirt workshops are gathering force and honour the ancient Greek practice of *ana-suromai*. Hunter takes women outdoors to flash their genitals literally to the four winds and make art about their experiences. 'After three days, the women have a much stronger relationship to their bodies,' she says. Then there's the growing wave of millennial instagram warriors such as Laura Kingsley, who uses her Clitorosity project to chalk strange wishbone shapes around America and then ask locals what they think they are. @Clubclitoris, @Clito.clito, @the.vulva.gallery, @Vulvalutionary and @thesexed, an educational platform dedicated to 'sex, health and consciousness', have similar celebratory messages and a growing mass of followers.

Back on the terrace in Las Vegas, Nadine makes it clear she isn't just a clit activist. She also works on the Raëlians' GoTopless Inc. campaign, which celebrated its eleventh birthday in 2018. Women supporting the non-profit group march bare-breasted in different cities for one day every August. Nadine accompanies them, although, 'I'm a high-school French teacher, so I can't allow myself to be arrested or I'd lose my job. I have a bikini that looks like boobies!' Her passion is admirable. She talks about being *engagée*, as the Existentialists used to say. But she is talking about being sexually *engagée*. She grimaces suddenly. 'So spicy,' she says, frowning again at the Bloody Mary. Nadine admits she gets unhappy when people refer to the Raëlians as a 'cult' when all other major religions have their weird side too.

'It's another sort of discrimination,' Nadine says sadly. 'These FGM women are discriminated against because they are women. We are discriminated against because we are Raëlians. We have to stop judging each other or we'll never have peace.'

And Nadine really wants love to rule because, just as Annie masturbates for world peace, the Raëlians do it because they want the clever Sky People to come back to earth and they won't if there's too much disharmony.

I suggest the Sky People might want to come back to Palm Springs. People seem pretty happy there. She says that actually, the Raëlians just held one of their retreats, known as a Happiness Academy, in Palm Springs. They hold them all around the world: Japan, Australia, Europe, for the growing number of believers. She says there are more than 100,000 at present. At the Happiness Academies, nudity is encouraged, although not stipulated.

The Sky People would certainly get a better Bloody Mary in Palm Springs.

'Shoot!' Nadine's smile finally disappears. 'That's undrinkable. Aargh!'

And then I have to be going if I'm to make the San Francisco sex party in time. I'm waiting for the moment I've been looking forward to all day: the kiss goodbye. I will be brushing the cheek cells of the woman who has brushed the cheek cells of the man with the shoulder pads who met the aliens.

But when her face touches mine, it is icy. It is the least sensual *bise* I have ever received. When I pull back from the cold embrace, Nadine's almond eyes are gleaming in the twilight. The Raëlians might take a while to come back to planet earth at this rate.

WANKY McJERKOFF

The drive back to San Francisco feels like a night in the ghost train. It's not so much the memory of the cold kiss goodbye, it's more my bad choice of CDs from the charity shop in Palm Springs. Listening to *Liza with a 'Z' Live from Carnegie Hall* is like eating cheese before bedtime. Liza segues off into a psychotic nursery-rhyme medley in the middle of 'It Was a Good Time'. She quavers to her baby about how daddy's gone off hunting and left them all alone and who knows what's going to happen now? In the blackness and loneliness of the Highway 15, with a brain already impacted with thoughts of miniature alien galaxies living all over my body, it makes for a traumatic drive and it only strikes me later that today is Friday the thirteenth.

I finally escape Liza Minnelli's musical nervous breakdown by pulling into the Rodeway Inn in Barstow for the second time. It's four hours since I left Lake Las Vegas. Nikki is on reception again. I'm hoping she doesn't ask me to sign my name on the dotted line before the lights go out and she starts to grind, because I'll be too knackered.

But the next day, as Valentine's Day dawns, I feel refreshed the minute I step out on the landing of room 123. The desert light of California can put you on a fantastic high. And yet after a few hours on the road I get hot (it's still unseasonably warm) and hungry and traumatised by what's happening on the radio. All the songs are about love and, because it's 14 February, all the DJs are saying things like, 'I hope someone's treating you real good today.' This message is being directed to women and men are being posited as the should-be Prince Charmings. Betty Dodson's philosophy about being a non-monogamous woman refusing to depend on one person for orgasms, money and happiness doesn't seem to have infiltrated very far.

Two hours outside San Francisco I stop off at a gas station full of screaming kids. I stagger out with a bottle of diet A&W Root Beer and go and sit under a tree in the picnic area. I'm thinking of calling Virginia, but I don't because I'm pissed off that she's decided to visit her brother in freezing-cold Nebraska instead of having a dirty weekend with me. So I call Hadji. It's nice because he's in a good mood. He says I sound grumpy and that I should write a song called 'Masturbation Blues'. He starts singing: 'Woke up this morning/Had another masturbation workshop to attend . . .'

He makes me laugh. I say it isn't going very well between me and Virginia. Even as I say it, I know it's a lame thing to say. I tell Hadji I'm going to a 'play' party in San Francisco, hoping he doesn't know what a 'play' party is. As we're talking, I notice that the trunk of the tree I'm leaning against has been stripped of bark in one area to reveal smooth, golden wood underneath. Like the lean, arching back of a beautiful boy. I tell him that this time last year, he'd brought me a tray of Veuve Clicquot, scrambled eggs and chocolates in bed. When I first met Hadji, he gave me a Made in China plastic bug filled with candy for Valentine's Day and I gave him a hard time. I trained him up.

'What did we do for the rest of Valentine's Day?' he asks. I probably sent you off to work so I could think about having sex with someone else all alone, I think. When it's time to say goodbye, there's a weird gap.

'Bye then.'

'Bye.'

I want to say, 'I love you,' but I don't know if that's allowed any more. I haven't got *Sex by Design: The Betty Dodson Story* with me, so I can't read her stupid rule book. Back on the road, I suddenly burst into tears. I'm so tired, so exhausted. I locate a handkerchief in a forgotten pocket of my rucksack, but when I blow my nose I cry even more. Love smells of Ariel Automatic. It's the powder Hadji uses to wash our clothes in back at home in London. I get stuck in a massive traffic jam on the Bay Bridge and then finally, after ten hours on the road, I stagger back into Jet's house.

My period has just started (what is the etiquette for a period at an orgy?) and a cough has developed. I'm really not in the best shape to go to a sex party. It's 6 p.m. and I feel like curling up and going to sleep forever, but I have to be at Raven's by 8 p.m. I heat up a can of organic lentil soup from Jet's cupboard and remember a line from Barbara Carrellas' *Urban Tantra*: 'Change your clothes, change your consciousness.' So after I've washed up my soup bowl, I take off my yellow Birkenstocks and slip into my army boots.

Raven seems nervous when I get to her house. I can understand this. As she's said before, sex clubs are work for her. She seems pleased with the present I bought her in Palm Springs. A short-handled broom from an HIV charity shop called Revivals. I'm hoping it might be like the 'heather broom' that Sade used in the notorious Marseilles incident of July 1772 when he was found guilty of sodomy and the accidental poisoning of prostitutes with some sweets containing the aphrodisiac Spanish Fly.

Raven is wearing a long black dress with leather feathers along one sleeve and shoulder and I change into the $3 gay-boy leather shorts that I also bought in Revivals. Raven cuts me up a white T-shirt, saying she's going to draw a heart on the front and do I want abstract or figurative? I say 'abstract', and she gives the T-shirt back with a red and black squashed thing on the front. She puts on some eyeliner for me, advising me to go for a 'fucked-up' look.

'Nice Palm Springs tan,' she drawls, as I parade around her apartment in my outfit, suddenly awake again now that the spotlight is back on me.

'Thanks,' I say. 'I haven't married the sun yet. We're just having an affair.'

She narrows her eyes. 'Are you sure you want to go to this club?'

My panicked expression must speak a thousand words.

'Don't worry,' she sighs. I'm about to take all my day clothes with me in my backpack, but she tells me to leave it at her place. She picks up her Paco Rabanne chain-mail bag, calls a cab and when we arrive at Kinky Salon, there's a woman in a grubby wedding dress getting out of a taxi accompanied by a man dressed like he's going to a corporate breakfast meeting. We follow them inside and Raven gives a flower to the man taking the money. He's a bit sniffy, which puts Raven in a huff. Then, before we can go up the stairs, a woman stops us to ask if we know 'the rules'. There's a board in front of her with a list of commandments. I note that one of them says something about not getting intoxicated.

'Name one of the rules and I can let you in,' she says.

'Don't drink too much alcohol?' I mumble, vaguely.

'Negotiate your boundaries,' Raven says, like a true San Franciscan. We are allowed in, and when we get to the top of the stairs we emerge into a cramped space full of women who look like Anna Wintour. Some people, men and women, are done up in latex crinolines and punky fairy outfits, but you can tell it's an aspirational crowd. I suddenly miss the plebs from Lash.

'I told you,' Raven groans as she surveys the room.

There's a female stand-up on a stage cracking jokes about her latest one-night stand. The crowd thinks it's great, but all I can think is, *Where's the sex room?* I wander to the bar but there's no drinking because you have to bring your own bottle. Then I see something billed as the 'Fungeon'. When I get there, five people are sitting around on the floor in a tiny room, talking as if they're in the middle of their breakfast meeting. A woman tied up to a Saint Andrew's cross (Raven has told me that this is the name for the X-shaped cross) is being half-heartedly whipped. A cute lesbian couple come to check out the Fungeon. 'It can be riveting looking at bad sex,' I say, and one of them giggles. Then I feel bad. This is the classic sort of thing someone who's not getting laid would say. I wander off, in search of the proper sex room. This isn't a BDSM club so, in theory, some actual genital congress might be taking place.

When I locate the sex room, it's very well-behaved. Two dozen mattresses are on the floor and naked couples writhe on each. It reminds me of a naughty school dorm. Mostly, it's men on top doing missionary on women, although some of the beds have two girls grinding together like Boucher paintings come to life. I realise I've never seen so much live human sex going on in front of me before. It's mesmerising. Both sexy and funny. But then a woman kills it by tapping me on the shoulder and announcing that 'unaccompanied lingering' is not allowed. This surprises me. I thought I was cruising. I later discover on the website that one of the Kinky Salon rules is 'Please, please, please don't hang out on your own watching people! It makes them feel uncomfortable and it makes you look like a Wanky McJerkoff!!'

I'm confused because unaccompanied lingering seemed to be encouraged at Lash. On the way back to look for Raven, I get talking to a twenty-something chick sitting on a wall wearing just a tutu and the expression of one who has seen all, suffered all. We get on to the subject of polyamory and the difference between that and an open relationship.

'With an open relationship there are usually no rules, so you don't feel safe,' she explains. 'Polyamory is all about communication and boundaries.' There she goes with that 'boundaries' word again. I finally find Raven giving some sort of breast massage to a woman who looks like an old colleague of mine from *Harper's Bazaar*. I'm surprised to feel a wave of jealousy. Then a man comes over with his girlfriend and introduces her to Raven. Maybe they want a threesome, or a twosome with Raven calling the shots. Raven doesn't seem to mind this sort of thing. Presumably, it's good for business. And anyway, by now I've twigged that Raven intends to take me to bed with her tonight. She pats my bum and I hear the man whisper, 'Nice ass,' which is very flattering. Raven nods as if I'm a bull she's reared for the ring.

Back at Raven's, I lie on the velvet couch with my army boots hanging over the arms. I tell her that I hate all the 'boundary' stuff. All the rules about gloves and honesty before you can get going on your orgy. There's a story in this week's *Bay Area Reporter* where a gay male writer says that the intimacy of 'insertive sex' is being sacrificed for what he sees as bogus safety concerns in kink clubs. Now that a pill called PrEP stops you getting infected with HIV, he says you might as well let it all hang out.

Raven says something sarcastic about what's so bad with honesty and communication, and have I told my 'various boyfriends and girlfriends' what I'm getting up to in San Francisco? She does, however, have a cynical take on the way some of the play parties are run. She recently went to one in Oakland, the Brooklyn of San Francisco, where the host was saying, 'I'm a trans man, I'd like you to refer to me as "they" and here are the rules.' Then 'they' announced that everyone needed to say out loud who they'd 'partnered with' lately and what sexual diseases they had.

'I mean,' Raven says, 'if you had full blown AIDS maybe but, you know . . .'

It reminds me of something I read on FetLife. A woman of twenty-two wanted to go to a 'hostage party', but she'd just been diagnosed with herpes and she'd read in the party organisers' FAQ that those with 'communicable diseases' would be asked to wear a certain colour wrist band. I wonder if Raven is going to ask me what kind of disease I might have, but she doesn't, nor does anyone else over all of the time I spend in San Francisco. I don't ask anyone either, although everyone I meet is very thorough about condoms on everything from dicks to dildos.

I'm soon lying on Raven's bed as she rummages around in a huge box. She eventually emerges, saying, 'Meet Janet!' It's very exciting being alone in bed with Raven on Valentine's Day night, but it's also a bit like being in a sex laboratory. Raven still hasn't released her hair from its black knot and she sometimes lets me kiss her and sometimes she doesn't. I hate the idea of someone 'letting me' kiss them, although I can see that if your job is being a dominatrix, it must be weird having night-off sex. I am astonished when she does let me kiss her. Her mouth is warm and virginal and longing. It feels a very dangerous thing to do. At one point, I'm kissing her and she's letting me touch her white-apple breasts at the same time and I get very turned on. 'Sit on my face,' I moan even though

I am wary about getting too intimate by smelling her smell. And she just laughs. 'What are you talking about?' she says, as if she's Estella and I'm Pip and I've just called a 'knave' a 'jack'.

She takes hold of Janet, her double-headed blue dildo. 'Are you ready?' she whispers in a voice that's just mean enough, and I'm not sure if it's her or the dominatrix. I clamber on her in shameless supplication. I murmur, 'Daddy,' in her ear and she plays the game. She says, 'Do you want me to fuck you with my big dick?' She tells me to 'surrender to Daddy' and the sensations wash over me. I forget about being cool; I let my body take over. And then the Hitachi Wand is on my clit. I haven't seen the mad vibrating rolling pin since Betty's workshop. This time, there's no spinning in space. This time I see a blue snake slithering through a leafy green tunnel, I see a glimpse of a small black bird under a pale white breast and then I pass out.

I jerk awake a few seconds later because I'm forgetting my manners. I know from the other weekend that Raven likes to be fisted so I heave myself up. I feel a wave of pride when Raven says I have 'little hands' and that they're 'perfect for the job'. Soon Raven is making her Popeye-eating-spinach sound. But it takes her such a long time to come that I fall asleep between her legs.

The next morning, she tells me that she wanted to prolong the 'little hands' sensation and later found she couldn't come. It's reassuring to know that even the pros have off days. We get out of bed and I meet Raven's flatmate at the sink in the kitchen. He's cleaning some hi-tech-looking rubber oblong with a tube coming out of it. I ask him if it's from the dungeon and he says that no, it's a water bag for his bicycle.

I ask Raven if I can buy her lunch. I still have the hire car. So I drive us to Presidio, while she screams (like everyone seems to do) about what a terrible driver I am and warns me that she doesn't want Mexican or Chinese.

We settle on a Thai restaurant and once we're sitting at the table, away from her neighbourhood, away from her dungeon, in front of a cuisine she approves of, she relaxes like I've never seen her relax before. It feels as if we're on a regular date. She says things like, 'Thanks so much for taking me out,' and declares the green curry to be 'excellent!' As we eat, she reminisces about how she used to love to shop at food markets when she went on holiday to Paris, how she wants to start writing, how we should go and see *Fifty Shades of Grey* one day for a laugh.

There's a common belief that all sex workers have had abusive childhoods and that's why they're into weird sex. Tutu had a grim childhood in many respects, but like she once said of her dominatrix years, 'All that shit could not have happened to me and I'd probably still be into rough sex – only I wouldn't have done it for money.' She also reckoned that she wouldn't have been so good at it.

I've preferred not to delve too much into the specifics of Raven's 'serious-not-joking white trash' childhood, but she's clearly wrestled with demons and conquered many of them. She's impressive. And she has taught me a lot. About pain, for instance. It annoyed me when my vulvodynia doctors used to trot out the 'What are your pain levels on a scale of one to ten?' line. They didn't finesse the question by asking, 'Is your pain burning, stabbing, aching, shooting, throbbing, electric?' But Raven goes even further. She says that certain types of extreme sensation – i.e. pain – can teach you to relax around fear or adversity in your life. Sometimes you just have to sit with your pain. Accept your pain – see where it takes you.

Mine has brought me to a Thai restaurant in San Francisco, eating green curry with an enigmatic woman. I can never be sure what mask Raven will be wearing, but sometimes glimpses appear behind it. When talk turns to *The Wizard of Oz* and I confess my suspicions that I am the Cowardly Lion, she looks surprised and says, 'You're not cowardly. You're brave,' and this feels like the nicest thing anyone has ever said to me.

I ask her which character she is and she smiles.

'The Tin Man, of course.'

'Why?'

Her eyes meet mine and she says, 'Because I don't have a heart, remember?'

It is a moment when, in the old world, I would have fancied I was falling in love with Raven. Should I nip this feeling in the bud? Raven once told me that lots of her clients came to her believing that they wanted to be tied up and dominated by a powerful woman. But often what they really wanted wasn't a cross-dressing scene in rubber, but rather some simple emotional intimacy where the other person was accepting of a few unusual 'additionals'.

For once, Raven doesn't say much as we head back up the hill to Jet's place. It's sunset by the time we get back to the view of orange and purple exploding behind the pine tree. Raven takes some pictures of me on the terrace. I take some of her. I kiss her. I feel the white orbs with the metal bars through. Damn. Fresh flesh is so compulsive. I wonder if she'll let me see the small black bird again. She pulls away. She must be used to nipping things in the bud.

'What are you doing next Sunday?'

'Seeing you, maybe?'

When she asks if I want to be her assistant in a demonstration she's doing at San Francisco Kink Weekend, I think, *When in Rome* . . .

PRE-DISCO TENSION

The night before the demonstration, Raven invites me to her house. But when I arrive, things are immediately weird. Dill is laying out chains and manacles and 'insertables', like a gym teacher sorting out bibs ready for an away netball match, and Raven is doing her Estella thing, saying she wants to go to sleep and laughing when I say, 'But I thought we were going to have sex.' I was half-referring to some kind of choreography sex to prepare for the 'show' tomorrow. But Raven just says, 'Look, sleep tonight and then I'll do what you want after the demonstration,' which makes me feel like one of her more annoying clients.

I lie next to her feeling scared/horny/pissed off. Like an oaf for wanting to hug her. Finally, I can't stand it any more. I get up, tiptoe into the living room and grab one of the demonstration insertables – three purple balls on a piece of string – from Dill's neat pile. Back in bed, I start masturbating on the sly next to Raven, which is pretty ironic because this is precisely the kind of situation I left London to escape from.

I sleep fitfully and get up early the next morning. I clean the purple insertables and put them back in their place in the living room. Then I lie on the velvet couch and flick through Raven's copy of the *Erotica Universalis*, trying to ignore the fact that I'm feeling incredibly nervous. I've been trying not to think too much about what being Raven's assistant might entail. From what I can work out, the San Francisco Kink Weekend is quite a big deal. It takes place at the Armory, a massive Moorish-style castle built in 1912 as a base for the United States National Guard. In 2006, Armory Studios, better known as Kink.com, the world's largest fetish porn company, bought the building for $14.5 million. In 2018, the Armory was sold for $65 million to a real estate company, suggesting that affluence is making San Francisco lose its hard-won kink capital status. Polly Superstar has also left the city and moved to Las Vegas, America's apparently new alternative-sex destination, where she has set up Kinky Salon.

Dill appears and goes over to the sex-toy pile to start quietly ticking off the checklist: butt plugs, Ben Wa balls (the purple balls on a string), batteries, rope, easy-wipe tissues. She starts to hum and the day begins to feel tranquil. I look over to Raven's bedroom and think of silver apples of the moon and golden apples of the sun. But then suddenly the shoes on the door rack begin to tremble and Raven emerges into the living room. She scolds Dill for not having packed the drag bag yet and snatches up a pair of bumless, crotchless fishnets from the pile. 'Here,' she snaps. 'You want to wear these at the Armory?'

I wish Raven could be a bit more nurturing. I'm thinking of telling her that in Spain, the bull gets treated just as well as the bullfighter before a *corrida*. Maybe I'm additionally tense because of Cliff Barnes. He's texted me a few times now since I first met him and I've discovered his profile on FetLife. His idea of a great night out is 'inviting a lady to dinner and, if she wears red heels, knowing that by the end of the night her ass is going to be as red as her shoes.' He called me at the beginning of the week saying, 'Hey pretty pony!' in the 1970s American TV voice and it all flooded back: the cashmere-mix jacket sleeve, the chewing-gum grin, the rough hands, the slapping-vulva motion, the 'Wow, I think we gave the best show!' He said he was coming to San Francisco on Thursday, but then on Thursday, he sent an email saying, 'Hi Sweetie, I hate to cancel but SF is a long way and I am kinda busy and a little under the weather . . . I know you are going home very soon. I will not forget a girl like you! Love to hear from ya!'

This was a bit too much psychological insight into Cliff Barnes. 'A little under the weather' is the kind of boring thing someone back home would say. I look at the bumless, crotchless fishnets that Raven is holding out to me. I take them. At least a day at the Armory will be a good story.

Soon I have my look: the fishnets under my Palm Springs leather shorts, my fancy black balcony bra that I still haven't washed from the weekend with Roxanne, proper leather manacles around my wrists that Dill has lent me, a leather strap around my neck, also from Dill, my army boots and an orange T-shirt with the word 'Giants' on the front. I bought the T-shirt from Revivals in Palm Springs because I liked the colour and the lettering, but I learn now that it's the name of the San Francisco baseball team. Raven applies some black eyeliner on me, standing back to announce that she's pleased with my 'punk rock Giants look'.

Then the doorbell rings and it's Terri who, I'm now learning, is to be assistant number two at this afternoon's demonstration. Terri is twenty-five, tall, slender and friendly. She's a journalist who specialises in sex writing. She's come with a young guy called Moses, who looks like a lesbian. They met at Lash the other week. Raven says to Terri, 'Can you come a lot?' Terri looks a bit taken aback by the question, but says that she can. Raven adds, 'But you have to wait until I let you, you understand?' Terri nods, assuring Raven that she's 'good at masturbating'. She goes into the bathroom to insert the purple Ben Wa balls as practice, but comes out saying that her 'vagina's too small'. I feel smug, but I also start wondering what exactly is going to happen in this show.

At around two, we set off to the Armory in Terri's car. Terri is wearing Lolita sunglasses and crunching sweets in her mouth. She looks in the rear-view mirror and says in a friendly voice, 'I'm looking forward to getting naked with you,' and then Moses offers me some of the sweets from a silver tin. I ask if they have marijuana in them, because everything in this town seems to. Terri and Moses giggle and say that they're just salted caramels. I suck on one as Raven sits next to me with the expression of one about to address the United Nations and Dill stoically guards the drag bag.

I'm still worried that we've had no dress rehearsal for the demonstration. All I want Raven to say is, 'I know this is your first time, but it'll be OK.' Clearly she's not going to say this so I try and pull myself together. This normally means having more Jolly Lolly but I think I've reached Jolly Lolly saturation point by now. *Oh well*, I think, *I knew this day would come: I'm running away to join the masturbation circus.*

MASTURS OF THE
UNIVERSE

We pull up outside an old castle with studded outsides. It feels like we're the kids from *Scooby-Doo* and I'm helping Dill lift the drag bag out of the Mystery Machine. There's a momentary hitch at reception when some cool-looking tattooed chick asks us for ID and I don't have any (the Palm Springs sex shorts come without pockets). But I'm back to feeling confident because Terri and I have bonded. 'I've never done this before,' I murmur to her as we walk up the Armory steps. 'Nor have I,' she whispers and we both grin.

The receptionist eventually lets us in because they're not going to turn away the performing seals, and we make our way up the grand staircase, fitted out with red carpet and stair rods. I heave the clanking drag bag (Dill has got her hands full with a foldable massage table) and sneak glances at the photo-realistic paintings that adorn the walls in gilt frames. My favourite painting shows a huge woman tied naked to a chair, legs splayed, mouth gagged, face defiant. Finally, we arrive at the top floor, the Armory's secret 'Edwardian Lounge', which is used for sex parties and educational events. It's all polished wood and red carpet and alcove rooms with formal chairs and more of the realistic paintings. Women having their breasts crushed between bamboo canes seems a popular theme. Raven disappears to find the organiser and I see a poster saying 'Fifty Skills of Grey – A Symposium' and realise that this is us. The poster explains that during the weekend, ticket holders will learn how to perform and enjoy the fifty BDSM skills mentioned in E. L. James's novel. Sessions include, 'Impact Play with Implements', 'Deep Kissing, Bathtub and Elevator Sex' and 'Adventure Scenes and Abduction Play' I'm disappointed when I see that our session is billed rather boringly as 'Adding Kink and Toys'.

I follow the sound of talking and end up in a large room that looks like a conference hall in a fancy Holiday Inn. Only there's a Saint Andrew's cross in one corner of the room and on the wall is an image of a blonde woman sucking the balls of a glamorous black trans woman with a cock. The erect black dick is flying up in the air. At the front of the room is a man who resembles a weasel. Skinny with greasy hair, he looks like he took the boat down the river of no return too. His assistant is a chick in her early twenties in immaculate black lingerie and heels. She's kneeling down in front of him next to a metal-framed bed. According to the programme, he's finishing up a session called, 'Dominant's Guide to Oral Sex'. He says things like, 'It's much more domly to be having sex with your clothes on,' and, 'Use the mouth as a masturbatory device.'

It's quite surprising when he unzips his black trousers and a huge, hard dick bounces out. The Weasel is quite nasty and very charismatic. I can tell he's going to be Rolodex material for later. He makes jokes. 'Excuse me, for some reason I can't think with my hand on my cock!' The audience chuckles. He tells them not to 'despair' if their 'sub' 'can't deep throat'. He talks of something called 'throat lube', thanks to a sphincter in the back of the throat. People are making notes. Of what? Maybe this is the secret that made Annie Sprinkle follow Gerard Damiano to New York all those years ago in Arizona when she asked him to teach her how to deep throat. The audience is a revelation. Not the raincoat crowd at all. About forty of them. They look like they're watching some black-and-white classic at the British Film Institute down on the South Bank. 'Give the sub feedback,' the Weasel is saying. 'Say, "Yes, that's right," or else you're going to leave them hanging there.'

One of the men in the audience appears to be a bit of a raincoat. He looks as if he should be on the pier in Scarborough sucking a Murray Mint with a handkerchief tied on his head. Would an image of him help get me off? Or is focusing on someone hideous just a reflection of my low self-esteem? I leave the room and walk around the hall for a bit. Terri looks nervous too, but she has Moses to calm her down. Then I see the Weasel leaving the room and I know our hour is near. I go to the loo and when I come back, I go to meet Terri at a table to the side of the stage next to some thick red curtains. They looked quite grand from a distance – all ruched and tasselled, but close up they look like they've seen better days. And it's not just the curtains. Everything looks a bit seedy now that I'm at the edge of the stage. The mattress on the metal-framed bed looks like some stained prison mattress. This is the time when what I'm about to do starts to sink in.

I perch on the table in what I hope is a cool manner, trying to ignore the butterflies in my stomach. I'm not sure when I have to take my clothes off. Do I walk on naked? The lighting isn't very flattering. Can I keep my boots on? I try out my looking-at-people-in-the-eyes-for-longer-than-is-polite trick. But nobody's looking at me and if they do, they're women giving me a sisterly smile, which doesn't feel porn-y at all. I've known for a while now that Raven has a highly tuned sense of the dramatic, but this afternoon she's been strutting around as if she's Liza Minnelli live at Carnegie Hall. She finally comes over and gives us some direction. 'Terri, you sit on the mattress and masturbate a lot with the Ben Wa balls. Stephanie, you're going to lie on the massage table and be the slow cum. I'm going to put a lot of dildos in you.'

Terri and I both nod then look at each other when she's gone. I do have flashes of confidence. I look out at the audience and think, *I'm about to drown you in a huge wave of energy.* Even people who wouldn't describe themselves as hippies or who've never taken a drug in their life know that orgasm takes you to an altered state of consciousness. It's like the Mick Jagger sensation at the Mama Gena weekend when I took my top off in front of 600 women and felt my energy raise their energy and their energy raise mine. Only this crowd doesn't look as friendly as the Mama Gena one. I realise I'm a bit nervous of their energy.

I walk over to the window and look out over the city, searching for courage. Tutu comes to mind and I find myself asking her for help. When she was dying of breast cancer, she woke up one night near the end and screamed, 'I don't want to fucking die!' So much for Elisabeth Kübler-Ross's five stages to the acceptance of oblivion. It was an intense time, but at some point during it all, I took on the idea or, rather, I made the resolution that I was going to live my life extra hard because she couldn't.

There's noise, and when I turn back to the room, Terri is already on stage. She's sitting naked and nervous on the stained mattress. She has a nice body, pale, no tats. I wonder when I'm supposed to go on. I decide to take off my orange T-shirt and keep on my fancy black bra. Then I take off the leather shorts and sidle onto the stage wearing just the bumless, crotchless fishnets, the black bra and my army boots. It feels cold around my vulva as I stand next to the massage table, as if my bits belong to someone else. And while I stand there feeling like a lemon, Raven devotes all her attention to Terri, introducing her to the audience as 'the beautiful Terri' (I wonder how she's going to bill me). Raven is very good on stage and soon gets the audience involved in a pantomime-type jive, saying, 'Shall we let her come?' There's a row of smart-arse young people at the front: butch dykes, a few trans men, an Asian baby gay boy. I stand there, looking at the eyes of the audience members and they're all looking at Terri. I can't blame them. I imagine I don't look as though I'm exactly 'owning the stage', as they say in the business.

Raven tells Terri to get on all fours because she's going to spank her and Terri suddenly starts acting cute. She plays up to the audience, going, 'Oh my God, I've never done this before!' (like everyone says in San Francisco) as she inserts the Ben Wa balls and giggles her way to her first orgasm. She really is entertaining. The audience loves her, 'Go girl!' they're all cheering.

Finally, Raven turns her attention to me. She says, 'This is Stephanie, the old granny.' She doesn't actually say that and Raven is not the type of person to favour young girls over old broads like me, but right now, that is what it feels like. I suddenly think, *What the hell was I thinking of, agreeing to appear naked on stage with a twenty-five-year-old?* Up to this point, I have had no qualms about my body. I've always despised that 'I hate my body' woman's magazine stuff. And all the amazing women I've talked to on the trip have rooted out any remaining doubts about my age or my shape. Until now. I feel like the one who's been picked for the school athletics team and then throws the discus backwards on the big day. I thought this was going to be like Linda Lovelace in *Deep Throat*, but as I mount the massage table and Terri emits another orgasmic scream, to the delight of the audience, I think of all the unsexy things in the world: knitting, shower caps, hairy nuns' feet in sandals. It gets worse. Raven tells me to lie on my back. She says to the audience, 'Shall we get her to take her army boots off?' There's a disinterested murmur from the crowd, who are on the edge of their seats, waiting for Terri's next orgasm. Raven pulls my boots off anyway. 'Oh my!' she says, thrown for the first time in the show.

I always wear a pair of green mountaineering socks under my army boots because they're too big for me. It's not a great look for a sex show. Raven pulls the woolly socks off. 'Now here,' she says to the audience, pointing at my pubic hair, 'we see that some women choose not to shave while some,' – turning to Terri – 'do.'

But nobody's interested in the slow-burn masturbator on the massage table. Raven picks this up and starts her Widow Twankey routine again. 'Shall we let Terri come?'

'Yes!'

'No!'

As all this is going on, she's using rope to tie my arms and legs to rings on the massage table. My legs are splayed open very wide and the rope is very tight on the left leg. I wonder if I should tell her. I might not be able to perform if it cuts off my circulation. My leg feels like it's going numb. This doesn't feel sexy at all. It feels like some weird gynaecological exam. *Oh well*, I think, *I wanted to know what this would feel like and now I know.* The show then turns into a biology practical and the smart-arse kids in the front are looking at me like I'm the frog in dissection class. When Raven starts mentioning names of sex toys like the Injoyus and the Eroscilator, they say things like, 'Is that spelled with an S or a C?'

I strain at the ropes and look out to the audience, desperate for someone who might turn me on, because Raven has told them that I'm going to add my massive orgasmic contribution soon. Raven takes her role as a sex educator very seriously and she's very thorough at her job. Right now she's informing the audience that a long build-up to orgasm can be even more exciting than the series of short, sharp shocks that Terri is demonstrating. Raven says to the audience, 'If you ask yourself, "Am I going too slow?" then you're probably not going slow enough.'

This is a great point, but unfortunately 'slow' isn't great theatre. Terri continues to have orgasms on the prison mattress (she was right, she can come a lot) but I'm having trouble on many counts. Firstly, my hands are tied up so I can't touch myself. Secondly, Raven has currently got the Betty Dodson Barbell inside me because I thought I'd be patriotic to Betty Dodson, so I told Raven it was my favourite sex toy. The heavy metal bar is great for private masturbation, but it's not that visual to watch when you're up against a twenty-five-year-old show pony pulling a string of purple sausages from her pussy every sixty seconds.

Raven seems to forget that I'm going to need more attention on my genitals if I'm going to come. She does a buzz here with the Hitachi Magic Wand, a thrust or two there with the Barbell, but then she goes back to Terri. I turn to the audience again but I can't see the man from the Scarborough Pier. There's one man at the back who I'm a bit scared of. I know he's getting turned on. He's like the Ricky Gervais bloke from Lash. Still, this is a fine time to realise I'm not an exhibitionist.

Raven remembers I need some bodily attention. She takes Betty's Barbell out and puts a finger slowly inside me and it's the best insertable to date. It feels really sexy. Suddenly there's life in my legs and pelvis. 'What does she want?' Raven asks the audience as she takes her finger away. There's a bit of mumbling and I want to shout out, 'She wants a dildo in her vagina!' But I don't know if I'm allowed to speak. Raven says, 'We're coming to a close now, Stephanie and Terri are going to climax soon.' And I'm desperate because how am I supposed to climax? I tug at the ropes holding my arms and by a stroke of luck, the left knot comes undone. When Raven comes back to the table, my left hand jerks up and I fondle her breasts. She's surprised at this, but fuck it – I'm going for it. And it works. I'm starting to slip down the slippery slope. I moan, 'I want to be fucked,' and Raven says, in her Estella ridicule voice, 'You want to be fucked? You want a man to fuck you?' I moan loudly, 'Yes!' because right now that would really do the job. She hesitates and says to the audience, 'She's having a fantasy.' But I'm thinking, *No, it's not a fantasy! If San Francisco is so transgressive, how come someone from the audience can't just get up from their seat and come over and do me?*

Raven tells people they can come closer if they like and a group of five or six gather at the end of the table, quite far off though. Some of them have their arms folded. Scaredy cats. That's when I realise I do have the power. There is one man I can see looking at me. Facing my cunt as I writhe around, straining at the creaking ropes. An audience at last.

Raven realises we're running out of time. She tells me and Terri to come in two minutes. Has Raven forgotten I still have nothing in my vagina? Maybe it's part of some clever idea about controlling your assistant's orgasm, but luckily I can cheat because I have a bullet-sized vibrator that she miraculously dropped on the table and that I'm using on my clit with my free hand as I flick through my fantasy Rolodex. I cannot conceive of leaving the Armory without having had an orgasm in front of this crowd. Cliff Barnes pushing his denim-covered crotch against a wipe-down table crosses my mind and then I realise about darkness. I thought I'd want my eyes open because I thought I'd get off on watching the audience. But when I close them, I stop being self-conscious. I hear myself breathing, I hear Annie Sprinkle telling me to breathe, to stay in the moment and then everything flashes before me: the eighteenth-century gents and their heather brooms, Thérèse the Philosopher and the venerable rope, Joycelyn Elders and her watermelons, Barbara Carrellas telling me to pull energy upwards from the pussy towards the heart, Raven saying that surrender is the gateway to serenity.

'Whose name shall we have her say when she comes?' Widow Twankey asks the audience of me.

'Saffron!' one of the smart arses shouts. But I'm far away from all that now. I open my eyes momentarily and look over at Dill. 'Fucked, I want to be fucked,' I say feebly, like a shipwrecked Robinson Crusoe washed up on a shore. Dill understands and comes over and penetrates me slowly with a dildo, much more skilfully than I did her that night in bed with Roxanne. I close my eyes and the bullet buzzes on my clit and I breathe like me and Annie Sprinkle did on Bernal Heights, like I realise I'm alive because my lungs can move like this. I can hear Annie say, 'Stay in the moment,' and so I do and there is breath and sensation and then the room disappears and I'm speaking in tongues, 'Tutu . . . thank you, T . . . I love you, Tu . . . Tu . . . T . . .' round and round in a black spiral until the energy rises up my body and a moan starts to fill the room. I am aware that I am making a very loud noise and occasionally I bob up for air thinking, *This will get their fucking attention*, but then I go back under. I am not having an orgasm – the orgasm is having me. It takes my body and drags it through a daze of landscapes, down dark velvety slides and unfurling tunnels to the days where me and Hadji would come in colour. 'What colour was it?' I'd say afterwards. 'A purple coming,' he'd whisper. 'A desert of black with a flash of silver lightning.'

And with another breath I shoot up to a place of light. 'Go to the light,' someone is saying. And, 'It's OK to let go.

Now it's the time.' The five of us around a bed, helping her get off, like willing a lover to come, to move her final orgasm up and out. It doesn't always work, but it worked with Tutu that day. It was the most terrible, most beautiful thing I ever saw. It reminded me of group sex. How I'd imagined group sex to be.

Another breath in, deep, for the day when she was all out of breath. And when the energy starts to pour out of the top of my head, the moan becomes a high-pitched howl in the room. Something that started deep down and spun through all my cells goes higher and higher until it goes through the roof. A fire, a baptism of orgasm or maybe of death. I feel the ro-ro-rope . . . I can't hold back . . . I am . . . dying.

I'm still howling when I hear, in the distance, Raven saying that it's time to stop. But I've arrived at the top of the rock and fallen all the way down and now I want to go up again. And I do. I realise now what Betty means by women having 'serial' as opposed to multiple orgasms. One after another. I hear laughter from a far-away room when a Raven voice says nervously, 'It really is time to stop now . . .'

I lie there, shuddering like a battery toy that seems to have run down, but then starts up again. And when I finally sit up, Dill is there and I put my arms around her and I cry. A crygasm, I suppose. I am totally spaced-out. I stagger off the table. I put my clothes on and wander around. I can tell that the energy in the room has changed. The smart-arse Asian boy comes up nervously and says, 'That was awesome, thank you,' and I think, *Yes, it wasn't bad for a finale.*

A man with a shiny head comes up and says thank you too. I don't know if he wants to cruise me or if he's a bit terrified of me. As we wait for Raven to get congratulated for the great show she's put on, me and Terri and Moses do a group hug that smells of warm salted caramels. Terri says, 'You are very open. I mean, not in a bad way. In a good way.' I wonder why everyone keeps telling me I'm open.

The Weasel catches me with his shiny eyes before I go, and Raven tells me, 'That was a proper, grown-up orgasm.' She is so happy with the enthusiastic reaction of the audience that she offers to take us all out for dinner. It's a feel-good drive to the restaurant because we've all shared something huge together. Out of the car window, I see a big green mound with trees on the top. I realise that it's Bernal Park, the clitoris of America, and it feels like a giant hour.

Terri is pink and post-orgasmic at the wheel. She asks us if we like funk and when we say yes, she puts on 'Strawberry Letter 23' by the Brothers Johnson. We all jig in the back of the car and it feels like we're the kids from *Scooby-Doo* in the Mystery Machine again, except we're also masturs of the universe. And if I was a drop of water getting bigger and bigger when I arrived in San Francisco, I'm now a tropical fruit so ripe it's split its skin and sweet juice is seeping out.

GOODBYE, PINKY TUSCADERO

I'm sitting on the top of a rock, feeling like the man from the Scouse mafia who just wants to stare at the fooking wall. After the big bang at the Armory, maybe this is the little death. It's a good place to die, here in the silence of the Californian desert, where you could be sitting on a rock tens of millions of years ago.

I'm reminded of a short story that Marco Vassi published in 1981 called 'Thy Kingdom of Come'. It's about a woman who gets fed up with the melodrama of sex for two and decides to dedicate herself solely to masturbation. Before long she is 'liberated into a strange prison' and her orgasms progress from cheeseburger affairs to the discovery of a connection between her clitoris and her third eye. She soars to the heights of sexual ecstasy, 'Unknown by all but those very few who have the courage to admit that sex is the sister of death and thus can only be known alone.'

In the end, God comes to visit her and wants to fuck her because he's so impressed by her sexual independence. He promises her eternal life if she'll give in, and not being one to turn down any new form of enlightenment, the woman reluctantly spreads her legs. Which seems to be a warning not to become addicted to the light. Or the limelight. Sex in public is a good experience because it makes you realise its huge power. But it also makes you self-conscious. It's hard to sail off into your own erotic world.

I'm spreading my legs right now. Doing my own genital show-and-tell right here on the rock. The author of *The Stoned Apocalypse* left New York to start his quest as Fred Vassi and came back as Marco Vassi, after Marco Polo, the first Westerner to explore the Far East. I'm going to change my name too – Pinky Tuscadero's, in any case. Squatting naked on this huge stone, I realise with shock that Pinky Tuscadero has left the building. She's not Pinky any more. My inner labia are now purple-tinged at the edges. I'm shocked at first but then I decide that she looks much more relaxed. She's been around the block, as Annie Sprinkle would say. Who is she now? Coco Tuscadero?

I stand up and scan the strange horizon for savages. Naked apart from a pair of Adidas high-tops, I'm channelling Raquel Welch from *One Million Years B.C.* Unlike the barren Nevada desert, the rocks in this part of the Californian desert are astounding: huge boulders like weird eggs that fell from the sky. I said that I wanted to get to the top of the rock and here I am at the top of the most beautiful rocks I have ever seen.

It's been a long climb. I suppose I should cry, but I've already done that. When Betty announced to the room in the middle of my genital show-and-tell that my cunt looked 'neglected', it felt like a punch in the chest. I was devastated that she had uncovered my terrible secret. Could you read a cunt, like reading tea leaves? I'd wondered who the dunce cunt was going to be and now it turned out that it was mine. I tried to hold it back but I couldn't. I hung my head and sobbed.

Betty was kind. She said I didn't need a vulva ballet, I needed a vulva hug. She told me to put my hand over my cunt and then she put her hand over mine. She asked everyone in the room to hold hands and send love and healing to my vulva. I had to write to my Canadian friend Natasha Salaash asking her to remind me of the scene because I'd blocked much of it out. 'It was a very powerful moment,' she said. 'I remember your face very clearly. I cried too.' Natasha later asked Betty how she knew about Pinky Tuscadero's secret and Betty said that she'd seen so many vulvas 'she could just tell'. Natasha has now set up her own Bodysex business, Embracing Pleasure in Saskatchewan in Canada. She's added some new elements, one of which is naked phototherapy. And that's pretty much what I'm doing right now: playing on the rocks, being naked on the rocks, pissing on the rocks, taking photos of my born-again cunt on the rocks.

I raise my face to the dazzling light and gulp it down like food. I catch my breath as the shock of a full Diogenes rush quivers through my body 'Don't get too high in the high desert!' Richard Dupont joked. When I bring my head down again to the place between my legs, it strikes me that my clitoris is bigger than it was at the Bodysex workshop. Maybe it was all the exercise. I wonder what Betty will say.

DEBRIEF WITH THE WIZARD

'To sex,' says Betty, clinking my glass.

It's April and I'm back in the Wizard's office. The sugar mice are still on her bookcase and here I am, three months later, making my triumphant return to recount my adventures. I tell her that Joycelyn Elders was eighty-one and amazing.

'Well, fuck that shit, I'm eighty-five,' she says, slugging back her vodka and pink grapefruit. She's curious about the watermelon though. 'So she'd sit on it and hump it?'

She tells me that I was right to be told off for 'unaccompanied lingering' at Kinky Salon. You can't have a room of naked people fucking and have a clothed person looking. 'You're sucking out the energy!' She tells me that lingering is OK with the 'BDSM people' because, 'They're exhibitionists and they need voyeurs.' I appreciate her insights and I'm keen to know her angle about the talking in the Fungeon.

'That's not great, right?'

'I wouldn't put up with it.'

It's great to talk to someone sane after only a few hours out of California. The man sitting next to me on the plane spent the journey checking out the East Coast weather report on his smartphone. I thought, *This is what normal people do*. I worried vaguely about what would happen when I went back to the UK and there were no people on tap for me to have sex with, no Raven, no spaceships, no lollipops.

It's after 4.20 in the afternoon, so Betty starts up a vape pen with wings on the side and red flashing lights at the top, which makes her look if she has flaring dragon's nostrils. As we smoke, I tell her about my Armory experience. She doesn't talk for a long time and I can't tell if she's impressed or terrified. Either reaction is not ideal from a guru.

'You're crazy!' she finally pronounces, which makes me feel better. 'I wouldn't do that on stage in front of an audience. That's . . . well, you're very vulnerable.'

'I know,' I say.

'You do that at home on your own time,' she scolds.

I think back to Marco Vassi's masturbation heroine and the conclusion that too much enlightenment can be bad for you. I rub my sunburned nose. By the end of his life, Rousseau was sick of the Century of Lights, believing that the dazzle augured a terrible blaze, as it did, in the form of the French Revolution. He reminds readers in his *First Discourse* of the satyr who wanted to kiss fire the first time he saw it, even though Prometheus warned that he'd soon mourn for the beard on his chin.

I try to explain to Betty that I had this idea about not saying no to anything. 'Well, good for you,' she relents. 'You're not damaged.' She asks if I had a 'complete release' during my orgasm and I say I'm pretty sure I did.

'Massive?'

'Massive.'

I tell her about the demonstration at the Armory and how I got really turned-on and wanted a man to come out from the audience and fuck me. She explains that unfortunately most men can't control an erection in a public situation. 'But that's where some sharp little dyke comes out on the stage with her dildo and fucks you blind.' She nods approvingly at her idea. 'That would have been quite a show.'

I'm glad we're back on the same page. When I tell her that I'm now really good at using dildos as well as vibrators, she drawls, 'Well, I'm proud of you, darling.' She asks how Pinky Tuscadero is doing and I tell her that she grew up. She chuckles. 'Well, she can have different names for different stages. Pinky Tuscadero was her high-school name.'

I tell her that I had big crushes on Susie Bright and Annie Sprinkle and she tells me I should have been more assertive.

'You have to come on strong and let them know where you're at and move in on their body and take a hold of them and then it's like, "Could we make an arrangement to spend a few hours together and have sex?"'

I like Betty's cruising advice. In my first interview she told me, 'Honey, don't get too hooked up on the gay shit. Every woman is available to have sex with a woman.'

I tell her that the 'arrangement' line is all very well but that I've read it's better to take the straightforward physical approach. She narrows her eyes. 'It depends on your style,' she says. And your age. 'When I was in my forties I could come on to a person physically . . . '

She stops as she recalls that she came onto someone physically only the other night. At a comedy club. A young guy she'd just been in a workshop with. The guy came over and said, 'Betty Dodson!'

'As he leaned over I cupped his balls and said, "I remember you from the workshop, honey."' She smiles at the memory. 'His friends are thinking, "Who the fuck is this old lady?"' She shrugs. 'He'll either call or I'll never hear from him again. Separates the boys from the fuckers.'

She's been thinking of getting something going with her twenty-seven-year-old gender-queer assistant, who she calls her 'dyke boi'. But a) she's always made it a rule not to mix work and sex and b) she's reached a stage where her best sex is with herself.

'God, I had an orgasm last weekend [*eyes to the sky*]. See, I'm really using the edging thing: I come up to it and I have to pull the vibrator away. Ahhhh [*breathes out*]. Then I go: "Go ahead and come . . . no, wait a minute . . ." Then I'm back on: Ahhh, ahhh, ahhh. Then, if I don't come, I'm going to lose it all together . . . internal conflict, and then I finally say, "I can't wait any looooooooong . . ." [*sound of Betty falling down a mine shaft*].'

I know my time is coming to an end. I sense Betty has one of her mystery rendezvous coming up. Before I leave, I'm hoping the great oracle will give me some advice on my love life from here on out.

She shrugs. 'Well, you're designed for sexual pleasure, whatever that involves. It was so much more fluid when we were doing it in the sixties and seventies. Most everybody was paired, but that didn't mean you were going steady. It just meant you were either living together or you had been, but when you came to a party you did your own thing.'

I tell Betty that all the women I met on my trip talked about her, raved about her, name-checked her, recognised that they wouldn't be anywhere without her.

'They love you, Betty.'

She tuts.

'You've been very important to a lot of people.'

'I know.' She shakes her head. 'It's an honour.'

The magic charm in Betty's life was her mother. She often talks about her. Says things like, 'My mother was a remarkable woman.' As her mother lay on her deathbed, Betty thanked her for the gift of always knowing that she'd been unconditionally loved. It gave her the strength to carry on with the mad career path she'd carved out for herself.

I ask her if I can take a selfie of the two of us and we go and sit on her couch. Tumble, actually, following the vodkas. Betty puts her arm around me and we tussle playfully and she sort of grabs my breast, which might have been an accident or a vodka memory or more of Betty's breached twenty-first-century sex etiquette.

As we walk to the door, she tells me to keep working on my sex drive. 'Put it in your diary like a date at the health club,' she says. 'You have to make the effort.' And then she can't resist going back to her native Kansas.

'Remember,' she says. 'It's like that movie: you *are* the Wizard. There's no one person who's going to say, "You are now orgasmic!" What are you looking for – a priest?'

The Marquis de Sade's black-and-white engraving people cross my mind, but they disappear when she reaches out and gives me a hug goodbye. I feel a wiggle of energy spinning round in her belly – the orgies, the emotion, the struggle, the ecstasy, it's all still there.

LAMINAK

Hi Stephanie,

Yes, by Jove, you've got it!!! An expanded awareness of what sex can be, beyond the obvious mainstream kinds of sex.

Energy sex! Ecosex! That's so exciting you experienced some of these. The nice thing is that one doesn't have to give up any other kinds of sex. It's an add-on experience.

I'd love to see your tree in the Pyrenees. And your other 'E-spots'.

May your masturbation sessions all run the gamut!

And back.

Keep it wet.

x

Annie

I've had a sort of aftershock. One of those orgasms that comes out of nowhere, just when you were thinking it was all over. I left America in May and flew straight to the Pyrenees to do another Vision Quest – the Duke of Edinburgh Award with a Carlos Castaneda twist that I'd told Annie about that morning by the clitoris of America. You're all alone in the hills and there's no food allowed, no mobile phone, just some water and whatever else you can fit in your rucksack. After a few days of immersion in nature, you're supposed to get a revelation, but so far my main 'vision' has been *steak frites* with Roquefort sauce and a glass of chilled Gamay.

Manex, the shaman, has placed me on an exposed rocky ledge at the top of a deserted ravine in the no man's land between France and Spain. All pink campions and heather and wild horses if you're in the mood, but actually it's just boiling hot right now and I'm starving.

My TV friend thinks I'm mad. 'Blimey, haven't you had enough self-discovery this year?' she said when I told her I was stopping off here on my way back to London. I'm trying to see my location as symbolic of my transition into letting my light shine. But there are loads of flies, really aggressive ones. And vultures. Their wings are like huge feather dusters that make a scary swish noise as they cut through the air only metres over your head.

Luckily, there is one place in my benighted paradise that I love. A mossy hollow in the side of the ravine. A bower, you could call it if you were feeling romantic. It's lined with soft green moss and daisies and tiny wild strawberries. The back wall of the bower is slightly cobwebby, so I only occasionally look at that. And the best thing is that at around four in the afternoon, the hollow gets some shade thanks to the old oak tree. You can lie on the soft green bed and it feels like a fairy's bed. The Basques call the little people *laminak*. Apparently, the little people do jokey things, like come by your tent in the night and slap it so it hits you in the face. Your friends back in the city will tell you it's the wind. And I've been trying to tell myself that too, at night when the tent side suddenly gusts inwards when there hasn't been any wind for days.

But I'm happy to lie in my bower at four o'clock in the afternoon under my parasol of oak leaves, even though I'm starving hungry. Apart from food, the other things I think about are the book I'm writing – I freak out, thinking that maybe I've let too much light into in my secret *arrière-boutique*. Also I think about wanking. I put it off. I write a letter to Virginia that I'm not sure I'll send, telling her I don't think my sexual peregrinations are over. Then, as usual, there's nothing to do except watch an oak branch sway in the baking-hot afternoon. Oak trees are ugly, like cobwebby fruit cakes with sticky leaves all covered in crud. I've always avoided them.

Like trees, you're not supposed to move around too much on a Vision Quest. 'Sink into yourself' Manex tells us. It's really irritating. Really hard. On the third day, I can't bear it any more. I take a long walk to a dried-up waterfall in the most beautiful shady spot. The water looks fresh but soon, back at camp, I'm crapping puddles of foetid diarrhoea into the ferns as bluebottles swarm around my bum. This is quite a testing point, but luckily, dominatrix rules hold up even at times like these. I decide to simply 'surrender'. I clean myself up and look on the bright side. Nothing worse can happen now. I might as well do my obligatory wank and get it over with.

I retire to the mossy hollow shaded by the parasol of leaves from the cobwebby oak above. The cone-shaped mountain to the south-west of my precipice seems an obvious object of desire. I'm feeling crabby as I take off my orange Giants T-shirt and lie on the cool moss wearing just my boxer shorts.

But as I lie there and start to smooth the hood of my clit, what catches my eye is not the mountain, but the arthritic oak branches in front of it. It's like looking through a window and seeing the stain on the glass rather than the stunning view beyond. My eyes fix lazily on the end of one of the skinny branches. There's a cluster of old, thick leaves, two brown and curled. The branch bobs up and down in the breeze. I watch it for along time. It comes to seem like a dick. Sort of phallic. But not. It seems to be looking at me, as if it wants to come inside and play, like a plastic toy snake that moves unstoppably and you never know which way it's going to twist next. The skinny branch watches me touch myself, sees me getting turned on in my green grotto.

And after a while it isn't just the gnarled old branch that is watching me, but the whole of the oak tree and then the valley as well and the cone-shaped mountain behind it and the trees in the forest on the other side of the valley. And suddenly I'm a huge exhibitionist and my legs are giant's limbs and my pussy becomes a Gulliver-sized cunt rippling and radiating over miles and miles of earth.

I take my boxers off and now I am completely naked on a mountaintop, sucking up the energy of the tree, the sky, the ground, into all the pores and holes of my body and giving back to them what is in me. And all the while, the oak branch watches, bobbing up and down, talking in the breeze. The skin of the tree, so thick and old and scaly, the cluster of leaves, two brown and curled. I want to clamp my huge cunt on the twisted oak. Wet . . . bark . . . rub . . . I feel a magnetic pull from the branch to the body and from the body to the branch. For the first time in my life, there is no human porn scenario churning in my head. Just the relentless branch and the scaly skin in this ancient valley that scares me a bit at night when I know no humans will come.

Then a moan comes from my throat as my colossal limbs open even wider to the valley. There's an explosion between my legs and when I return I think, *What the hell was that?* Just as there's a kind of energy that comes between a performer and their audience, so there is an energy that can come between a human being and a tree. An exchange of some kind.

Then the bastard flies come back and I retire to my tent thinking, *This is all very weird, even by my standards.*

The word 'dryad' comes from the Greek word *drus* meaning 'oak tree'. When Rousseau said he wished he could believe in dryad tree spirits, maybe he was just sitting under the wrong tree. Mainly, my experience in the mossy bower has left me feeling that you never know where masturbation is going to lead you. I think back to Annie Sprinkle's line about how enlightenment, sexual liberation and masturbation are like a game of tennis. Some days you'll have a great game and sometimes you're going to get all your balls in the net. The point is to keep practising.

EPILOGUE:
PRIVATE TIME

18 October 2018

When I finally arrived back in London four months after I'd left, my first feeling was that my clothes had shrunk. Or maybe they were too big now. While Hadji helped me carry my suitcase along the Blackfriars Road back to the flat, he talked about the Chekhov play he'd just seen at the National Theatre and I wondered if there were any rooms you could go off and have sex in if you got bored. I was trying to hang on to my American life by chewing a piece of root beer float gum, but in London it just tasted like a mouthful of chemicals.

I wasn't sure I was up to this game of tennis. I was horrified by the grim British mentality of, 'Well, life's a bit shit, isn't it, but we'll just have to get on with it.' I felt like Marco Vassi when he returns from his Stoned Apocalypse. He feels as though a high fever has passed, 'And yet a disquieting greyness had seemed to settle over everything.'

People didn't get the masturbation thing at all. They'd make lame jokes. All they wanted to know about was, 'What's happening with Hadji now?' and 'Are you still with the New York chef?' All that romance crap, as Betty would say.

To start with, things were raw between Hadji and me, although actually they were no worse than the old Sunday mornings with the croissants. At least things were out in the open. We knew a change was coming – that it had come already. I started to think more about the romance crap too. I was back to sharing the flat with Hadji. We didn't have sex, but we were sleeping in the same bed and it felt nice to hold each other. I thought about steak and how savage and bloody it was in the beginning. And then the years passed and it became the comfort of beef Wellington and now here I was, ten years later, curled up with him in a warm puff-pastry blanket. Maybe all sex descends into affection and love. That conundrum again.

Masturbation is easy in a way. You don't need anyone else to do the work. It makes you grounded and self-aware and for me, it really worked as a springboard back to health. But you need to work out a balance or it just becomes a way to avoid intimacy with others. Sometimes, physical pleasure alone isn't enough. Sometimes it feels good to connect with other people. Sometimes you don't know what impact a sexually unsatisfying relationship is having on your life until you make the decision to get out there and explore. The important thing is to keep pushing things forward. Relationships per se aren't a bad idea, but we need to talk about different ways to have them. We might as well try.

Now that it's 2018, Hadji and I have become very modern. The other night over stir-fry, I admitted that the booty call I'd been having with a new woman had become a bit more than a booty call. He said that actually he hadn't been to the cinema at all that afternoon but rather to the sauna in Waterloo, where he'd had an agreeable encounter with a Cuban man called Homer. My fork did freeze momentarily over my tofu, but then it felt amazing to be able to have this conversation without feeling too much uneasiness. It felt like sort of a breakthrough.

Mainly, I have been thriving ever since I came round to Annie Sprinkle's bed-sheets philosophy – the idea that being whole is more important than being relentlessly sexual. I've also learned that it's important to keep your vibrations high, as they say in California, which is why I make sure I spend time alone, refreshing myself in a place that I love. My Cannes friend says that she dreams one day of going off and being the mad old lady on the hill, but I am her already.

I go to my bolthole in Spain, where in the afternoons I write and in the evenings I drink Campari and lemonade and eat squid. Sometimes I do some 'homework'. Sometimes I feel like one of those Japanese wagyu cows that spends its life being massaged and fed beer. I try and enjoy sensation rather than fear it. Even when my skin feels inflamed, I see pain as a backbeat rather than the only song I can hear.

Every morning I cycle up to the arid hills, breathing huge draughts of air into my lungs, sucking it in, feeling the clean sweat on the back of my orange Giants T-shirt. I stop under the olive tree in the shade and breathe in and out, in and out, panting but feeling alive as I look over the hillside – the horses, the scrubby old trees, the Med down below. Then I ride up higher, hauling in more air and then I sit on the rocks and try to think of no one, not Hadji or booty calls or anyone. I close my eyes and do the butterfly meditation: a bird tweet here, a plane noise there, the creak of a cicada, the sound of my breath. Fluttering over everything and landing on nothing. Then I bob back into the world, jump back on my bike and fly down the hill very fast, scudding past trees and more trees until I pass the Chino supermarket and the strange Catalan bun shop. Some days, when I'm singing, I actually hit the top note on 'A Little Respect'.

When I finally arrive at the beach, the Bay of the Glittery Fish Food, I plunge into the sea. Having a sardine swim past your naked body on an early summer morning is almost as sexy as being the only human on the beach at a seal orgy. I must email Annie to ask her if she thinks this is a three-way: the sun, the sea and me.

This is what I have learned: that I am powerful. That there is such a thing as an aura and that you can charge it up. My favourite part of the naked swim is walking back to shore. You stride out of the water raising your knees high and feeling the white foam spread out behind you like long, luxuriant skirts. You can do this on the level of it being a great Pilates core exercise or you can feel as if you are bringing the sea back with you, its might, as if you have taken something of the sea inside you.

When you are striding out of the sea, a stark-naked fifty-two-year-old, you don't give a fuck, not a single solitary fuck. And if some scrawny old perv comes up, you will look him in the eye and he will shrivel before you because this is the aura you have at this moment, an all-consuming strength. You don't have to go swimming on a nudist beach in the Mediterranean to get this power (although I recommend it). You can just do your thirty-five minutes a day (the length of time Natasha Salaash recommends masturbating) and you'll start realising, remembering, what you have.

One morning the doorbell rang and two plumbers were standing there. The Xhamster plumbers! I'd become so sidetracked with truck drivers during my trip across America that I'd forgotten about the humble workmen of my earlier homework sessions. The communal water tanks on the roof had broken and Jordi and Chavi had come to fix them. They wanted to shake my hand, know what my name was. It wasn't until they'd left that I realised I had no bra on and I was wearing my vest with the naked cowgirl on the front. When they came back later that afternoon to finish the repair, Chavi had put on a clean shirt: red check with an anchor on the sleeve.

It's details like these that are important when you've adjourned to the movie theatre in your head. I took my clothes off and went and lay down on my bed, my hands resting on the vulva formerly known as Pinky Tuscadero. I'm not going to tell you what happened next, because my greatest desire right now is never to write about my sex life ever again. It's time to close the door on my secret *arrière-boutique* and I moan as I slide back into that easy, oily, blissful place, going, *Oh yes, yes, here we are, coming home* . . .

ACKNOWLEDGEMENTS

I would like to thank the following people who encouraged me, inspired me, housed me, fed me, bedded me, befriended me, taught me, humoured me, edited me and generally reminded me that it is OK to follow your bliss (and your blisters) and to go in a direction that some might see as out there. One of the many things I learned during the writing of *Sex Drive* (and during the two-year aftermath when I tried to sell it to a series of risk-averse mainstream publishers) is the importance of community. Without the following friends and supporters, this book would never have come to light and I would probably have given up and written a crime novel instead.

Thank you to: Jake Arnott always; Lisa Luxx my 'poet friend', who pointed to a brewery sign one night in Camden, London that said, 'Take Courage'; to C, who first set me on the road to healing – thank you for being sexy and joyful and putting up with me. To Tutu, who still sends me strength; to my parents, Roy and Veronica Theobald, for the gift of unconditional love.

Thanks to Annie Sprinkle, Joycelyn Elders, Susie Bright, Nicole Daedone, Barry Komiseruk, Regina Thomashauer, Veronica Vera, Barbara Carrellas, Nadine Gary, Whitney Wolfe Herd, Carol Queen, Eve Minax and Ham. Thanks to

Beth Goldstein for San Francisco hospitality beyond the call of duty; to Gina Buhl and the memory of your lovely, sex-positive mum, Alice Lee Buhl. I heart Arizona. Thanks to V.S. for the Los Angeles dumpster dining; Fanny Harper who said, 'Just write it anyway, you never know'; and the amazing and brave women at the London Vulval Pain Support Group. Thanks to Meg Maccini, Natasha Salaash, Olivia de Haulleville, Julia Petrisor, Patrick Califia, Gayle Rubin, Kathy Silberger for the pad in Boston where the idea germinated, Valerie Wirschitz for the Suffolk writing haven, Richard Dupont, Ted McIlvenna, Grace Robbins, Krissy Eliot, Suzann Gage, Rod Tedder, Erika, Jo Walters and Lisa McNulty in New York, Pincus Corcoran, Clay Corcoran, Alison McNaught, Vic Boydell, Jami Weinstein, Emma O'Kelly, Circe Hamilton, Phillipa Dabell and Genavieve Alexander, who handed me £40 over a table in Knightsbridge and got my crowdfunder rolling. Thanks to Manex Ibar, Carlin Ross, Anna Ziman, Anne Philpot, Nicola Canavan, Alan Dolan, Anne Larue, Amandine Brûlée, Odile Fillod, Polly Rodriguez, the founders of Omgyes.com: Lydia Daniller and Rob Perkins, Long Boy, Shawn Blevins, Stephanie Rafanelli, Will Spicer, Guinevere Turner, Polly Superstar, Britt Collins, Caroline Michel, Garth and his Place in the Californian Desert (I extra heart California), Mishelle in Texas, Lori Dovi, Buck Angel, Meena Khera, Julia Hobsbaum, Bidisha, Jessie Brinton, Fleur Britten, Jane Beaufoy for the Latin and Greek, Lydia Lunch, Cathy Unsworth, Cathy Peace, Linda Riley. Thanks to Prince for the music and Marco Vassi for the enlightened filth. Thanks to Pinky Tuscadero and B.A.D., obviously.

Many books were inspirational while researching *Sex Drive*, but notable ones were *Solitary Sex: A Cultural History of Masturbation* by Thomas W. Laqueur (2003), *Mighty Lewd Books: The Development of Pornography in Eighteenth-Century*

England by Julie Peakman (2003), *The Story of V: Opening Pandora's Box* by Catherine Blackledge (2004), *The Stoned Apocalypse* by Marco Vassi (1972) and *At Home with the Marquis de Sade* by Francine du Plessix Gray (1998). Thanks to Harriet Poland for sweeping in at that snooty publishing party and showing an interest in a book about – shock, horror – sex. Thanks to Kary Fisher, Maggie Hanbury and all connected to Unbound: the crowdfunders, John Mitchinson, Georgia Odd, Amy Winchester, DeAndra Lupu and especially the incredible Fiona Lensvelt, who totally understood this book from the very beginning and breathed new life into it just when I was running out of steam.

Thanks to all the kinksters and sexual pioneers I glimpsed or met along the way. Most of you are way more interesting and smart than the respectable people who hint that what you do is frivolous or unimportant. Thank you for going against the flow and for forging ways of being that help people feel free. Thanks to Ganesh and Corn Woman, the Goddesses and the Angels. Here's wishing all readers a 11:11 day and some supersonic Private Time.

ABOUT THE AUTHOR

Stephanie Theobald is a British novelist, journalist, public speaker and broadcaster known for her playful and thoughtful work around sexuality and alternative feminism. She writes regularly for the *Guardian*, the *Sunday Times*, *Elle* and *Red*. She is the author of four novels: *Biche*, *Sucking Shrimp*, *Trix* and *A Partial Indulgence*.

Unbound
Liberating ideas

Unbound is the world's first crowdfunding publisher, established in 2011.

We believe that wonderful things can happen when you clear a path for people who share a passion. That's why we've built a platform that brings together readers and authors to crowdfund books they believe in – and give fresh ideas that don't fit the traditional mould the chance they deserve.

This book is in your hands because readers made it possible. Everyone who pledged their support is listed below. Join them by visiting unbound.com and supporting a book today.

Bronwyn Cosgrave
Anna Cottis
Betsy Crane
Nicole Daedone
Lydia Daniller
Olivia de Haulleville
Tanya de Villiers
Tim Delaney
Kate Devlin
Shari Diamond
Lori Dovi
Stella Duffy
Shaun Duggan
Jane Dunford
Charlotte Dunleavy
Roger Eaton
Amanda Eliasch
Sara Ellis
Benjamin Elwes
Roxanne Escobales
Robert Fairer
Almudena Martínez Ferrer
Anabel Fielding
Simon Finch
Amy Finegan
Louise France
Caroline Gibbs
Lucy Gibbs
Kath Gifford
Nicola Godwin
Alexandra Roumbas
     Goldstein
Beth Goldstein

Harriet Green
Tanya Green
Sarah Gresty
Anouchka Grose
Fanny Harper
Bridget Harrison
Birna Helgadottir
Lucy Hillier
Lara Hoad
Alexander S Hoare
Julia Hobsbawm
Belinda Hollows
Mary Horlock
Iris Horsey
Steph Hulsmann
Manech Ibar
Laurel Ives
Jody Johnson
Jon and Deborah
Adam Jones
Pip Jones
Stefan Jovanović
Dan Kieran
Anneka Kingan
Henry Krokatsis
Eva Laeverenz
Tracy Laval
Fiona Lensvelt
Alison Levy
Tiffany Lin
Hanna Lindermuth
Claire Lowe
Sarah Lucas

Tobias Luther
Genevieve Madeira
Agnieszka Makar
Ruth Marshall
Francesca Martin
Caitlin Mavroleon
Katherine McMahon
Alison Mcnaught
Jocelyn Meall
Nick Mellish
Erin Meyer
Ross Mills
Kate Misrahi
John Mitchinson
Kamin Mohammadi
Polly Morgan
Paul Moss
Gaelle Mourre
MysteryVibe
Carlo Navato
Farah Nayeri
Sanjay Nazerali
Clare Nobbs
Emma Okelly
OMGYES.com
Cathy Peace
Gabrielle Pedriani
Rowan Pelling
Julia Petrisor
Justin Pollard
Alison Potter
Marianne Power
Heidi Preen

Stephanie Rafanelli
Ann Rafter
Julie Read
Emma Reynolds
Linda Riley
Christina Robert
Andrew Roberts
Wyn Roberts
Polly Rodriguez
Peter Rook
Sheree Rose
Ian Russell
Joanna Russell
Eva Sahn
Fernando Salazar
Naomi Schogler
Tom Shakespeare
Don Shewey
Carole Siller
Nach Smith
Annie Sprinkle
Julie Street
Clover Stroud
Henry Sutton
Alex Swallow
Justine Taylor
Roy Theobald
Regena Thomashauer
Adam Thompson
Amelia Troubridge
Rebecca Trowler
Tom Usher
Sharon Walker

Jane Walsh
Joanna Walters
Robert Ward
Lydia Watson
Assia Webster
Abbi Whitcombe
Charlotte Williamson
Jane and Louise Wilson
Louise Wolfson
Sara Woodford
Sarah Woodhead
Ali Wren
Katie Yirrell